New Horizons 10/11 £14.99

The **Fashion Careers**
Guidebook

The **Fashion Careers** Guidebook

Julia Yates

A QUARTO BOOK

First published in 2011 by A&C Black,
an imprint of Bloomsbury Publishing Plc.
49 - 51 Bedford Square
London
W1CB 3DP

www.acblack.com

ISBN: 978 1408 146 620

Conceived, designed, and produced by
Quarto Publishing plc
The Old Brewery
6 Blundell Street
London
N7 9BH

QUAR.CFAS

Editor: Liz Jones
Art Editor: Joanna Bettles
Picture Researcher: Sarah Bell
Art Director: Caroline Guest

Creative Director: Moira Clinch
Publisher: Paul Carslake

Colour separation in Hong Kong by
Modern Age Repro House Ltd
Printed in China by 1010 International Ltd

9 8 7 6 5 4 3 2 1

Contents

Continued overleaf >>

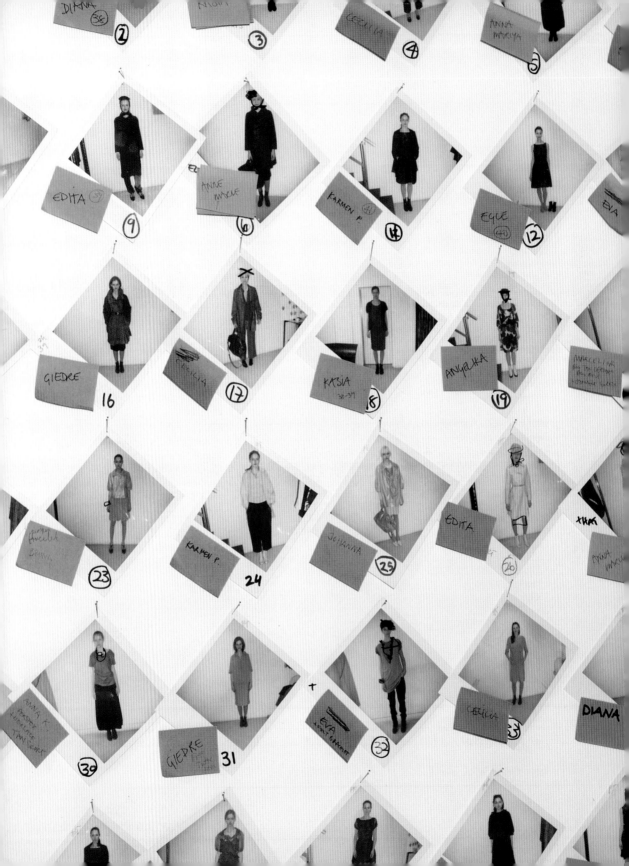

Foreword

Fashion – that glamorous, giddy world full of gorgeous people having fun and looking cool. No wonder so many, young and not-so-young, want to be part of it. But as you should know by now (if you have opened this book) it's a bit more complicated than that. Those gorgeous, glamorous people are usually the consumers, not the clever, hardworking, committed people who make this vast and complex industry tick.

Clothes are part of our lives, whatever our age, whether we protest that we have no interest in 'fashion' or not. For those who can read the signs we each reveal a part of who we are by our choice of what we wear. It is the industry's task to meet these different needs and make enough profit to survive. Increasingly our society also wants us to do that sustainably, not damaging the environment or exploiting other human beings or animals irresponsibly.

I often hear the cry 'I want to work in Fashion but I don't know what to do!' Scratch the surface and you will soon see the infinite variety of roles and skills that are needed to make the whole thing tick. All it

needs is to find the right slot for the particular set of talents
we each possess.

That is always hard at the beginning, not least in recognising
ourselves and what exactly we have to offer. This book is packed
full of useful information and sound advice, and keeping an open
mind, looking for unexpected opportunities, researching, listening to
advice and above all being practical will ease you onto the starting
blocks and into that first proper job.

There are plenty of challenges ahead for our fascinating, volatile,
global industry that will demand imaginative and industrious
people who love the fashion business – and who also want to have
fun. See you there.

Professor Jane Rapley OBE
Head of College
Central Saint Martins College of Art and Design

about this book

The fashion and textiles industry is one of the most exciting, creative and dynamic industries you could imagine. It's huge, worth a lot of money and is constantly changing.

Part 1

The first part of this book is here to help you with the process of actually getting a job. It will explain the different ways in which people find work within the industry. The first article is about education and covers the kinds of courses you can follow, how you should go about choosing the course and where to study, and how you can make the most of your time at university. Next, the role of internship is examined. This section explains some of the advantages of work experience and gives some tips on how to give yourself the best chance of converting two weeks of internship into a paid, long-term job.

The next few articles cover the mechanics of job hunting. How to write a great CV, how to put together a winning portfolio and how to make sure that you do yourself justice at an interview. There are tips on how to find all those jobs that are never advertised, including some advice on networking.

Within some specialisms, freelancing is more or less essential. The article on freelancing will give you some insight into being self-employed and will make sure that you are clear about the range of different skills and knowledge you'll need to make your freelancing career a success.

Part 2

Part 2 is a directory of some of the most common, most popular and most interesting jobs in the industry. One of your first challenges is to work out which particular sector and specific role within this huge, diverse and complex industry is going to suit you best. The many different jobs at different levels mean that if you want to work in the industry somewhere, there is probably a job out there for you. But working out which is the right one is not always easy. . . This section of the book is designed to inform and inspire you.

If, after all this, the choice still seems overwhelming, see the flow chart on page 12 to help clarify things for you.

A short introduction gives the flavour of the job being discussed in this directory entry.

Print designers may be employed by fashion retailers, fabric manufacturers and printers, or interior design and production companies. The industry is beginning to acknowledge that the print can 'make' the garment.

print designer

The print designer will usually be given a brief by the buyer, but will then be expected to interpret that in their own way and with their own style. The brief from the buyers might be quite broad. They might, for example, ask for something that fits with a vintage 1950s trend, and the designer might be given a colour palette and some swatches of fabric. The designer will then go and do some of their own research, in markets or even overseas. The designer then sketches out some ideas and brings them back to the buyer, and when they reach agreement the designer works up the designs in more detail, usually using Illustrator or Photoshop.

Once the designs are signed off, the artwork for the designs needs to be prepared, ready for production. This can be quite an involved process and the designer needs to be technically capable as well as artistic. Artwork needs to be different depending on whether it is a repeat design, half drop, placement print or a border design.

Production of fabric now mostly happens overseas, in China and Bangladesh, and the print designer may be involved in travelling to the factories, or may do all the work via email.

Not every design ho[...] in-house art staff. Freel[...] sell their artwork to ind[...] studios represent a larg[...] original work to design[...] value the fact that the p[...] piece of artwork is sold[...] the profit. Print designe[...] do this print preparatio[...] for the studio. Most of [...] CAD, which makes adj[...] Numerous art studios a[...] at large print shows.

Routes in
Print designers can hav[...] training may be in grap[...] illustration or fashion d[...] following your degree [...]

LEFT [...]
ABOVE [...]

Sample adverts give you an idea of the types of qualities and qualifications a potential employer is looking for, as well as the kinds of tasks and responsibilities that come with the job.

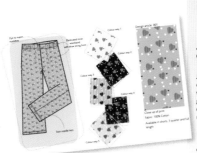

Illustration for a print design showing different colourways and examples of how it might be used.

CASE STUDY:

Janine is a print designer for a UK chain store.

Janine did a degree in multimedia textiles that focused on designs for all different sorts of surfaces including fabric, wood and leather. Janine then applied for a job doing graphic design – for a fashion supplier, providing graphic design for prints for Top Shop and other mass-market retailers. She didn't particularly enjoy working for the company, but the job was interesting.

After a couple of years she decided to do another degree, in textile futures, in London. This was a hard course but really interesting, and it allowed her to develop a different perspective of textiles; London was also the best place to be for the fashion industry. During her course, Janine did a lot of work experience with a whole range of different designers. She networked all she could during this time and had some brilliant experiences.

Eventually she got herself a paid job working for Nissan – designing interiors for cars. This proved to be much slower paced, and Janine soon realised that she missed the fashion world, so eventually, after applying, applying and applying, she got a job with the design team at Alexander McQueen. This was a tough environment to work in, but she found it inspirational and did some of her best work there, a real highlight being when some of her designs went onto the catwalk in Milan.

She then got a job as a print designer for New Look and has been there now for two years. Her advice to anyone looking to work in the fashion industry: 'Network, network, network.'

Case studies and 'day-in-the-life' features give an insight into what it is like to do a particular job on a daily basis, what kind of person it might suit and routes into that career.

Best bits
- ▲ You can be very creative; you can inject your own style and personality into your designs
- ▲ Seeing people wearing your designs

Worst bits
- ▼ As an artist you want to work on your designs until they are perfect. But as a print designer you don't have the time; it's easy to end up working very long hours

Skills needed
- A love of fashion
- A good eye for colour
- An understanding of garments and their construction
- Good artistic skills

Study
- Print design
- CAD, Photoshop, Illustrator, U4ia
- Colour, different media
- Art history
- Drawing, painting and illustration

Links
Association of Suppliers to the British Clothing Industry (ASBCI): for industry news and making contacts. www.asbci.co.uk
British Interior Textiles Association: includes directory of manufacturers. www.interiortextiles.co.uk
Can U Cut It? Careers information and case studies. www.canucutit.co.uk
Drapers The industry magazine. www.drapersonline.com

Rating
Average salary: ● ● ○
Entrance difficulty: ● ● ○

Typical salaries and difficulty of entrance to the career are summarised on a scale of one to three.

Stand out from the crowd
Draw, draw, draw! Some production and design jobs do not place an emphasis on drawing, but this is one area where an artistic capability will really set you apart.

There are tips on how to shine at an interview and positively differentiate yourself from all the other candidates.

Links to useful, career-specific websites are suggested, with a short description.

Ideas for key courses of study to follow in pursuit of the career.

before you start

Are you really committed to working in the fashion industry, and are you prepared to work really hard?

Yes – Great! Think about what aspect of the industry you'd like to be involved in – **choose from the tags, right.**

No – Maybe you don't have what it takes.

1. Creating products

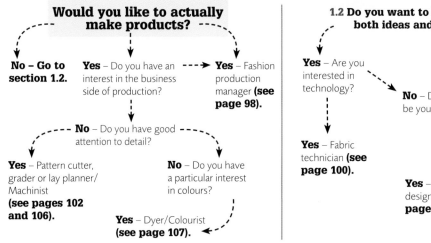

Would you like to actually make products?

No – Go to section 1.2.

Yes – Do you have an interest in the business side of production?

Yes – Fashion production manager **(see page 98).**

No – Do you have good attention to detail?

Yes – Pattern cutter, grader or lay planner/ Machinist **(see pages 102 and 106).**

No – Do you have a particular interest in colours?

Yes – Dyer/Colourist **(see page 107).**

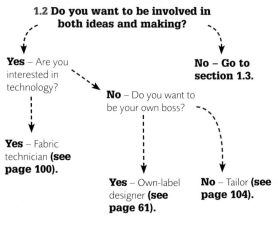

1.2 Do you want to be involved in both ideas and making?

Yes – Are you interested in technology?

No – Go to section 1.3.

No – Do you want to be your own boss?

Yes – Fabric technician **(see page 100).**

Yes – Own-label designer **(see page 61).**

No – Tailor **(see page 104).**

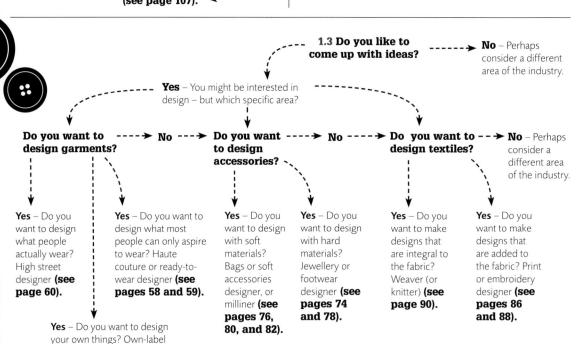

1.3 Do you like to come up with ideas?

No – Perhaps consider a different area of the industry.

Yes – You might be interested in design – but which specific area?

Do you want to design garments? ----→ **No** --→ **Do you want to design accessories?** ----→ **No** ----→ **Do you want to design textiles?** --→ **No** – Perhaps consider a different area of the industry.

Yes – Do you want to design what people actually wear? High street designer **(see page 60).**

Yes – Do you want to design what most people can only aspire to wear? Haute couture or ready-to-wear designer **(see pages 58 and 59).**

Yes – Do you want to design your own things? Own-label designer **(see page 61).**

Yes – Do you want to design with soft materials? Bags or soft accessories designer, or milliner **(see pages 76, 80, and 82).**

Yes – Do you want to design with hard materials? Jewellery or footwear designer **(see pages 74 and 78).**

Yes – Do you want to make designs that are integral to the fabric? Weaver (or knitter) **(see page 90).**

Yes – Do you want to make designs that are added to the fabric? Print or embroidery designer **(see pages 86 and 88).**

Do you want to be involved in creating products? **Go to panel 1.**

Do you want to be involved in selling products? **Go to panel 2.**

Do you want to form a bridge between the fashion industry and the public? **Go to panel 3.**

2. Selling

Do you want to work directly with the customers?

No – Do you have a strong head for figures?

Yes – Merchandiser **(see page 130).**

Yes – Sales assistant/ Store manager/Personal shopper **(see pages 122, 124, and 138).**

No – Retail designer/ Visual merchandiser **(see pages 134 and 136).**

No – Are you visually creative?

Yes – Do you have a strong interest in business?

Yes – Buyer **(see page 126).**

3. Bridge with the outside world

No – Go to section 3.3.

Do you want to inform people?

No – Go to section 3.2.

3.2 Do you want to influence people?

Yes – Using words. Fashion journalist **(see page 160).**

Yes – Using pictures. Photographer/ Illustrator **(see pages 148 and 152).**

Yes – Through events. Fashion show producer **(see page 162).**

Yes – What people buy, through showing the clothes. Photographer/ Fashion shoot producer **(see pages 148 and 158).**

Yes – Through campaigns. Fashion marketer **(see page 146).**

Yes – By influencing what people think. Fashion PR **(see page 144).**

Yes – Using fashion to influence other things/create a certain look. Make-up and hair professionals/ Stylist **(see pages 164 and 170).**

3.3 Do you want to educate people?

Yes – Do you want to teach young people?

No – college lecturer or work with adult learners **(see page 178).**

No – Do you want to work in an educational environment?

No – Do you want to work predominantly with the public?

To enhance the performing arts? Costume designer **(see page 110).**

Yes – Teacher or college tutor **(see page 178).**

Yes – Technician **(see page 185).**

No – Work predominantly with collections – Curator/ Archivist **(see pages 180 and 184).**

Yes – Museum education officer **(see page 182).**

The fashion industry is a unique and incredible place to work. The trouble is, there are many people out there who think so, too. And this means that you are going to have to try that bit harder to get your first job. ✦ There are certain exceptions, and as you go through the book, you can see from the ratings where the less competitive areas of the industry are. But for the majority of the industry, getting a job, and a paid one at that, can be quite tricky. ✦ The usual route to the more competitive jobs is through an internship. ✦ This section is here to help. It's been put together with the help of employers who are recruiting and professionals with success within the industry, so there is plenty of expertise and credibility behind the advice and tips. It can seem that there is a lot of luck involved in getting your foot in the door, but you can sometimes make your own luck, and you can certainly put yourself in the best possible position to take full advantage of opportunities when they do come your way.

What kinds of skills do you need to be successful in the fashion industry?

There are of course different skills and attributes required for different specialisms within the industry: for example, PRs need a winning way with words, tailors need great skill with their hands and embroiderers need endless patience. There are also some skills that are important for pretty much every role within the industry, for example, creativity, teamwork, and great people skills. You also need to be resilient, able to cope with setbacks and rejection without letting them affect your self-belief or your motivation to work in the industry. Most job hunters in the fashion industry will meet with many rejections before they are taken on. The important thing is to try to learn lessons from rejections but not to let them put you off. You'll also need tenacity. You need to be the kind of person who doesn't let it lie. The kind of person for whom 'no' does not mean 'no' – it just means 'not right now' or 'not in exactly this way'. If they say 'We're not recruiting right now' you need to be the kind of person who thinks 'okay then, I'll try next week' or 'okay then, I'll try another department'. Then you'll need to be a bit creative: not just artistically but psychologically. You need to be able to think of a new avenue that hasn't yet been explored, an approach that feels fresh or a technique that they haven't come across before. And finally, you need a little bit of luck. You need to be in the right place at the right time, or strike up a conversation with the right person over coffee or happen to have a friend who goes on holiday just when a great opportunity comes up.

You shouldn't be put off. But you should be realistic about the challenges ahead, and perhaps more significantly, you shouldn't think that a few rejections means that you're not cut out for this business. It doesn't. It just means that you need to try a bit harder or stick with it for a bit longer.

How do you know when to quit?

This is a hard one to answer as you are the only person who can judge it. There will be many people each year who make the decision that they aren't prepared to wait for their lucky break, or who aren't willing to, or simply can't, go through the steps it takes to get there. We all have our breaking point. For some it will be a few months after finishing college. For others it may be years down the line. You are the only person who can say if and when that moment will come for you. Make sure that you get and take all the advice you can – it would be a waste for you to spend months sending off a poorly crafted CV to hundreds of employers, or to fail to make a good impression while on work experience for a lack of understanding of what the employer might be expecting. It might also be helpful to give yourself a timescale. You might, for example, think that you can manage to work for free for three months and then make a decision to reassess at the end of that period. You might not be ready to give up at that point, but it may be useful to have a clear point in time in mind after which you'll review your progress, see if you've made any headway and think about new strategies or other people who might be able to give you advice and support.

What else could you do?

As a student of fashion, you will have developed all sorts of skills that will be useful in many other arenas. Before you make any decisions, it's worth writing yourself a list of all the things you're good at and all the things you want from a job or career. Most people interested in fashion, for example, will be quite creative. There are many ways to be creative: for you it might be drawing, or a great sense of aesthetics, or colour, or good problem solving. Perhaps you're very good with people. Think about what exactly you mean by this: are you a good listener, are you great at persuading people to see your point of view or are you an expert in identifying what other people want? Spend some time working out which of these skills you would really like to use in your work and then try and work out which other kinds of jobs you might enjoy. You might need to speak to your tutors or careers adviser to help you with this.

education

This is where it all starts. The right course can set you up with a great range of skills, a good knowledge of the industry and a network of peers that you will keep in touch with all your working life.

Knowing exactly where to start can feel a bit daunting, but don't let this paralyse you. It is important to make sure you do your research properly but the industry is not one that tends to put you in a box and make you stay there. It's very common to change direction after you graduate, and success tends to be dependent on enthusiasm, creativity, hard work and an ability to get along with people, more than on the specific degree you've got and where you got it. Do what you can to make the right choice in the first place, but don't feel anxious that you're committing yourself to one particular role for the rest of your working life.

A good piece of advice for any prospective student is always to do what you enjoy. Usually, if you're enjoying something, you'll be good at it, and there's no way you'll make it in this highly competitive industry if you're not working on something that means a lot to you.

Why study?

Traditionally, most people in the fashion industry learned their trade through an apprenticeship of some sort, or by working their way up from the bottom. There were many entry-level jobs for people with no specialist skills or knowledge but plenty of enthusiasm. Today the picture is a little different, for a number of reasons.

First, the degree of technical knowledge required of fashion professionals has increased drastically over the last few decades. Whether you end up working in design, manufacturing, retail or communications, the industry is far more technically and academically sophisticated than it was a generation ago. Marketing managers are expected to understand a lot about the psychology of the customer, designers need knowledge of fine art and textile designers must be able to use and manipulate specialist software.

The second difference is in the range of subjects that you can study. A generation ago, students were quite limited in the subjects that were open to them in further and higher education, with subjects as 'mainstream' as psychology and computer studies being considered a little daring! These days students can opt for more or less whatever they want, and within the arena of fashion, there are hundreds of special courses to choose from that will equip graduates with the skills and

The degree of technical knowledge required of fashion professionals has increased, and this trend looks set to continue. To get a job in today's industry some form of study is almost essential.

CASE STUDY:

Jacob always knew what he wanted to do. Concentrating on business studies and art and design at school allowed him to get onto a course in fashion marketing and promotion, which included some work experience in the PR department of a major high street retailer. Although this didn't lead to a job after graduation, he was able to go back and get some more experience there, and after a few months, his tutor got back in touch with him, saying that she'd heard of an opportunity that he should go for.

knowledge that they need for all aspects of the fashion industry. The third change over the last 50 or so years is in how fiercely competitive it is now to secure a job in the industry. There are far more job seekers than there are jobs; employers can really pick and choose and will always cream off the best of the applicants. So why would they choose a candidate who left school straight after school when they can get one with a degree?

A degree on its own is not enough, though. The best way to look at a degree is as a springboard. There are lots of opportunities that come to you while you're studying, such as the chance to learn skills, develop networks and find out about the industry, but it's up to you to seek these opportunities out and make the very most of them. Getting a BA should be about far more than the letters after your name.

Types of course

The number of courses available is quite overwhelming. The typical route for a fashion designer might be to take some creative art courses at GCSE and A level, or the equivalent, and then study fashion design at university. School students frequently take additional classes in fine arts or design, which helps them to develop their creative skills and build a strong portfolio for application to the top universities. Working in varied media, and two- and three-dimensional art forms is important in developing a good eye and strong artistic skills. Universities look for that diversity in a portfolio, as well as good grades, when reviewing applicants. You could also start with a more generic course of study at school, then transfer to a college specialising in art and design. Many art and

When you're thinking about where to study, do make sure you go along and visit. You'll get a chance to see all the facilities, but more importantly you'll get to meet the teachers and some current students, and this will give you a good sense of what it's actually like to study there.

Decide what aspects of a course are important to you and use that to guide your decision about where to study. Different universities will have different strengths.

design courses require the student to have completed an art foundation course that focuses on a broad range of artistic skills. Interdisciplinary courses are frequently offered and encouraged (for example, a fashion design course with elements of textiles or graphics). Many universities have excellent courses in fashion design, as well as a diversity of other courses, offering a broad educational experience. Then, on top of this, there is a wide range of adult education courses and evening classes, which can allow you to specialise, improve your skills or experiment with design as a career choice.

Where should I study?

There are some universities that have great reputations for particular subjects, but one university is not necessarily going to be the best for every course relevant to the fashion industry. A course with a strong reputation can be a great advantage for a number of reasons. A good reputation will often encourage inspiring teachers and great fellow students to work there, and of course it will make your CV stand out, quite apart from the fact that the reputation may be well deserved in its own right and you may just get a great education there! Having said that, some very well-known courses and institutions might have established their reputation some time ago, and may keep that reputation alive simply through attracting great students who go on to achieve great things. Don't rely on reputation alone. One university might have great facilities, another might have a very strong set of contacts and another might give you some interesting opportunities for work experience.

Most faculty are graduates of the courses they teach. The top schools have the top faculty and therefore the top design

QUALIFICATION ROUTES: EXAMPLES

Jessica is now working as an associate designer for a high street retailer

- Art classes in secondary school
- Weekend course in fashion drawing
- Accepted to art and design college
- Art foundation program
- Selected fashion design course at university
- Interned at sportswear company
- Graduated with BA in fashion design, specialising in womenswear

Jason is now working for a small independent menswear designer

- A levels in art, Spanish and science
- Accepted at large university
- Studied architecture
- Interned for a tailor during summer holidays and loved it
- Transferred to fashion design
- Graduated with BA in fashion design, specialising in menswear

Amber works for a large high street retailer as a floor supervisor

- At secondary school, took business courses in spare time
- At sixth form, studied business studies and psychology, while working at an upmarket clothes shop on Saturdays
- Promoted to Saturday supervisor at shop
- Graduated with a degree in business studies
- Hired full-time by high street retailer, worked up to floor supervisor

CASE STUDY:

Rachel always excelled at the creative subjects at school, but although she did really well in her art subjects, she knew she didn't want a career as a fine artist. So she ended up studying psychology at university. This course wasn't at all what she thought it would be – far more science-based than she'd anticipated, so after the first term she knew it wasn't right. She dropped out of the course, went back home to live with her mum and dad and got a job in a local independent boutique to earn some money while she decided what to do. The owner of the shop designed some of the collections they stocked and gradually Rachel began to learn about the process of fashion design. She was a quick learner and found that she was genuinely talented at this. She spent 18 months working there, as part-designer, part-sales assistant, and then decided that she should go back to university. She had to take a foundation course before she could get onto a fashion design course, but once she had started she never had a moment's doubt.

talent, as well as all the top connections in the industry. The quality of the faculty is often an indicator of future job leads.

What if the course is wrong?

Don't panic, but do act. Mistakes are usually much easier to rectify the earlier you start. Work out why it's wrong. Is it studying altogether, that particular course or that particular university or college? Is it that you've realised you don't want a career in that field, or that you're struggling to keep up with the workload? When you've got that clear in your mind, go and see your adviser. It may be that there is a straightforward solution (for example, changing modules, extra support, swapping to another subject at the end of the year) that your tutor or careers adviser can help you think through. Don't forget that for most jobs in the fashion industry, employers are quite happy with a degree that is 'fashion-related' and doesn't need to be directly related to the job itself.

How do I make the most of my time at university?

Work really hard! Be open to your tutors' input and be motivated to learn and grow. Get a good degree. A degree on its own isn't enough, but it goes without saying that a good degree is going to be more helpful than a bad one! The best students are likely to have strong relationships with their tutors and your tutors are great contacts. Build your own network. Your fellow students can become some of your best and longest-lasting contacts, and will become professional connections later in life. Good friendships with your university peers can give you an important support network to get you through the tough early years and

Checklist:

1 What do I need to know about a university's fashion course?

2 What is the curriculum; what courses are offered?

3 What did last year's graduates go on to do?

4 How big are the classes?

5 What facilities will I have access to?

6 Who are the faculty – have they had good experience?

7 What's the reputation of the university?

8 What are the student demographics?

9 What are the compulsory courses I must study?

10 How much academic advisory support is there?

11 How much time will I get with my tutors?

12 What support will I get with finding work experience?

as your careers progress they can be a great source of industry information and opportunities. Make some mistakes. This is your time to try things out and is often the best way to develop your own style. Get as much work experience as you can. Most careers within the fashion industry entail at least a period of unpaid work experience. The more you can get under your belt when you're a student, the more quickly you'll be ready to get a paid job when you graduate.

work experience/ internships

Work experience presents you with two main challenges – how to find it in the first place and how to deal with it to get the best out of it.

Why do it?

There are four main reasons to consider getting some work experience:

- **It's going to help you decide on your career path.** You may feel very certain that you want your career to go in one direction or another, but the only way to know for sure whether you'll thrive in one particular sector is to try it out.
- **Work experience is a brilliant opportunity.** You can try a few different kinds of employers or different aspects of the industry before you make your final decision.
- **You'll learn some more skills.** You will probably have learned loads of very relevant skills from your course, but sometimes the skills that you develop at university need to be adapted to make them directly applicable to the workplace. For instance, the software or machines that are used in the industry are often more up to date than those you are taught with at university, and employers often comment that graduates need to up their game in terms of the pace of work expected in the industry.
- **You'll start to make and develop your network.** There will never be a time in your career where your contacts are unimportant. Almost every job opportunity that ever comes your way will be at least in part attributable to your networks – whether they employ you, put you forward for the job, give you a lead on an opportunity in the pipeline or give you some advice. Your networks are

your professional lifeblood, and work experience is a great place to start building yours.

- **It's really the only way.** Even if you aren't convinced by the reasons above, this one is the biggie. There are some people every year who manage somehow to waltz into a paid job right from the start, but for most, internships – often unpaid – are a way in. Within the fashion industry profit margins are often tight, businesses are often small and professionals are working very hard. Against that context, every week dozens of CVs come through the door, from enthusiastic and highly skilled hopefuls offering to work for free. Well, what would you do?

Undergraduate internships

Many colleges offer internship programmes for students. They maintain relationships with companies who use students as a resource for both free work and possible future employment. These internships are very valuable introductions to careers in the fashion world, and give hands-on experience that can help build your CV as well as your skills. Discuss internship placements with your adviser or department head.

Recruiters

Recruiters from large and moderately sized companies will often visit universities to recruit final-year students, interviewing them for internships, current jobs or

'We'd got a load of photos and names of readers but the two piles had got separated, so we had no idea who anyone was. Our work experience girl was amazingly resourceful in getting the photos matched up with the names.' Fashion journalist

As an intern, you will learn an enormous amount from the glamorous professionals you'll work alongside.

positions that might open up in the future. This also gives them the platform to introduce the students to their companies and to promote them as exciting career opportunities. Even if the company is not your first choice for your first job, it is worthwhile to go to these presentations, listen, learn about the company and introduce yourself to the human resources team. Discussing your portfolio and CV with them will give you good feedback, and might help you find your dream job.

Training programmes
Many of the larger companies (Abercrombie & Fitch and Urban Outfitters, for example) actively recruit final-year students from the best universities for their internship/training programmes. These internships are sometimes unpaid, but often the interns are paid a small salary. During the training period, interns are rotated through different departments and given specific challenges and very real learning experiences. The programmes, which usually last for three to six months, give the companies a chance to evaluate their interns' skills, motivation and fit within the company, and full-time positions will often be offered to the best of the interns after completion of the internships. Competition for these internships is intense, and you should aim your CV and portfolio towards the specific

company. Often, these companies will ask students to do a project that will give them an insight into the students' talent level, their presentation skills, their ability to align their sensibilities with the brand and their follow-through. Research into the company's aesthetics and customer is essential to success, as well as the ability to take your project to the next level.

Should I accept unpaid work?
Unpaid postgraduate internships are often the first step in getting a paid position, and they give you the opportunity to prove that you can contribute to the success of the team. It is up to you to make the most of the experience. You have three choices:

- You can refuse to work without compensation.
- You can allow yourself to feel exploited.
- You can work unpaid, learning everything you can and giving your all to prove that you would be an asset to the company.

The third option is the best. In general, what you get from an experience is equal to what you put in. Be clear about what you want to gain from the internship, and give yourself a time limit for advancement. Discuss your goals with your employer, as well as your realistic chances for working up to a paid position if a vacancy arises.

While you intern, stay in touch with your contacts, because other opportunities may open up for paid positions.

What's the difference between an internship and shadowing?
Shadowing is more about watching someone else work rather than actually getting your hands dirty. It's usually done

The best path to a satisfying and helpful work experience placement is to accept that this is likely to be your first step into the industry, and it's up to you to make the best of it.

for a much shorter period of time – one or two days at most – and you might be able to arrange to shadow some relatively senior people. Shadowing is a great way to find out more about the industry and may lead to longer-term work experience.

Ways to find internship opportunities

Internships are sometimes advertised, but employers will rarely opt to pay to advertise for an internship placement, so the usual sources of vacancies are unlikely to yield much. Fashion-oriented university websites are often a good place to look for students and alumni, but the best place to look is on a company's own website.

Alternative ways to find work experience/internships

Most people find their placements in less formal ways. Have a look at 'CVs' (page 26) and 'Creative job hunting' (page 40), as all the tips there apply equally well to looking for internships as they do to longer-term (and better paid!) jobs. In general there are three typical routes:

- Use your networks: ask your tutors, your friends and your family if they know anyone who works in the field you're aiming at that you could talk to. Arrange to speak to them to get some advice (in person tends to be better than by phone if it's feasible) and see if that leads either to some experience or some other contacts.
- Contact organisations you're interested in working for and ask if you can apply for an internship. It's always a good idea to call first to get the right name (and right spelling!) of the person to contact, and in your application be specific (but not too

specific) about what you're after: 'I am particularly interested in learning more about the process of setting an exhibition up but would be very willing to work at any task that would ease the pressure in your office.' Many companies will ask you to apply through their website. You will be asked to email your CV, so have a company-specific CV and covering letter ready to send them.

- Find out about some projects that are coming up in the industry and see if you can offer to help. During Fashion Week, many designers and PR agencies are swamped with work and might need some extra help; the run-up to Christmas is a busy time for retailers; and the months preceding a new exhibition at a museum might be just the time they're looking for an extra pair of hands. Be explicit about what particular skills you can offer and keep your fingers crossed.

How to handle work experience

Attitudes to work experience vary tremendously. Employers can range from the very appreciative 'thank goodness there's someone who is able to help me out for free', to the supportive 'I'd like to help this person get their foot in the door', through to the pretty sickening 'they should be grateful for the opportunity to do my photocopying at 9 o'clock at night'.

The attitudes of the interns themselves also vary from the indignant 'I've got a degree! Why am I expected to be the "gopher"?' to the enormously grateful 'thank you so much for the opportunity to sweep your floor'.

There is some validity to all of these opinions. It does seem unfair that you are expected to work for free, but it is also

'I wasn't completely sure which direction to take after university so used the holidays to get as much varied work experience as I could. I worked for high-end designers, high street stores and a small partnership of a couple of recent graduates. It really helped me decide on my route.' Junior designer

worth accepting that this is simply the way the industry works and that actually, having a big name on your CV genuinely does improve your chances of getting a job.

Negotiating a contract

Once you are on your placement (and it is also perfectly acceptable to try to do this before the placement starts) one of your first tasks should be to set up a meeting to get a kind of 'contract' agreed. Not necessarily anything formal or in writing, but just to have the chance to find out what your employer wants to get out of you, and to have the opportunity to make it clear what you are hoping to gain. Start off by asking if there are any particular tasks or projects they want you to take on, and see if you can gain a sense of what kind of attitude they expect. Your employer is likely to be impressed with your professional attitude and willingness to adapt to their needs, and it'll help you because you'll know exactly how they want you to behave. You can then take the opportunity to explain exactly what you want to get out of your time with them, whether that's a particular skill you want to try out, a person you'd like the chance to talk to or a particular event you'd like to attend. Telling them what you want to do is a much better way to make it happen than waiting and hoping, and even if they say that they can't provide it for you, they are likely to be impressed with your proactive attitude and clarity of thought.

How to make the most of your time:

DO

▲ Do find out how everyone likes their coffee and make a note of it.

▲ Do the things they've asked you to do before you do the things you want to do. But make sure you get around to doing the things that are important to you as well.

▲ Do spend some time observing your new colleagues and try to mirror their behaviour: if they are frantically busy, make sure you work fast and find out what else you can do; if they're all wearing jeans, don't come in your suit; if they are all working until 8pm, make sure you are willing to stay late.

▲ Do be nice to everyone – if people don't like you, they won't ask you to stay, or recommend you to their friends, no matter how talented you are.

▲ Do be proactive, and really think about how you might be able to help. If someone mentions some photocopying – offer to do it for them. If people seem really busy, offer to pop out and get them a sandwich for lunch.

DON'T

▼ Don't act entitled: if the floor needs sweeping and the coffee cups need washing up, don't give the impression that you think you're above it.

▼ Don't complain – if you don't like what they're asking you to do, just grit your teeth, do it well and remind yourself that you're only there for a short time.

▼ Don't say no. Even a seemingly meaningless task might have positive outcomes in that it might teach you something, lead to something or at least it might give you a chance to show how willing you are!

▼ Don't ask too many questions. It's really good to be curious and interested, but don't forget that these are busy people with a lot of work to do. Ask questions about assignments you are given, and write down the answers so you don't need to ask again.

▼ Don't let them treat you badly. If you feel they are taking you for a ride (and only you can judge when the balance tips from reasonable request to something inappropriate), then it's time to stop and talk about it.

▼ Don't gossip.

CVs

Headings should be consistent – use the same font size and style for all of them.

Your CV could be seen as your most important marketing tool. It won't get you a job on its own, but you can certainly be rejected on the strength of it.

In most cases, when an employer sees your CV, that (and your covering letter) will be all they have to go on, so it's really worthwhile spending time making sure your CV does you justice.

Starting off

The most useful thing you can do before you even put pen to paper is to put yourself in the shoes of the employer for a few minutes. What are they going to want to see? What skills and experience are they going to be impressed with? What sort of thing will put them off? Scrutinise the job description (or, if you're not ready to apply for a particular vacancy, spend some time researching on the Internet) to find out what skills, experience and personal qualities are needed for a particular role, and then think about what you've done in your life that could provide the evidence that you're what they're looking for.

How to structure your CV

There are no hard-and-fast rules about how to structure a CV. There is a traditional convention, but if you have a good rationale, then breaking away from the standard form can be very effective. The traditional CV would start with personal contact information and then have either your education section or your work history section next (whichever is the most recent). Then work chronologically backwards within each section (ie, starting with your most recent experience). You would then traditionally have a section on interests

and end with the names and addresses of two referees.

So that structure might be your starting point, but what is going to work best for you will depend on two things: what your own experience has been and what the employer is going to be most impressed with. Essentially, you should put the most important things on the first page near the top. And don't feel that you need to be bound by the headings mentioned above, if you think your own story can be better told in a different way.

So, for instance, if you've had a lot of really relevant work experience but most recently have been employed doing something quite different, you could split the 'Work' section into 'Relevant experience' and 'Other work experience' – then put the relevant section on the first page and the 'other' could be relegated to halfway down page two. Or you could have a section that you call 'Fashion design experience' (or whatever is appropriate), and in that you could pull out your degree course, your bits of relevant paid work and anything else that seems directly related. You could then have sections called 'Other education' and 'Other work experience' for everything else.

It's common to have a section on 'Key skills' or 'Achievements' near the beginning of the CV, and this will allow you to pick out the best bits from everything you've ever done and show how it relates to the role you're applying for. Choose achievements and skills that you can talk

Suzanne Player

T 07794 568202 **E** s.e.player@hotmail.com

A fashion designer with great technical abilities and people skills, excellent work ethic and attention to detail.

key skills

Great sense of colour and exacting attention to detail
Huge passion for gorgeous, wearable clothes for women
Willingness to work very hard
Love of people: customers, colleagues and suppliers

education

2007 – 2010 Central Saint Martins, University of the Arts London
BA Fashion Design (womenswear) 2:1
Loved every minute of this gruelling, challenging and iconoclastic course. Final year collection was inspired by the architecture of the City of London, and won me some warm press coverage at London Graduate Fashion Week.

2006 – 2007 University of Westminster
Foundation Studies

2004 – 2006 St Francis Xavier Sixth Form College
A levels in Art and Design, English and Drama

work experience

February 2011 – present: CHANG MAI DESIGNS
Assistant Designer for this small but very creative design team. Assisted with all aspects of the design, particularly specialising in embellishments, and was involved in trend spotting for the upcoming season. I enjoy getting involved with all levels of work from cleaning the floors right through to designing the collections. Honed Photoshop skills.

October 2010 – February 2011: ALVERSTONE
Full time Internship. Learnt how a big label is organised and was involved with the collection from concept through to finished product. Learnt the value of meticulous attention to detail and demonstrated great people skills, working closely with designers, manufacturers and the PR team. Had the opportunity to create some print designs that were used for the catwalk collection, and demonstrated accurate pattern cutting.

July – August 2009: DEBENHAMS
Intern for the design department at Debenhams. Great opportunity to learn about design for a mass market, and I learnt a lot about the commercial side of the creative business.

June 2006 – present: Various retailers including MARKS & SPENCER and TOP SHOP
Sales assistant. Enjoyed working with the customers and gained a real insight into the way that people buy clothes. Teamwork skills have proved to be useful in all settings, and combining this part-time work with a full-time degree required effective time management and good organisational skills.

interests

Painting, walking, exhibitions, baking, chatting, laughing, karaoke, dancing, France, cycling, cheese.

references

Upon request

Sample CV

Make sure your contact details are clear to read and prominently placed.

You don't need to write in complete sentences. Lists and bulleted points may get your point across more efficiently.

List work experience or education in chronological order, with the most recent experiences first.

with enthusiasm about, and ones that the employer will be interested in.

The sections on interests and referees are optional, so keep them in if you have space and think they are relevant.

How long should my CV be?

The standard CV would be one or two pages long. It's worth considering a single page – these are busy employers and a one-page CV means that a) they are more likely to actually read everything; b) your ability to get it down to a single page will suggest to the employer that you are well organised and able to prioritise; and c) having to cut it down to a single side will have made you really consider what experience to include and what to reject, and the result is likely to be a highly relevant and punchy CV.

If it's too much of a struggle to get it down to one page, don't worry. Just make sure that your most relevant and impressive experience goes on the first page. Don't ever make it longer than two pages, and don't leave it at a page and a half – this gives the impression that you haven't done enough in your life to fill two sides, but aren't sufficiently well organised to get it on one.

What makes a CV go straight in the employer's bin?

- 'Poor spelling'
- 'Lack of care and attention to detail'
- 'When people spell the name of our company wrong – or get the name wrong altogether'
- 'When the covering letter is clearly generic and doesn't really refer to either the particular job or the company'
- 'Anything over-designed. I'm just interested in what the CV has to say'
- 'Times New Roman'
- 'A CV that bears no relation to the job'
- 'Candidates who waste lots of space telling us all about their scuba diving qualifications or their trip around India'

What to include

The rule of thumb here is include it if it is relevant, says something important about you or if it helps tell your story. Ask yourself 'so what?' about every single thing, and if you can't justify its inclusion, get rid of it. The suggestions below are general guidelines – you need to judge whether or not they are applicable in your particular situation.

1

Personal details

Your name, and some contact details – email, mobile number, perhaps landline and address – are typical. You don't need to put things like marital status, date of birth or nationality, unless you are trying to make a particular point – for example, if you are from China and the organisation has great links with China, it might be to your advantage to mention your nationality at this stage.

2

Education

You would usually only include the two most recent educational stages. For example, if you are currently at university or a recent graduate, you would list the name of your university and the subject you studied, and your year of graduation. You would also list your school, as well as your A level and GCSE subjects and results, especially if they were outstanding. You need the name of the educational institution (not address – although country might be interesting). Then say something about your course. You could pick out one or two modules that were particularly relevant or you could say a couple of things about a particular project that you liked, especially if you did one that could relate to this job. Or perhaps something about the relevant skills that you developed while studying.

Work

Make sure that you don't leave any substantial gaps in your work history, but you also want to make sure the list isn't endless. If you have had lots of similar jobs, you could group them all together, saying something like '2008–2010, a range of part-time and temporary jobs in restaurants and bars to fund my way through university.' With work, it's useful to give a flavour of the role, but guard against listing all the different tasks you did as it's not very interesting and probably not relevant. Instead, you could start by explaining your job in a single sentence and then follow up with just a few statements about some of your achievements, or some of the skills you learned or demonstrated. Try always to back your skills up with some evidence: 'I demonstrated excellent negotiating skills' is not nearly as convincing as 'I negotiated a number of deals including getting a five per cent reduction on a major purchase, saving the company £500.'

Try out a variety of fonts and learn which work and which don't. For instance, Times New Roman is the default font in Word, and using it looks like you haven't tried very hard; Comic Sans is for mimicking handwriting and doesn't look serious. Display type such as Zapfino might work for the heading to your CV. Make sure whatever you use is easy to read and will reproduce well. Use a classic sans serif font, like those shown below.

Times New Roman 11pt

Comic Sans 11pt

Zapfino Regular 11pt

Gill Sans Regular 11pt

Helvetica Neue Roman 11pt

Myriad Pro Regular 11pt

Optima Regular 11pt

4

Personal statement

This usually comes at the beginning of the CV – immediately after the personal details – and is a short paragraph summarising your current situation. The most common mistake that people make with their personal statement is that it ends up being generic and bland, along the lines of 'highly effective self-starter with excellent communication skills, now seeking a challenging position in a well-reputed company'. Now, the problem with this is that it is so general that it could be referring to almost any person, wanting almost any job, in almost any organisation.

A statement such as 'A fashion design graduate, with a passion for knitwear and a great sense of colour, now looking for a work experience placement with a designer (specify the name) whose knitwear designs have been an inspiration to me throughout my degree course' will sound much more individual, will give the employer a real sense of your personality and will make you sound genuinely keen to work for that organisation.

5

Key skills

This can be a very useful section. It would usually go pretty near the start of the CV, but you could slot it in wherever you think it works best. It is a good way to highlight a few important pieces of information that you don't want the employer to miss, and it allows you to bring together the most impressive and relevant things you've done from all the different parts of your history. Again, try to back things up with evidence and be as specific as you can: 'great communication skills', although it may be true, is so broad and so commonplace as to be almost meaningless, but a statement such as 'I can communicate effectively with a wide range of people and have developed good relationships with clients, managers and colleagues through having a genuine interest in others and their work' feels much more believable.

6

Interests

Employers seem fairly split on this section. Some feel it's quite unnecessary – they are looking for someone to work with, not someone to spend their weekends with, so why would they care what you do in your own time? Others find interests revealing, and point out that colleagues are whole people, not work robots, so getting along with them does matter. The upshot is that it's really up to you to choose. Include this section if you have something interesting and relevant to say.

Have a think about what impression your interests will give: 'Long-distance running, reading and fishing' isn't going to suggest you're going to shine at teamwork, while 'reading, socialising and going to the cinema' isn't going to mark you out as someone who is out of the ordinary. You can always combat the assumptions directly by saying something like this: 'I enjoy long-distance running with a local group' or 'Reading – I particularly love Victorian literature but have had my eyes opened to more modern books through my book group'.

7

Referees

Names and addresses of referees can be a bit of a waste of valuable space. Employers usually won't contact a referee until they've decided to offer you the job, and certainly won't get in touch with them until they've asked your permission, so there's plenty of time for you to give them the details further down the line.

Candidates sometimes write 'names and addresses of referees are available on request' as a way to address the issue but not waste too much space, and this is fine – it marks the end of the CV quite nicely – but is not needed. However, if you haven't got quite enough information to fill two pages, it can be a good filler, or if you have a really impressive person as one of your referees – for example, a senior manager within the organisation or a personal friend of the employer – it may also be a good idea.

How to deal with things that might look bad

Most of us have at least one event in our career history that might not show us in our best light. Whether it's a period of unemployment, a false start or a disability that we're nervous about disclosing, it's hard to know how best to deal with this on a CV. While you should not try to mislead your potential employer, it's often worth waiting until you've met with them before you confess your darkest secrets.

There are three ways of minimising the impact of a piece of information:

- **Don't mention it.** If your concern is around something like a work permit, or an issue with mental health, then you can easily get away without mentioning it on your CV. An omission such as this won't be obvious. You could choose to not mention it at this stage but then bring it up either after you've been offered the job or at the end of the interview – either way they will by then have something more than a piece of paper to judge you on so are more likely to be open-minded.
- **Bury it.** Busy employers will often only skim-read the second page of a CV, and you can use this to your advantage. If you relegate the piece of information to page two, then quite possibly the employer won't take too much notice of it, or even if they do, they will probably be so impressed with the amazing skills and experience you've demonstrated on page one that they decide to give you a chance.
- **Explain it.** Given that most people have made a career mistake themselves, they are often quite willing to forgive one, especially if it's clear that you understand what happened and have learned from it. A brief line of explanation will often go down very well.

How it should look

It's tricky to come up with any firm rules about the appearance of a CV. It needs to be clear and it needs to be consistent, but beyond that it's up to you to decide how you're going to lay it out and design it. As with everything in the CV, the look and feel needs to reflect you as well as the organisation you're applying to.

The CV should look tidy – this will mean that it is easier for the reader to see the information, and it will convey the impression that you are well organised, have good attention to detail and care about the job. Tidy means making sure that your margins all line up, that your headings are all the same type (in terms of their size, use of bold, underlines and so on), and that your font is the same size throughout. Give it the 'arm's length' test: hold it up with your arms outstretched, and see what kind of impression it gives. Are the sections clearly demarcated? Is there enough white space?

Good-quality paper always leaves a positive impression, but avoid bright colours – even if the reader notices and appreciates your creative approach, they may well have to photocopy it for colleagues, and bright colours don't photocopy well.

Think about the font you're using. Times New Roman is the default font for many PCs, but it isn't a great one for CVs, as it looks quite old-fashioned. Play around with the fonts available and see what you think conveys the right impression. Font size is important. Try 11 point as a start, but what looks good will vary with the font.

How creative can my CV be?

If you're a creative person and you're trying to demonstrate your creativity to a potential employer, it would seem like a wasted opportunity not to try and get some creativity into your CV. Exactly how far you take it should be guided by the kind of role and organisation you're applying to. Your CV should reflect the character of the company and the role. Regardless of how edgy and creative the employers are, if the design obscures your message, they're not going to be impressed, and they may well miss the key messages. Do also consider logistics. If you want to send something out to a large number of employers (and in this industry it's not at all unusual to send over 100 CVs before you get a positive response), then avoid a CV that is too expensive to produce or that may get damaged in the post.

You might want to think about more subtle ways to show your creativity, such as a flash of colour, a few thumbnail images of your work, a personal logo or even an unusual layout. Employers are quite polarised in their views on creative CVs – they love them or they hate them – so it is always going to be a risk. The plus side of an unusual design is that it will stand out, and some employers may love it. The downside is that it may put some people off. If you make sure that the design of your CV reflects you as a person, then it is likely that employers that you would be most happy working for will be drawn to your CV, and it is those you wouldn't be compatible with

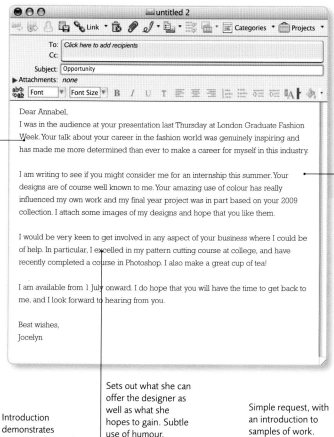

A covering letter for a CV with the aim of landing an internship.

Introduction demonstrates interest in the work of the designer.

Sets out what she can offer the designer as well as what she hopes to gain. Subtle use of humour.

Simple request, with an introduction to samples of work.

anyway who are more likely to be turned off.

Covering letters

You will almost always need to send a covering letter, or email, along with your CV. The covering letter really needs to be tailored to each individual job – if you receive a lot of applications, a generic letter can be spotted a mile off, and they do not go down well.

A covering letter should be quite short – no more than one side of letter paper in total. You should introduce yourself and maybe highlight one or two items from your CV to draw the reader's attention to. You should then explain why you want this particular job in this particular organisation. If you really think this part through, your cover letter will stand out.

Bullets or paragraphs?

Either is fine. If you go with paragraphs you must keep them pretty short and snappy,

but it's a good way to show off your writing skills. Bullet points tend to look quite neat and punchy, and they lend themselves more to the active language that can work well in a CV.

Do I need to tailor my CV?

It's quite common for people looking for work in the fashion industry to be applying for some quite different kinds of jobs concurrently. You might, for example, find yourself applying for work experience with a magazine at the same time as looking for some retail work to earn money. In this situation you would certainly be better off having two quite different CVs, as you'd want to highlight different elements of your history. Even when you are applying for two fairly similar jobs, you might want to just cast your eye over the CV to make sure that the right elements stand out.

Should I send some examples of my work along with my CV?

Yes. If you are applying for a job as a designer, a photographer or a writer, it would seem crazy to miss the opportunity to show the employer what your work is like. After all, that is really what they're going to base their decision on. If you're emailing your CV, you could quite easily include a link to your website. This is probably the best way to do it, but you could also print off some images to enclose with the CV and send a CD. Hard copy may seem old-fashioned but it may be more attractive to the potential employer, and more immediate. Try to make the examples that you send relevant to the employer, and don't send too many – just two or three. Leave them wanting to see more.

If all this sounds daunting, it should. A good CV takes a long time to create, and tailoring each covering letter and CV to each individual job can feel like a chore. But it will pay off. A well-constructed, well-designed, relevant and tailored CV will get your job search off to a great start.

portfolios

A portfolio is a collection of your work, or images of your work, in a portable form that you can carry around to show employers. Portfolios are common in all visually creative spheres, so if you are interested in the design side of the industry, illustration or photography, you will need to spend some time getting one together.

The physical case for your portfolio can be bought from any good art supplies shop. You can buy them in lots of sizes, but for interviews try either A3 or A2 size. There are two key elements to portfolios. You need to give some thought to how you're going to put one together – which images to choose and which order to put them in. You also need to practise talking about your work. The images aren't enough on their own – an employer wants to understand the process, to find out how you created your designs.

Practical considerations

If you are going into the design or illustration side of fashion, your sketching skills and ability to communicate your ideas with clarity are very important. Your fashion figures should be compatible with each collection you design (for example, an elegant figure for an evening collection, or an edgy, bold figure for a clubwear collection). In design presentations, the clarity of your design ideas is the priority, so use flat sketches, or 'flats' (a slightly more animated drawing of the design shown without the figure), to show all of the accurate details. Having a mood board, with conceptual visuals and fabric swatches, helps to show your creative process. Your presentation should be artistic but also well thought out, so that your interviewer can see both your design talent and your organisational skills.

You may want to include some photographs of your finished garments or collections so that you can show how the two-dimensional concepts evolved into final, wearable designs. This is especially useful if your design process is more three-dimensional, or your construction skills are stronger than your sketching abilities. It is very important to have high-quality photographs, and it is worth having a professional photographer take them if you

Cyclamen

Delphinium

Hollyhock

DO	DON'T
▲ Do make sure all the images are oriented the same way.	▼ Don't make it any bigger than A2 size – it needs to be easy to handle and carry around.
▲ Do make sure it's not creased or scratched.	
▲ Do keep your portfolio up to date. If you want to keep in anything more than a year old, you should have a very clear rationale as to why it's still relevant.	▼ Don't keep your only copies of any pieces in your portfolio – you should be able to replace it without too much cost or effort if it gets lost or damaged.
▲ Do tailor it to the particular job.	
▲ Do make it varied. It will give you a chance to show off your skills better and will be more likely to keep the employer interested.	▼ Don't put your best work at the end. The employer might not have time to make it that far!

can afford it. You might have a friend who is a great photographer and who knows how to set up shots to make your work look its best. If you are taking photographs yourself, think about the background (white is usually best, as it will show most items clearly) and the lighting, to ensure that it highlights the object in a flattering way. Take a range of images in different settings and make your decisions once you've seen them printed out.

The images should be mounted on plain card and should all be oriented the same way – either all portrait or all landscape – you don't want the employer to have to keep turning the whole portfolio around or craning their neck to see it properly.

A table of contents is a nice thing to put at the beginning – it makes the whole thing look very professional. Put your name and contact number or email on each page. Make sure the portfolio is clean, tidy and consistent, and don't make it too long – 12 or so well-chosen images is plenty.

Choosing what to include

As when putting your CV together, you need to start by putting yourself in the employer's shoes for a minute. Opening your portfolio with a couple of collections that specifically relate to the aesthetic and customer of the company you are interviewing with is a good idea. They are looking to see if you can fit into their team, and this will show that you have done your research and are excited about the product they design. Think about what the employer is going to be looking for, and see what you

can do to meet their requirements. If they are looking for a very versatile designer, then make sure the work represented in your portfolio is diverse. If their designs are known for their bold use of colour, choose images that highlight your understanding of building up a palette.

Include images that you are really proud of – partly because these are likely to impress the employer, but also because these are the projects you're most likely to be able to talk about with passion.

As well as images of the final product, it's good to include some indication of the thought process. Many interviewers like to see your sketchbook, which will show them a lot about your design process. This sketchbook should reflect who you are as a designer and can contain rough developmental drawings, swatches, clippings, handwritten notes – anything that you use to develop your ideas. Carry it in the pocket of your portfolio and be ready to share it with them if requested. When recruiting for a junior designer or intern, employers are often looking for potential, and an understanding of how you come up with your ideas can be very revealing. You could include some initial sketches or a mood board.

Having some variety within your portfolio will make it more interesting for the employer to look through and will give you the opportunity to demonstrate a range of your skills.

Your portfolio should be tailored to the particular job and organisation you're applying to in just the way that your CV is.

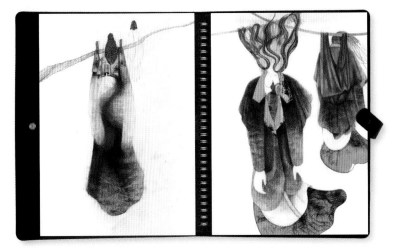

Your portfolio should be coherent – think about the order of the pieces carefully so they tell a story, and make sure you can talk about them fluently as you flick through.

Show a range of techniques and how you arrived at an idea. For example, below on the left the technical flats complement the styled photograph of the finished dress. On the facing page, a selection of illustrations demonstrates a line.

It's useful to have a larger number of images of your work, and then when you are going to an interview you can just choose the particular ones that are most relevant for that opportunity.

Do I need an online portfolio?
These days having an online portfolio is becoming increasingly important, but it's definitely something to have as well as, rather than instead of, a physical hard copy.

Could I just take my laptop?
Most employers seem to like having something tangible that they can hold and like to be able to flick backwards and forwards. It can also be hard to position the laptop so that you and the employer can both see the image at the same time. A hard copy makes a better impression and is easier to manipulate.

Can I put in anything other than images?
Yes, the more variety the better. Put mood boards, swatches of fabric, CAD printouts and sketches; you can also use words if you want. These will all contribute to showing how you work and will make the portfolio more interesting for the employer to look through.

Do the projects in my portfolio have to be from my course?
No. You can include anything that you think says something about you and the way you work. If you're really keen to work for a particular organisation, you could set yourself a brief based on that company, or one of their clients, and come up with some designs or images that relate specifically to them. This is a great way to show how keen you are on the job and can show how well you understand their brand.

What if they ask to keep it?
This is not usual, but an employer might be keen to show your work to a colleague before making a final decision. It would usually be a good sign, so don't blow your chances by making a big fuss. It is, however, completely reasonable to say you can't leave it but are very happy to come back at another time when their colleague is available to show it again.

Talking about your work
The portfolio is a very different marketing tool from the CV. When an employer looks at your CV, that is all the information they have at that point. It needs to stand on its

Your portfolio should be packed full of what you consider your best work, but keep it recent and make it relevant to the particular interview.

own. A portfolio works a little differently. You would usually bring your portfolio with you to a meeting or interview with an employer, and you will present it. This means that you need to get used to talking about your work. Remember that your portfolio gives you the opportunity to talk about what you can do. For example, that eveningwear collection is a chance to tell them about your experience draping in bias chiffon, or creating beading designs. Those perfect flat drawings give you the opening to talk about your love of Photoshop and Illustrator.

Employers like to hear you talking about your work for a number of reasons. First, it gives them a much better sense of the process behind your designs. Second, it lets them get to know a bit more about you – with any luck, you'll be quite relaxed and natural talking about something that means a lot to you, so it can be quite a revealing process. Third, it can be quite useful for employers to see how you talk about your creations. In your future job, you will need to be able to communicate your ideas with all of your colleagues, regardless of whether they are creative types themselves, so listening to you talk about your work will give the employers an indication of whether you'll do this effectively.

Some employers will want to look through your work at their own pace though, and ask questions if they have any as they go through. So the first thing you should do when you get your portfolio out is to ask the employer whether they would like you to talk through your work, or if they'd prefer to look through on their own.

Talking about your work is something that you do need to practise, so have a good think about each individual image in your portfolio and about what you might say. The suggestions below are just ideas to get you thinking.

1 You would probably want to start off with an overview of your work before launching into the first image. It's hard to describe your work in just a few sentences, but it's a really useful skill to perfect.

2 Once you've given the overview, you can start going through the detail. Two good starting points are a description of the concepts and a critical analysis of the work.

3 When you talk about an item, let the employer know how you came up with the idea. What the brief was, your inspiration, and how you developed your ideas. If you have a mood board or some initial sketches, you can use these to explain the process you went through and talk about how you got through the brief to the final product. Employers are likely to be interested in how you developed, so talk about anything you learned during the process.

How long should it take to present?

You could ask the interviewer upfront how long they have for this, or you could just make sure you're picking up on cues and that you speed up whenever you get the sense that they're ready to move on. As a guideline, don't expect to spend more than about ten minutes.

What if they steal my ideas?

Really, this is something you're just going to have to risk. In most cases, if the employer likes your work enough to pinch your ideas, they'll probably want to get you on board so that you can come up with more amazing ideas for them.

Should I talk about every image?

It's fine to move fairly quickly over one or two images to allow you more time with your favourites. You should still have done some thinking about what you might say about each one; if the employer seems intrigued, you need to have something to say about it. If you wouldn't want to talk about a particular item, consider whether it should really be included.

interview skills

For every job you ever get you're likely to have to go through an interview. There are all kinds of interviews, and of course every employer is looking for something different, but there are still some general rules that can help you whatever the context.

Interviews can range from the very formal (two-day assessment centres with very structured exercises and lots of people observing and analysing you) right through to the almost shockingly informal – a brief chat over coffee that doesn't appear to touch on anything related to the job. But for the most part, interviews will be semi-structured conversations with one or two members of the team that cover something of your skills and experience, the role that you're applying for and your reasons for wanting to work there. If appropriate you will probably be asked to show and talk about your work, and you should have a chance to ask any questions you have about the job and organisation and maybe have a look around and a chance to meet some of the team. In many cases, you will meet first with human resources personnel, who 'edit out' the applicants who are not the best fit for the position.

First impressions count

Impressions are based 70 per cent on body language, 23 per cent on how you talk and only 7 per cent on what you say. This doesn't mean that you don't need to worry about what you say in an interview, but it's worthwhile spending some time thinking about how you come across. Think hard about what you should wear to your interview. The usual guideline is that you

should be wearing an outfit along the same lines as the sort of thing the staff wear, but one level smarter. So if they usually dress casually, you should go for smart casual, and so on. Aim to dress like the company's ideal customer/muse to fit in. This gives the impression that you understand the brand and will be a seamless fit.

Think about your posture – it says a lot about you. Have a look at yourself in the mirror as you walk into a room and as you sit. You're trying to aim for relaxed but confident.

If you can bear it, record yourself answering a typical interview question, and as you play it back think about what impression you are giving through your voice and language. When you are nervous, your voice is likely to become faster and higher pitched, so in the interview make a conscious effort to slow down and lower your pitch.

Research

To try and ensure that you come across as well as possible, it's a good idea to spend some time thinking and researching before the interview itself. Research on its own isn't going to guarantee that you'll be able to answer every question perfectly, but it increases your chances of having thought about the answers a little and means that your experiences and achievements should at least be at the forefront of your mind. Here are some ideas of the sort of research you could do before the interview itself.

- **The sector:** Read the trade press and find out what's going on in the sector. What are the trends, who are the major players, what are the latest developments, who's won awards? What about the competition – what are the other similar companies out there and what distinguishes them from each other?
- **The organisation:** Read the organisation's website and make sure you know it backwards. What does it say about the organisation – what are they proud of and what does it say about their values? What do you like about the organisation – why would you like to work there rather than for one of their competitors? What do you think about their work – which of their products are you particularly impressed with and why? Do a Google search and check out the archive websites of the press to find out what other people are saying about them.

Research isn't going to guarantee that you'll be able to answer every question perfectly, but it increases your chances of having thought about the answers.

- **The job itself:** Have a good read of the job description and try to get a really clear idea in your mind about what the job would actually entail. What skills are they looking for? What kind of person would do this well?
- **Your motivation:** So why do you want the job? Why have you picked this industry and this particular role? If you can talk with conviction and enthusiasm

about your reasons for wanting to do that particular job for that particular organisation you're going to put yourself head and shoulders above many applicants.

- **Your skills:** Your skills and experience are likely to be the things on which the decision is based, so it's worth spending some time thinking about them and how they can be useful in this role. You could start off by thinking about yourself and the things that you're genuinely good at – if you struggle to come up with much, have a think about what your teachers or tutors have said about you, or ask your friends and family and see what they come up with.

Once you've got yourself a list, you need to get some evidence. For every skill that you might claim to have in an interview, you need to be able to back it up – when you used it, and what makes you think you're good at it. In addition to the skills that you believe are strengths for you, you need to think about the skills that you need to do this job. With any luck, the two lists of skills will overlap, but even if there are some skills required for the job that you feel you aren't strong at, you still need to have a line prepared for the interview.

If you haven't particularly excelled at a skill, then maybe you can provide evidence of one component of it. If, for example, you've never done much project management, you might be able to talk about how well organised you are, or how well you've always managed to meet your deadlines. Alternatively, if there is something that you're lacking you might want to think about either starting to gain some experience in it or at least talk with enthusiasm about wanting to learn. 'I haven't as yet had a chance to really learn much about Photoshop, but I've just started an evening class to learn the basics and am really excited to develop my skills' will make you sound far more motivated and able than 'I've never used Photoshop'.

Common interview questions

- Why do you want this job?
- What skills and experience do you think you could bring to this role?
- Why are you interested in our company?
- Tell us about one of your university projects.
- What did you learn from your work experience placement?
- How have you enjoyed your course?
- Give us an example of a time when you've had to work in a team.
- What do you think this role will entail?
- Where do you see yourself in five years' time?
- Which designers (or whatever profession you're applying for) do you most admire?
- What do you think you'll find most difficult about this role?

- **Your experience:** Have a look over your CV and think both about what the employer might want to ask you about and what you would like to tell them. If you've done any relevant work experience or a relevant course, consider how you could talk about it. Not just a list of your duties or what you studied, but what you learned, what you loved and one particular project that you can talk about that might give the interviewer a sense of how you work.
- **Social media:** One additional factor in the job search process is awareness of your representation online. A good candidate's chance for a job can be destroyed by careless postings on social websites. That pub-crawl snap showing you in a compromising position may be fun to share with your friends, but can be a red flag to potential employers, and they do check Facebook, YouTube and MySpace to see whether there is any irresponsible behaviour in your postings. Also, make sure your voicemail greeting on your mobile phone is appropriately professional, not strange or immature.

There might be negative things in your CV that come up for discussion. If you have left any gaps in your history, the interviewers may well ask what you were doing. If you dropped out of university before finishing your course or had an

Uncommon interview questions (that you may still get asked!)

- What colour was the door to this office?
- What makes you laugh?
- Who would you invite to your fantasy dinner party, and why?
- What else have you applied for?
- When did you last get angry/cry?
- Tell me a joke.

extended period of unemployment, you should come up with a good, credible explanation of what happened. Employers are human and will usually forgive a mistake, but you need to be honest and open about what happened and make it clear that you have learned from the experience. In these cases a false start or change of direction can even be a positive as it can illustrate how you have made your career decisions in a convincing and personal way. Don't blame other people – research has shown that this is not a way to impress the interviewer. Instead, be honest about your mistakes, but make it clear that this is not something that you are likely to repeat. 'I started on a business studies course, but soon realised that it was a great mistake – I'm a very creative person and although I found some of the subject matter interesting, I felt stifled and quite unmotivated. I decided to give up the course and spent the rest of the year gaining a variety of different work experience placements and really thinking about what I wanted to do. And I haven't looked back. I'm loving my course in fashion design and have got some excellent feedback from my tutors, and some great marks!' This kind of response will always go down better than 'I was given terrible advice at school and my teachers on the business course were horrible to me so I dropped out.'

'Have you any questions for us?'

At the end of the interview, the employer will usually ask if you have any questions for them. Always have at least two questions ready (everyone will have one, so two will stand out and make you appear engaged and interested in the company – as long as they're good). If you don't, it can give the impression that you're not genuinely interested in the organisation or the job. Although this is a good opportunity to ask some potentially quite senior insiders about their views, do think about the impression that your questions will give. This is still part of the interview and can make quite a difference.

Don't ask about practicalities such as pay, conditions and working hours. It can make it seem as though you're only interested in the job if the package is right. It's important to be clear about the practicalities before you start, or even before you agree to take the job, but save it until you've convinced them that you're right for them. Use this opportunity to show that you've done some research or perhaps that you've got some understanding of the bigger question. If there was something that intrigued you about their website, or something interesting that you've read about them in the trade press, this is a good time to find out more.

Can I lie in an interview?

This isn't a good idea for a number of reasons. First, most people are terrible liars, and even if the employer isn't quite sure that you're lying, they may well end up with a vague feeling of mistrust. Second, if they find out (and it's an astonishingly small world), then your reputation will be greatly damaged. Finally, if you end up believing that your job offer is based on a lie, then you're not going to feel very confident about your ability once in the position. Make the best of your experiences in the interview by all means, but steer clear of outright lies.

What should I do if my mind goes blank?

This is quite common, and on its own is often not a great problem. The key is to make sure it doesn't put you off for the rest of the interview. Here are a few ideas that might help you deal with it while retaining your composure! You could ask the interviewer to repeat the question or to rephrase it. You could repeat it back to them to check your understanding (and buy yourself a bit of time in the process). You could be truthful, tell them that your mind has gone blank and ask for a few moments, or you could ask them if they would mind coming back to that question towards the end of the interview when you've had a few minutes to mull it over.

Should I shake hands?

This is a nice, professional, and warm thing to do. Do practise your handshake with a critical friend beforehand – interviewers can read a lot into the way you shake hands, so you have to be sure yours isn't too weak or too strong! Face the interviewer directly and make eye contact.

Is it okay to bring examples of my work, or references, along with me?

If you're applying for a creative job, you should definitely bring some examples along with you. Otherwise you should only bring something along if it has a direct bearing on the job you're applying for, and don't bring a reference along unless it's particularly pertinent.

What should I do after the interview?

As the interview ends, it's polite to thank the interviewer for their time, and it's certainly okay to find out when and how they're going to let you know the outcome. If they don't get in touch when they say they will it's perfectly within your rights to give them a call. If you don't get the job, asking for a bit of feedback is a really good idea. Lots of employers won't be prepared to offer that service, but it shows that you're eager to improve and if they are happy to talk to you, you might learn some very valuable lessons. Finally, write to them afterwards (a handwritten note, not an email, and mention something specific to your conversation), thanking them for their time, saying that you were really impressed with them, and asking if they could keep your CV on file and let you know if anything comes up.

creative job hunting

For a lucky few, they finish their course, see an advert, send off a CV and before they know it, they've landed a job. For the majority of those trying to get into the competitive areas of the fashion industry, it is more complicated.

Why be creative?

Most jobs are never advertised, and the vacancies that you might get to hear about are usually greatly oversubscribed and often end up going to people who already have links with the organisation. It may feel like an uphill struggle, but with an understanding of how recruitment works in this industry, you can make sure that you give yourself a great advantage and put yourself ahead of the competition.

This chapter looks at a few creative ways to expand the number of opportunities you find out about, minimise the competition and increase your chances of getting noticed.

There are two key principles that are going to make your job search more effective:

1 Look for job vacancies in many different ways
2 Spend a good amount of time on each application

Stick to these two guidelines and you will get a good return on the time you've invested.

Where to look

Most graduates are looking for vacancies in one or two places. For example, they might look in *Drapers* (or the online version) and their university careers service site. Both are very good options but with thousands of young people reading *Drapers* every day,

any job you see here will also have been spotted by hundreds of other enthusiastic, well-qualified candidates. However well you put together your application, and no matter how perfect you are for the job, your chances of being invited for an interview are slim, as the employer reading the applications will give your CV only a few seconds before making a decision. And your university careers service site? Far less competition here (although you can be sure that everyone from your course will be looking); but how many relevant jobs are you finding each week? It's likely that it's not many.

The importance of networking

One of the most effective ways of finding a job in the fashion industry is through networking with previous graduates from your university who are working in the field you are trying to enter. Universities usually have alumni organisations that can provide you with contact information. Reach out to these alumni, introducing yourself as a recent graduate of their college. Ask them if they know of any companies who might have upcoming openings or are expanding. Most alumni are happy to help 'one of their own', and they usually have an ear to the ground about their industry. Ask them if they would take a brief look at your CV/portfolio/website and give you feedback. After you have established a rapport with these alumni, stay in touch every couple of months to re-establish that bond. After you

The person who reads your CV should be left with the impression that they are the only company you've written to, so your CV needs to be carefully tailored to that particular organisation.

have found your position, it will be your turn to offer assistance to new graduates. And of course, always remember to write a thank-you note to your benefactors and let them know once you have got your first job (whether it was through one of their leads or not).

Another avenue for networking is the people with whom you have interned while studying. Because you have developed relationships within those organisations, asking for feedback and advice is usually comfortable and effective. While interning, try to form mentoring relationships that will support you in your search upon graduation. Many companies offer paid postgraduate internships that serve as both training programmes and a test period for both the employee and the company. These internships frequently turn into full-time positions if there is a good fit between the new employee and the company.

Unadvertised vacancies
You may decide to send a CV to an organisation that has not advertised a

vacancy, on the off-chance that they are really impressed with it and want to meet you. Lots of people do this, and although it is not a bad approach, it needs to be done strategically to make it worth your while. The mistake that most people make is to design one good CV and covering letter and then send it around to as many companies as they can think of. It is clear to most employers which CVs and covering letters are generic (that is one CV and letter that can be sent to any number of different organisations – they usually start with 'Dear Sir or Madam' and incorporate phrases such as 'hoping to work for a dynamic, successful business with a strong brand such as yours'). This kind of letter stands out a mile for all the wrong reasons and will rarely get a response.

The person who reads your CV should be left with the impression that they are the only company you've written to, so your CV needs to be carefully tailored to that particular organisation (see CVs, page 26). You need to call the company to get the name of the person to send your CV to, and

Using agencies and collective websites
Most jobs are posted on the website of the particular company looking to fill a position, and looking for jobs online is the most effective way to search. You may have to look through a lot of individual sites, but it is worth the time.

You should also keep an eye on other universities' websites and the general websites for the fashion industry. Do a Google search and see what other sites come up, as well as searching general job sites like Monster. Sign on with recruitment agencies, freelance centres, job banks and clothing industry job sites. The following sites are a good place to start:

- **www.fashionpersonnel.co.uk** Allows you to search by sector, salary and location; covers all kinds of fashion-related jobs

- **www.fashionunited.co.uk** Allows you to search for paid jobs and internships by type, and register your CV

- **www.freelanceuk.com**
- **www.peopleperhour.com**
- **www.freelancers.net**

Find out what a company's products or services are like and what they think their particular strengths are. Give serious thought to exactly how your skills, experience and style can fit in and help them.

you need to do some research into the company so that you can make it clear that you are genuinely interested in them and would really fit in.

Get a dialogue going

If you really want to improve your chances, you could try to develop a relationship with the employer by talking to them on the phone. This is most likely to work for a small company where the key people are involved in all aspects of the company, including hiring for entry-level positions.

The main problem with sending a CV is that if the employer isn't looking to recruit someone right away, then your CV, even if it is perfectly tailored, is likely to be filed away and quite possibly forgotten about altogether.

So, how about this as a scenario: you call up and find out the name of the person heading up the specific department of your interest; you get put through to them and explain (briefly) that you are passionate about the company and that you're looking for work at the moment. Ask if it would be okay if you were to send your CV to them: they may be slightly irritated at the interruption but possibly impressed that

you've gone to all that effort. More importantly, you've got a dialogue going.

If they come back with 'I'm afraid we're not recruiting now' or 'all these things go through our HR department', then you can pursue it by trying to find out when they think they might be recruiting, where they would advertise if they were, or ask if they would mind having a look at your CV just to give you a bit of feedback on it.

Depending on how that goes, you might either leave it there, for the time being, or try your luck with something else. If you get the impression that the person you're speaking to isn't all that intent on helping, or you feel that the two of you just don't click, then you need to be sensitive enough to leave it there. You should keep in touch – send them an updated version of your CV once you've made the changes they suggest, with a card to thank them for their help, and make sure you send them an invitation to your end-of-year show. It's also a great idea to ask them for someone else's name. If they say that they aren't recruiting at the moment, ask if they know of any other organisations who are (and for a contact name). Once you've got through to someone on the phone, make sure you take full advantage of the opportunity!

Be persistent

You've picked a tough field to get into. If you're not really motivated, there are plenty of others lining up behind you ready to take your place. Getting your foot in the door is not easy. You need to be confident in yourself and in your abilities, and you need to stick at it. Use your creativity to find new and interesting ways to approach organisations, and keep at it.

freelancing

The fashion industry employs many, many freelancers at all levels and in all areas, and this is in part because it allows businesses to be more flexible.

Even though you work for yourself, you will often still be required to fulfil an exacting brief for a client, as a freelancer. Here, a designer pins a garment on a dressmaker's dummy.

Businesses can hire professionals with different skills depending on the particular project, and don't need to go through complicated and costly processes of selection and training for their workforce. When times are tough, they can reduce their salary costs, and when a big project comes in, they can hire the exact number of staff they need for exactly the duration of the project.

What does it mean?

Working as a freelancer, or being self-employed, simply means that you are your own boss. You may get your income from selling your wares, either directly to the public (for example, selling your own jewellery, accessories or garments at a market stall, or from a website) or supplying to another business, such as selling to a shop. The other typical way to make your living freelance is by selling your services or expertise, working on a variety of short-term contracts for different employers. You might, for example, be commissioned to write a particular article, take photographs for a shoot or design some fabric prints for a particular collection. You might be asked to work on a project because you are known to have a particular skill that is needed, or you might be asked to cover for someone who is on holiday or maternity leave. Freelance contracts might be as short as half a day's work or as long as a year.

Some freelance work can be done from your own studio or office, while some clients want you to work on site so that you can interact with other members of a team. An example is a technical designer who will do sample fittings on models, making decisions with the design and merchandising team before sending corrections to the factory in Hong Kong. Or an illustrator who works directly with the art director on a new sales campaign.

Why would I want to work for myself?

One of the most fun parts of working as a freelancer is the variety of assignments and clients. You are seldom bored because you are continually taking on new challenges. The most common reason for people to want to work on a freelance basis is to gain autonomy when it comes to making decisions. For others, working freelance is simply a requirement of the profession they have chosen, or a necessity at a particular point in their career. Working for yourself means that you can do the work your own way. If you are marketing your own designs, you can design the items that you want in the way that you want; you aren't answerable to anyone else. Freelance rates tend to be much more generous than standard employee salaries, and you can pick and choose the work that you do and the people that you work with. At least,

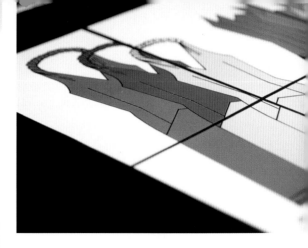

Have you got what it takes to make it as a freelancer?

- Independence
- Confidence
- Belief in your product and yourself
- A good product
- Great organisational skills
- Resilience
- Tenacity
- Willingness to learn
- Good people and networking skills
- Self-promotion
- Professionalism
- Drive

that's how it is when it's working well. In reality, at the start of a self-employed career, freelancers may find themselves in the position of having to do whatever work comes their way, when it comes their way, or having to make the products that people want to buy, rather than the ones they want to make. You may find that although you no longer have to do the work that your boss has asked you to do, you are having to do the work that your clients ask you to do. And clients can be every bit as demanding and unreasonable as managers!

One of the most fun parts of freelancing is the variety. You are seldom bored because you are continually taking on new challenges.

In some areas of the industry, freelancing is more common than in others. The retail sector is less likely to be enthusiastic about freelance sales assistants and managers, whereas if you want to make your career as a photographer, then setting up as a freelancer is more or less essential.

Freelancing is not an easy option, but it does give you a degree of freedom and flexibility that you don't have as an employee, and ultimately you know that you are working for your own benefit and not for the benefit of your managers and shareholders.

Salaries and benefits

As a freelancer you would usually charge around double the wage that you get as an employee. Although this might seem like a lot, it's not quite as lucrative as it sounds. As an employee, you get a lot of extra benefits that you don't get when you're freelance. The most obvious ones are holiday and sick pay. Employees take it for granted that they don't lose a week's pay when they go on holiday, or a day's pay if they are ill. You also lose the infrastructure that is available at work, so the cost of a new PC, a training course or even a ream of paper will all need to come out of your freelance daily rate. Retirement contributions are not something that people always think a lot about at the beginning of their careers, but in the current climate, it seems increasingly important not to assume that there will be a state pension for you when it comes to retirement. As a freelancer is it more difficult and more costly to pay into a pension, but it is very important, so don't neglect it.

Getting commissions

Freelancing is based on reputation and networks. Jobs are given to professionals that the employers know, or those who have been recommended to them by trusted colleagues. It can feel quite ruthless, as a single substandard project or a difficult relationship with a client can mean that you struggle to get more work. Although some people start their careers as freelancers, some find it easier to start off as an employee and make the transition to self-employment a little way down the line. This will allow you to learn about the industry, and start to build relationships with clients – or at least find out how that side of things works – and will allow you to start to

As a freelancer, you will be responsible for buying and maintaining your equipment and office supplies yourself.

develop your own network of colleagues and gain a reputation. Freelancers are most often hired by people they've worked with before, as the employers feel confident that they know the freelancer's work and have some confidence in their professionalism, so it's usually easier to get established as a freelancer once you've made a bit of a name for yourself in the field.

There are also companies who specialise in supplying freelancers. These companies take care of finding projects and negotiating fees with clients, and they take a commission from the compensation you receive. If you sign on with one of these companies, and perform well at the jobs they send you to, you can anticipate fairly regular work. Many new graduates start out in this way while they are looking for a full-time position.

Business skills

To be a successful freelancer you need more than creative skills. The exact skill mix that is going to be the winning combination for you will depend on your particular circumstances, but you can be confident that you will need to develop some degree of expertise in self-marketing and finance at least. How much marketing you need to do will vary tremendously. For some it might just be a case of making sure that all your contacts know that you are available for freelance work and keeping in touch with them from time to time. For others, especially those wanting to sell their goods directly to the public, the promotion, PR and marketing side of the business might end up being quite significant.

The other key area is finance. As a

freelancer, you need to do two crucial things to stay afloat. The first is to stay solvent. An important factor to consider is determining how much to charge for your freelance services and making sure you get paid. Create a contract defining exactly what services you will provide, in what time frame, the amount you are to be paid, and when. Some commissions are paid by the project, and some are paid on an hourly basis. It is up to you to work out in detail what the compensation details will be and demand that the client sticks to that. One suggestion is to ask for a retainer upfront, and pull payments from that, with your client renewing the retainer as work progresses. Another possibility is to ask for a portion of the money at regular intervals as segments of the project are completed. That way you will not invest months of work with a client who always promises to pay you next week, but never does.

The second thing is to make sure that you're paying your taxes. Although business finances and tax law can be incredibly complex, don't allow yourself to be so daunted by it all that you just bury your head in the sand and hope it all works out. It won't work out unless you make it, and if you leave it, you will be storing up significant problems for yourself that are only going to get worse and will become more time-consuming and more expensive to sort out. Besides which, you can choose to make your finances fairly straightforward. Being solvent, in essence, is about making sure that you make more money than you spend. In terms of tax, you need to remember that you will have to pay a fairly significant proportion of any profits you

Going freelance: checklist

Before you make a decision to go freelance, work through this checklist and see how well prepared you are:

1 Who are your customers?

2 How are you going to let them know about your products or services?

3 Who are your competitors?

4 What's unique about your product or services?

5 How well organised are you?

6 What are the risks?

7 How are the finances going to work?

8 Have you put a business plan together?

9 Who can help you?

10 How will you build a client base?

make to the government. If you can keep those two concepts in your mind and keep very careful track of what you spend (keep hold of all receipts!) and what you earn, then you'll know where you are and be in a position to make the right decisions. Do take advice. HMRC has advisers available at the end of the phone to help.

With both of these fields, and any other non-creative aspects of your business, there are professionals out there who can help. You can buy in the help of accountants and marketing experts who will do anything from giving you a small bit of advice right through to managing that part of your business for you entirely. Most freelancers choose to at least work with an accountant who will do their taxes once a year.

Sole trading

Another difference between employment and self-employment is that as a freelancer there is no one else to do anything. There is (usually) no one to delegate to, no one else to pick up the pieces and if you don't do it, then it won't get done. The amount of time that you will need to devote to non-creative parts of your business can take you by

surprise. If your computer needs to be fixed, there is no helpline to contact; if there is a problem with a payment, there is no payroll department to sort it out for you; and if you run out of pens, you have to go to the shop yourself. It's all up to you.

The other issue that people sometimes face as freelancers is the isolation of the work. Although you will inevitably have clients and suppliers that you will be dealing with, many freelancers say that they really miss the camaraderie and banter of the office, not to mention that having a team around you means that you have other people to bounce ideas around with, and other brains are available to help you solve problems or listen to you moaning about a difficult client.

What's the difference between freelance and self-employed?

Nothing, really. They're just different terms for the same situation, which is that you are paid directly for a particular piece of work, rather than working as an employee on an ongoing basis.

Can I be employed at the same time as being freelance?

Certainly, and many people are. It makes your tax return at the end of the year a little more complex, but it's very common for people within the fashion industry to be employed part-time and to then work freelance on their other days. This can be a great way to combine or at least compromise between a stable income and creative freedom. However, it is important to check with your primary employer that there isn't a conflict of interest or a non-compete clause in your contract.

What's a portfolio career?

A portfolio career is the term for someone who's got their fingers in lots of pies, professionally speaking. So if you work part-time as a designer, teach at an evening class twice a week and take on freelance commissions in your spare time, you could call yourself a portfolio worker.

What do I need to know about tax?

Call HMRC, or go to the www.hmrc.gov.uk website. As an employee, you pay your income tax and National Insurance through the PAYE scheme, whereby money is deducted automatically before you receive your payslip. As a freelancer, you are responsible for making these payments yourself – bi-annually in the case of tax, and quarterly for National Insurance, based on your own (or your accountant's) assessment of your earnings for each tax year. Make sure you anticipate this and withhold the appropriate amount of money from your commissions, or you will be caught short when you have to file your yearly tax return. But the good news is that as a freelancer you can deduct many of your expenses, utilities for your office or studio, your equipment, your supplies, your transport and so on, from your taxable earnings. However, taxes are an inevitable part of the picture to be considered.

Do I need a business plan?

You don't need one to start up as a freelancer, but it can be really useful for you, and if you want to borrow money from anyone, then it's a pre-requisite. A business plan doesn't need to be very complex. If it's just for your own benefit, then it can be as straightforward as working out how much money you're going to need to charge per day or for each piece of work, and how many days each month you're going to need to work in order to pay the rent. If it's for a bank loan, they will want quite a lot of detail as you will need to convince them that you have done all your research and have some good evidence that your idea is going to make some money. It's worth talking to the bank before you start putting pen to paper to find out what format and what level of detail they will want.

How do I copyright my designs?

You don't need to do anything active to copyright your ideas – they are copyrighted as soon as they are created. What's more tricky is proving when you created it, so keep an account of the work as it is created and put the © copyright symbol plus the date and your name on everything you produce. As an employee, your employer holds the copyright for your work, but if you are freelance it is your copyright unless you have made an alternative arrangement.

Some freelance work will involve working on-site, so you can work with other members of a team or perhaps use specialist equipment.

It's not always easy to work out exactly where the industry starts and ends. The government, for example, wouldn't classify selling clothes, or writing about clothes, under the banner of 'fashion and textiles', and you could argue that museum curation and teaching lie firmly within other industries. But if you've decided to read this book, then you have an interest in fashion or textiles, and included are all of the main jobs that you might find interesting, regardless of which 'sector' they fall into. ✦ The jobs in this directory are divided into the following broad sections: design, textiles, production, costume, retail, communication and education. But even then things aren't always clear-cut. Technologists and tailors, for example, belong in both the design and the production sections. ✦ For each of the jobs in this directory, the kind of information that you are going to need to make a realistic choice about your own future is included. This information is a mix of factual data and anecdotes, the kind that you might not find in a conventional careers book but that paints a real and vivid picture of what the jobs are actually like.

Descriptions of the different jobs are backed up with case studies and 'day in the life' features, and examples are given of how the roles might vary between one organisation and another. The best bits and worst bits of the job are highlighted, and the sorts of skills and attributes that make people more likely to succeed in the role are discussed. There are tips on what to study, places to go for further information and some indication of how lucrative and how competitive the jobs are.

Finally there are tips on how to get your first break in the business and how to stand out from the crowd. Don't worry too much if you haven't made your mind up at this stage. It can take years for people to decide which specialism is the right one to pursue, and even if you think you're quite clear now, it's not at all uncommon to change your mind as you learn more about the industry.

After all, the industry has changed beyond recognition over the last decade or so, so who knows what changes are to come in the next few years, or indeed what new jobs will exist by the time you finish your training? The industry is not one that pigeonholes people, and although employers like to see that you are committed and motivated to one particular field, they're also keen to see flexible staff with a broad range of interests, so keeping your options open at this stage is often a good plan.

If you do think you have an idea of the direction that you might like to take, that's great. The earlier you start working towards a clear career goal, the sooner you're likely to get there.

CHAPTER ONE

fashion design

Fashion design is one of the most well-known career areas within the industry. Most people interested in fashion probably think they have a fairly good idea of what the life of a fashion designer is like, but the reality may be a bit more complex than they imagine.

Backstage at a fashion show at Fashion Week, making last-minute adjustments to an outfit.

The term 'fashion design' covers a whole range of different jobs and, if this is your chosen career path, then you will need to make a number of decisions about which area of fashion design is going to suit you best.

With all of the available specialisms it is possible to change your mind and shift your direction later on in your career, but if you do know from the start exactly which area of the design industry attracts you, then you're going to be in a better position to get relevant work experience, target your portfolio and student collection most appropriately and make some of those all-important connections in exactly the right field.

You can split the fashion design industry up in all sorts of different ways, but some of the key distinctions are:

- Type of business
- Kind of employment
- Garment categories

There are three main types of business – haute couture, designer ready-to-wear (prêt-à-porter) and high street – and within each of these there are different kinds of employment; you can be employed by someone else (an individual designer, a supplier or a retailer), work freelance (working on a variety of short-term contracts for a range of different employers) or set up your own label. The third distinction is based on the kinds of garments you design. The most obvious distinctions are between menswear and womenswear, but designers can also specialise in areas such as childrenswear, lingerie, bridal, sportswear, knitwear and tailoring, along with many others.

There are some differences both in the process and the culture associated with these different sections of the industry, which we will look at in the following sections, but the jobs will be variations around a common theme. Essentially the designer is employed to come up with ideas for garments, a range or a collection that will sell.

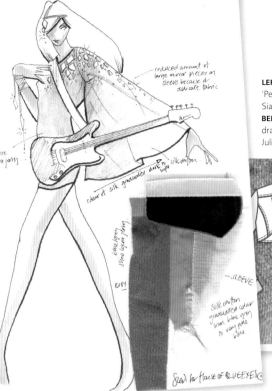

LEFT Sketch entitled 'Performance piece' by Sian for Tallulah Rendell.
BELOW 'Flats', or working drawings, of a jacket by Julie Armstrong.

The fashion design process:

- Research into trends, lifestyle, customers and competitors (could be done in conjunction with buyers, merchandisers and forecasters).
- Come up with the concept for the collection, and develop mood boards.
- Work on design specifics for the collections – sketch silhouettes and details (pockets, fastenings, lines), and select materials and trims. You might visit trade shows to look at yarns and fabrics.
- Draw up a technical flat and a spec (working with garment technologists) including measurements, colours, construction details and all information needed to make the garment.
- Send the spec to a factory to make up samples.
- Check the samples (you might make small changes to the fit or details such as pockets at this stage).
- Talk to buyers and merchandisers to check that they think the garments will sell – make changes if needed.
- Get the samples signed off and start either taking orders or getting clothes produced.

Time lines will vary enormously, with this process taking anything from 18 months right down to six weeks for the fast-fashion chain stores. Different designers will work with a different number of seasons each year (usually four, three or two). Different companies may have a varied number of delivery periods within each season, sometimes delivering a new assortment each month or one large collection a season.

Junior designers in large companies will be more likely to focus on one or two parts of this process, as they will work within a clear hierarchy of designers and colleagues who specialise, for example, in forecasting or colours, whereas in a small design team or if you work by yourself, you could get involved in the whole process.

> *The fashion industry is built on who you know, and you will only get work if people know you and like working with you.*

What makes a good fashion designer?

All fashion designers need to have technical know-how, commercial sense and interpersonal skills. Technical know-how includes an understanding of colour and how to build a colour palette, knowledge of fabrics and how they respond to the shape of the body, comprehension of the engineering needed to create garments, the ability to sketch well and familiarity with CAD (Photoshop and Illustrator).

A designer also requires creativity, research skills and the ability to translate fashion trends. These talents will be used across the board in fashion design, but their relative

A designer checks the fit of a complicated fitted bodice on a dressmaker's dummy.

importance will vary from one design role to another (for example, fabrics might be thought of as particularly crucial in menswear, shape in womenswear and engineering in bras and suits).

Commercial sense is an intuitive understanding of what designs will work on the catwalk or the sales floor. You need to know who your customers are, what they wear, how they wear it, why they wear it, what they will pay and who else they might be buying from. And you need to be able to apply this analysis to your designs: How can I make this outfit more cheaply? How can I ensure that my customers like my designs more than those of my competitors?

Finally, interpersonal skills are more important than you might imagine. You will never be working alone. The kinds of relationships will vary from one role to another, but they will always be critical to success. Designers work in teams with other designers, buyers, suppliers, merchandisers, pattern cutters, garment technologists and many others, so you need to be able to work effectively with these people, recognise and respond to their expertise and explain your own ideas clearly and with passion. Even if you are designing and making by yourself, your relationships with your fabric suppliers and your customers are key, and however you work, your work will be better and more widely known if you can foster good relationships with those around you.

More perhaps even than this, the fashion industry is built on who you know, and you will only get work if people know you and like working with you.

Two illustrations from designer
Nicholas Ashburn's portfolio.

Best bits

- ▲ Being able to be creative
- ▲ Seeing your design ideas being worn
- ▲ Travelling – suppliers, factories and customers are often all over the world

Worst bits

- ▼ Hours can be unpredictable and you can feel that the job is taking over your life
- ▼ You can never be sure that your designs will be successful; it can be very disappointing when something that you have spent months working on does not sell

Routes in

A relevant degree is more or less essential and there are institutions worldwide where you can study fashion- and textiles-related courses. Work experience – usually unpaid – is commonplace, though even this can be competitive; experience of any kind on the retail side of the business is very useful. A strong network is your greatest asset, so make sure that you keep in touch with all colleagues and contacts from your course and any work experience that you do, and go out of your way to meet and keep in touch with new people who might be able to send some work your way in the future. When applying for a job, you should always show a portfolio that addresses the particular brand's aesthetic. If the interviewer sees potential, they will generally give you a project to complete to see if you are a good match for the company.

Links

The Appointment has job vacancies in fashion, as well as retail and hospitality. www.theappointment.co.uk

British Graduate Fashion Week: have a look at what graduates are producing this year. www.gfw.org.uk

Can U Cut It?: for careers information and case studies. www.canucutit.co.uk

Drapers Online has industry news and job vacancies. www.drapersonline.com

Womenswear as a whole is the biggest area within fashion design. One of the designer's main roles is to interpret current trends in a way that is going to appeal to the customers.

womenswear designer

Trends are key in this field, so timing is everything. Although many high street and ready-to-wear designer collections can take up to 18 months to prepare, some fashion-forward retailers get garments into their stores within six weeks. This makes working in womenswear highly pressurised. Customers have become more and more demanding and these days like to see different clothes in a shop every time they visit it.

Routes in
There are a lot of fashion design courses and the vast majority of fashion design students specialise in womenswear, from ready-to-wear to high street. If you want to make a career in womenswear design, you need to start thinking about your own niche. Do you want to work on designer ready-to-wear collections, or would you prefer to work for chain stores? Are you interested in the fast pace of the fashion-forward retailers (such as Top Shop and Zara), or would you prefer to work at a more moderately paced, traditional label like Marks & Spencer? The clearer you are about your preferred market, the better. You can aim your portfolio and collections towards the place you ultimately want to work, and you can try to get an internship in the kind of place you hope to end up – this will allow you to start making the right contacts and it will make you look committed and focused on your CV.

CASE STUDY:

Maria is the VP for Armani Exchange Womenswear.

Images and pieces from Armani's collection.

Maria studied on one of the most prestigious fashion courses in the world. One of the main things that Maria feels she got from the course was a great network of like-minded people at the same stage in their careers. She got a bit of freelance work during her course, and then when she had finished her final collection, she invited these contacts to her show and managed to sell some of her ranges on a sale-or-return basis. Maria has worked in a really interesting range of roles. She's worked for Top Shop, All Saints and Gap and has owned her own label. She now works at Armani Exchange. Her advice to someone thinking about womenswear is: 'Be true to yourself. Develop your unique vision but be open to experiences.'

Best bits
- ▲ You get to use all your creativity: colours, shapes, fabrics
- ▲ If you love ever-changing trends, it's fantastic to work in the heart of the industry

Worst bits
- ▼ It can be highly pressurised, and working with colleagues who are also all under pressure can have its drawbacks

Skills needed
- Ability to cope with pressure and high volumes of work
- An interest in and instinct for trends
- Strong design skills
- Resilience

Study
- Research methods
- Flat pattern cutting
- Modelling on the stand
- Garment construction
- Tailoring processes
- Technical specification
- Illustration

Links
Drapers Online: for industry news and opportunities. www.drapersonline.co.uk An excellent range of **entry-level design jobs**. www.arts.ac.uk/student/careers/creative-opportunities.htm
Careers information, advice and links. www.prospects.ac.uk

Rating
Average salary: ● ● ●
Entrance difficulty: ● ● ●

Stand out from the crowd
It's all about fashion. Know your trends and think about how these could work for your customers.

The menswear market has grown dramatically over the last few years, with magazines and high-end fashion stores promoting a more image-conscious generation of men.

menswear designer

The design process for menswear is broadly similar to that for womenswear and other areas of design, but there are a few differences that are worth noting. First, although menswear has become much more fashion-conscious over recent years, it is still nowhere near as trend-led as womenswear. This means that the turnaround time for menswear tends to be far longer than for womenswear – collections are likely to be planned months rather than weeks before they are seen in shops, and there tend to be fewer deliveries, or 'drops' per season. While styles don't always change dramatically from season to season, designers create subtle, but important, changes in proportion and detailing. Although their collections usually do carry variations of traditional jackets and trousers, many young designers are very innovative and creative in silhouette, styling, and combinations of fabrics and textures. An understanding of fabrics and yarns, as well as a knowledge of tailoring, can be a real advantage. Finally, the culture of menswear departments (in general) is often thought to be less aggressive than womenswear because it is often a little less pressurised and a little less competitive.

Within menswear you can specialise in men's suiting, knitwear or formalwear, and there are also opportunities to work in sportswear, specialising in areas such as surfwear and cycling.

Routes in
Specialise as early as you can and get as much menswear work experience in as many different places as you can while you're studying.

Best bits
▲ Although still a long-hours culture, menswear is in general run at a more moderate pace than womenswear
▲ Longer lead-in times and changes that are less dramatic from one season to the next makes this a relatively less pressurised environment

Worst bits
▼ You may end up feeling that your creativity is being limited
▼ Garments are not usually as on-trend as in womenswear, so this may be frustrating if you are really interested in the latest styles

Skills needed
• General fashion design skills
• A good understanding of fabrics
• Attention to detail

CASE STUDY:

Jason works as a senior menswear designer for a cycling clothing company.

Jason did a degree in menswear design and started off with his own label of menswear sports clothing. For a few years he was really successful, but things stopped going so well and he found that he needed to get himself a job. He spent some time working as a designer for a small surf brand, but found that he didn't really enjoy this; it's more difficult to be as creative as when designing under your own name. Jason finds that he is much more suited to designing cycling wear. Within this field there is a real sense of a design community all passionate about the same thing. His advice? 'Don't rush to get your own brand. Learn from the place you're working first. Make contacts – they might invest at a later date.'

Study
• Research methods
• Flat pattern cutting
• Modelling on the stand
• Garment construction
• Tailoring
• Technical drawing
• Illustration

Links
British Menswear Guild
www.british-menswear-guild.co.uk
Drapers Online: for industry news and opportunities. www.drapersonline.co.uk
Entry-level design jobs. www.arts.ac.uk/student/careers/creative-opportunities.htm

Rating
Average salary: ● ● ●
Entrance difficulty: ● ● ○

Stand out from the crowd
Love your textiles. It's all about fabric.

Haute couture is seen as the pinnacle of fashion design. Top-end designers produce catwalk collections each year that are enormously influential, without being wearable or affordable for most.

haute couture designer

Image from Jean-Paul Gaultier's Autumn/Winter Haute Couture show, Paris Fashion Week.

Haute couture designs are perhaps most usefully categorised as art, not fashion, and are often used by a designer as an opportunity to try out ideas before putting together a ready-to-wear collection. Pieces are created as custom, one-of-a-kind items, tailored to the particular person who will be wearing them. Couture designers include Jean-Paul Gaultier, Christian Lacroix and Valentino.

Collections are shown on the catwalks in Paris, and this contributes to the status of Paris – generally acknowledged worldwide – as the home of fashion.

Debates continue to run about the need for the haute couture collections, as they are time-consuming, vastly expensive and not profitable. Designers look on them as a sort of 'loss leader' – a way to cement their brand and give them the exposure and coverage that then allows them to sell ready-to-wear collections and perfumes at a great profit.

Routes in

The haute couture designers in Paris are always looking for graduates to come and work in their studios. They will often employ a number of interns at any one time, so if you go over to Paris with your portfolio, some charm and quite a bit of persistence, you may well get lucky. Whether or not you enjoy yourself is another matter; it's sensible to consider what you want to get out of your time with the designer and negotiate that with them at the beginning.

It's rare to work your way up from such a placement. The

designers like the fresh enthusiasm and the cheapness of new graduates, but few get taken on permanently. Your experience will teach you about the process, the suppliers and the techniques – and will look brilliant on your CV.

Best bits

▲ You will get to work with incredible designers on some of the most influential collections in the fashion world
▲ If you are talented and skilled, you may get to make design contributions

Worst bits

▼ Intern roles are almost invariably unpaid, and you are usually expected to work extremely hard, do long hours and get your hands well and truly dirty – sometimes quite literally

Skills needed

• Creativity and hard work
• Charm
• Persistence and a good dose of luck

Study

• Fabric types
• Research methods
• Flat pattern cutting
• Modelling on the stand
• Garment construction
• Tailoring processes
• Technical specification
• Illustration

Links

Chambre Syndicale de la Couture Parisienne
www.modeaparis.com
Claire Shaeffer authors books on couture sewing techniques.
http://claireshaeffer.com
The Victoria and Albert Museum
www.vam.ac.uk

Rating

Average salary: ● ● ●
Entrance difficulty: ● ● ●

Stand out from the crowd

Actually going to Paris with your portfolio and CV is probably the best way to get noticed. Send colour copies of your work as a 'teaser'.

High-end designers and design houses produce catwalk collections that are shown at the fashion weeks in Milan, Paris, New York and London. These collections are on sale in designer shops, boutiques and department stores and inspire the rest of the apparel industry.

ready-to-wear designer

L ead times for ready-to-wear tend to be fairly generous, with collections being planned as much as 18 months before the catwalk shows, and budgets are substantially more generous than for high street fashion. These are the clothes that are seen on the rich and famous, and are occasionally bought by ordinary consumers on sale. The design process within ready-to-wear is usually a very creative and conceptual one. The collections will be led by concepts and personalities, and can be inspired by anything that the designers choose – from architecture and film to landscapes.

The designers who produce haute couture collections will also usually produce ready-to-wear collections, but in addition there is a vast number of other designers who will showcase their ready-to-wear collections on the catwalks. This could range from the cutting-edge anarchy of Vivienne Westwood and Alexander McQueen to the quintessentially English looks of Gieves & Hawkes and Paul Smith.

Routes in

Design houses have a great tradition of using interns. As an intern you will have the opportunity to work with some incredible designers, and you may even get to see some of your ideas appear on the catwalk. The work is hard, hours are long, you will usually not get paid and you are expected to accept this and work with good humour and gratitude. Intern jobs are rarely advertised so you need to approach the design houses on spec. Make sure your letter and CV is tailored to the particular designer. You will almost always need to follow up with a phone call and a visit, always trying to tread that fine line between getting yourself noticed and being pushy.

Best bits
▲ Pushing yourself creatively
▲ Working with creative colleagues
▲ The glamour!

Worst bits
▼ Not nearly as well paid as you might imagine
▼ Longer hours, harder work and tougher competition than the rest of the industry

Skills needed
• Lots of creativity
• An interest in high fashion
• Tenacity and resilience
• Good technical skills

Study
• Research methods
• Flat pattern cutting
• Modelling on the stand
• Garment construction
• Tailoring processes
• Technical specification
• Illustration

Links
Drapers Online is the newspaper for UK fashion, with industry news and job vacancies. www.drapersonline.com
British Graduate Fashion Week: have a look at what graduates are producing this year. www.gfw.org.uk An excellent range of **entry-level design jobs**. www.arts.ac.uk/student/careers/creative-opportunities.htm

Rating
Average salary: ● ● ●
Entrance difficulty: ● ● ●

Stand out from the crowd
Don't give up. There are plenty of stories around about successful designers who made 20 or more applications to the same design house before being accepted. One application is usually not enough.

Image from Paul Smith's Spring/Summer show.

The demands placed on high street chain store designers have changed a lot in the last few years. Across the board, fashion is moving faster, and customers are expecting more variety, more change and more speed.

high street designer

The culture and working conditions will vary greatly depending on what kind of chain store you work for. Fast-fashion chains such as Top Shop can turn clothes around remarkably quickly, with versions of ready-to-wear designer collections appearing in shops just a few weeks after they are seen on the catwalk. Their customers are young and fashion-conscious and won't wait. Some large chain stores have more mixed customers; their fashions do not need to provide such instant gratification, so lead-in times can be months rather than weeks.

Different companies will have different structures, in part dependent on the size of the organisation. You might be asked to specialise in a broad area such as formalwear or casual wear, or something more specific such as knitwear or tailoring.

Designers work in multi-disciplinary teams with buyers, merchandisers, technologists and fabric suppliers. It will usually be the merchandisers who give the designers a brief for the collections, which they will base on fashion forecasts, catwalk trends, sales histories and knowledge of their customers. Designers will then work to produce collections that are affordable and that will appeal to their customers. Profit is the bottom line for high street designers and the key to success is a high turnover, so designers need to know their customers well. Profit margins are small and timescales are tight so the job can feel pressurised, and creativity takes second place to sales figures.

Routes in
Getting into this area of fashion design really depends on knowing the right people. The way to do this is to look for unpaid work experience and then, once you have a position, make yourself indispensable. From there you might hope to be offered a junior position and work your way up.

Best bits
▲ Your designs are made into thousands of garments
▲ This is one of the best-paid areas of fashion design

Worst bits
▼ This would usually be seen as a less creative place to work than the catwalks, as you need to follow the trends that have been set, and produce designs to suit the budgets and particular needs of your customers

Skills needed
• Teamwork, communication and negotiation
• An understanding of your customers
• A interest in the business and sales side of things
• Strong organisational skills

Study
• Research methods
• Flat pattern cutting
• Modelling on the stand
• Garment construction
• Tailoring processes
• Technical specification
• Illustration, CAD

Links
Drapers Online is the newspaper for UK fashion, with industry news and job vacancies. www.drapersonline.com
British Graduate Fashion Week: have a look at what graduates are producing this year. www.gfw.org.uk
An excellent range of **entry-level design jobs**. www.arts.ac.uk/student/careers/creative-opportunities.htm

Rating
Average salary: ● ● ●
Entrance difficulty: ● ● ○

Stand out from the crowd
Work on the sales floor, and get to know your customers.

Many fashion design students dream about owning their own label. For the lucky few the rewards are great: fame, fortune and creative autonomy. But success relies on great design, excellent business skills and a lot of luck.

own-label designer

Grey and white 'Napoleonic' coat from Amin Anthony Phillips' Spring collection.

The biggest issue facing designers trying to set up on their own is finance. The upfront costs can often be prohibitive: one useful way to get some exposure for your collection is to exhibit at a trade fair, but it will cost you upwards of £10,000 just for the exhibition space and to make up your samples. Added to this, buyers are usually very risk-averse and may want to wait until they've seen you there for a couple of years before they're prepared to take a chance on you.

As an employed designer, you are part of an infrastructure. Even in the smallest of companies, there will be someone else who will buy your desk, set up the website and arrange for you to get paid. If it's your own label, then it's all up to you, and you either need to do it yourself or arrange for someone else to do it.

Routes in

There are many different ways to start your own label. Some of the most successful designers started their careers as employed designers and learned about the business side of things from the inside before setting up on their own. Others managed to find some funding from a venture capitalist (think *Dragon's Den*), or win a competition. Market stalls can be good places to start too; places like Camden and Spitalfields where you can sell your wares once a week with very low overheads. The Internet is another great resource for those with low budgets and is an excellent place to get some exposure. Do get yourself some business advice – if you have a good business plan, some understanding of the tax system and an idea of how to market yourself, you will stand a much better chance of success.

Best bits
▲ Creative freedom; you can design what you want
▲ Being involved in all aspects of fashion – not just design

Worst bits
▼ Trying to make ends meet
▼ Not being in control of things like the cost of materials and the strength of your local currency

Skills needed
• A range of business skills
• Flexibility and the ability to respond to opportunities
• Self-belief
• An innovative design sense and strong design skills

If it's your own label, then it's all up to you, and you either need to do a task yourself or arrange for someone else to do it.

Study
• Research methods
• Flat pattern cutting
• Modelling on the stand
• Garment construction
• Tailoring processes
• Technical specification
• Illustration

Links
Lots of **information, advice and support** on setting up your own business. www.ecca-london.org
National Council for Graduate Entrepreneurship www.ncge.com
Support for emerging fashion designers www.fashion-enter.com
HMRC www.hmrc.gov.uk

Rating
Average salary: ● ● ●
Entrance difficulty: ● ● ●

Stand out from the crowd
Get blogging. It's a great way to raise your profile without spending any money.

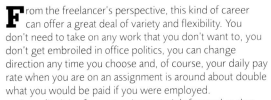

It is very common for designers to work as freelancers at some point in their careers. Many retailers and suppliers use freelancers as they can be a more flexible and less expensive solution to staffing logistics.

freelance designer

From the freelancer's perspective, this kind of career can offer a great deal of variety and flexibility. You don't need to take on any work that you don't want to, you don't get embroiled in office politics, you can change direction any time you choose and, of course, your daily pay rate when you are on an assignment is around about double what you would be paid if you were employed.

In reality it is often not quite as straightforward as that, and although you might think that you're going to be able to choose only jobs that inspire you, in practice you might find, certainly at the start of your freelance career, that it's sensible to accept any work that comes your way. On top of this, freelancers often find that they miss the security and companionship of being employed, so do think hard about the lifestyle implications of this route.

The major difference between the day-to-day work of a freelancer and that of the employed designer is the breadth of focus. As a freelance designer, you are often commissioned just to design, for instance. You are given a brief and asked to produce some ideas and sketches, but your role finishes when the buyers accept your designs. Or you might be working at a computer doing flats all day. As an employed designer you are much more likely to be involved in the whole process.

A successful freelance career is about more than being a great designer, it's about selling yourself as a great designer.

Routes in
The easiest route to self-employment is to start your career in an employed capacity. Get a job first and you will learn about the industry, find out what an employer wants from a freelance designer and the best way to sell yourself and make some solid contacts. You can also list yourself with agencies.

Best bits
▲ Freedom, autonomy and independence
▲ Diversity of design projects

Worst bits
▼ Professional and financial uncertainty
▼ Having to do your own tax return
▼ Lack of work-related benefits

Skills needed
• Self-promotion and networking
• Self-motivation
• Understanding of accounting (or get a good accountant)
• Strong design and technical skills
• Ability to adapt to new situations quickly

Study
• Research methods
• Flat pattern cutting
• Modelling on the stand
• Garment construction
• Tailoring processes
• Technical specification
• Illustration, CAD

Links
Lots of **information, advice and support** on setting up your own business. www.ecca-london.org
National Council for Graduate Entrepreneurship www.ncge.com
Support for emerging fashion designers www.fashion-enter.com
HMRC www.hmrc.gov.uk

Rating
Average salary:
Entrance difficulty: ● ● ●

Stand out from the crowd
You need to sell yourself and your work to potential employers. Brush up on your networking skills – it's all about who you know and who knows you.

Designers who are employed (as opposed to freelancers) usually work either for a brand (to be sold as 'private label') or for a supplier, doing licensee work.

designer for a supplier

An example of a supplier is Courtaulds, who design and make all the hosiery for Marks & Spencer in the UK. The supplier isn't usually a very well-known brand for fashion itself and may be making garments for different brands and retailers at the same time. Courtaulds, for example, as well as making the M&S lingerie range also make Pretty Polly tights, and make hosiery for about a dozen other retailers.

While the design process will be fairly similar whether you are an in-house designer or you design for a supplier, the nature of the day-to-day job, the culture, and the skills needed are usually quite different. As a designer for an in-house brand, you are more involved in every stage of the process, so where an in-house design team would work with the buyers, merchandisers and directors to decide on the concepts and trends for the new season, the designer for a supplier would be simply presented with a brief by the merchandiser. In some cases, the supplier designer then needs to win the business. In that case, they would work up some ideas and sketches for the client, and at this stage might be competing with other suppliers who have also been asked to present ideas. The designers who succeed working for a supplier tend to be those who are very commercially savvy, good at negotiation and who have excellent customer service skills. You can't rely on your design skills alone in this arena.

Routes in
Getting some work experience for a retail in-house designer is a good idea so you can demonstrate that you understand the clients, and getting exposure to different areas of the industry can really stand you in good stead. Beyond that it's about making contacts, impressing people and not giving up.

Best bits
▲ You can often work your way up the career ladder relatively quickly
▲ Combining business skills with creative skills

Worst bits
▼ Can be cut-throat and stressful

Skills needed
- Strong negotiation skills
- Expertise in handling client relations
- Sales skills
- Strong design skills

Study
- Research methods
- Flat pattern cutting
- Modelling on the stand
- Garment construction
- Tailoring processes
- Technical specification
- Illustration, CAD

Links
Drapers Online: for industry news and opportunities. www.drapersonline.co.uk
An excellent range of **entry-level design jobs**. www.arts.ac.uk/student/careers/creative-opportunities.htm
Careers information, advice and links. www.prospects.ac.uk

Rating
Average salary: ● ● ○
Entrance difficulty: ● ● ○

Stand out from the crowd
Think hard about your clients and your customers and understand what the differences in what they want are.

The concept of 'underwear as outerwear' and the development of casual loungewear have taken lingerie and sleepwear in new directions. Lingerie design now has to work at the fast pace that used to be reserved for womenswear.

lingerie designer

The process of lingerie design is broadly similar to any other area of design, but there are some key differences both in the culture and in the technical side of things. The lingerie industry is far smaller than the womenswear industry, so designers may find it easier to develop and maintain relationships with suppliers and other contacts. The design process, particularly for bras, is highly technical and is perhaps more complex than for other areas of womenswear as the focus needs to be on a combination of lifestyle, fit, function and fashion.

Routes in
A degree is not essential, but given how competitive the field is, you may well struggle without one. Bras are the most technical aspect of lingerie design and for this you would be better off with a specialist degree, but for other areas within lingerie a more general fashion design degree is enough.

Best bits
▲ The challenge of dealing with such a complex area of fashion design and the variety this provides
▲ Working with clothes that are so important to women

Worst bits
▼ Still having to work hard to convince senior managers of the importance of lingerie compared to other areas of womenswear

Skills needed
• Passion for the product
• High degree of technical knowledge in specific production techniques
• Meticulous attention to detail

DAY IN THE LIFE:
Lingerie designer

Victoria has designed lingerie for high street stores and a designer brand. Her speciality is bra design.

9.00AM CONCEPT DEVELOPMENT
Victoria selects fabrics, colours, prints and trims, then creates a concept board with photos and swatches.

10.30AM SKETCHING PHASE
Satin balconette bra designs are drawn. Victoria's finished drawings are very detailed and precise.

12.00PM TECHNICAL MEETING
The design studio has an in-house moulding facility and bra-making machinery, so the first sample can be ready this afternoon.

1.00PM MEETING PRINT ARTISTS
After purchasing three prints, Victoria requests recolourations, providing colour chips matching her palette.

2.30PM MODEL CALL
Victoria chooses three models to be measured and fitted.

3.30PM FIT MEETING
The first sample of the new bra is ready. Another sample is requested and the measurements revised.

3.30PM SPEC PACKAGES
Victoria prepares a comprehensive spec package for the factory in China.

Study
• Primary research, drawing and design development
• Pattern cutting
• Design
• Production
• Bra construction
• Contour design and illustration
• Computer-aided design (CAD) for contour fashion
• Style and colour prediction

Links
De Montfort University: the only specialist lingerie BA course in the UK. www.dmu.ac.uk
Drapers Online is the newspaper for UK fashion, with industry news and job vacancies. www.drapersonline.com
An excellent range of **entry-level design jobs**. www.arts.ac.uk/student/careers/creative-opportunities.htm

Rating
Average salary: ● ● ○
Entrance difficulty: ● ● ○

Stand out from the crowd
Lingerie is different from other areas of fashion. Think about your customers and their relationship with their lingerie.

A successful career within fashion design is often about combining focus towards a particular goal with the ability to notice opportunities and take advantage of them, even if they're not quite what you originally had in mind.

fashion design – other specialisms

This is an industry where skills are transferable: a degree in fashion design, specialising in womenswear, will teach you about fabrics, silhouettes, techniques, trends and customers, which can be applied equally to designing suits for men, pyjamas for children, sports socks or bridal lingerie. People do recognise the transferability of these skills, and the industry is full of people who started off here and ended up there. Having said that, it is a very competitive business, often built around personal networks. If you specialise in one field then you are going to meet lots of people within that area, and you're going to be able to give potential employers some proof that you have already done exactly the sort of thing you're applying to do.

The degree to which your role is narrowed down is partly determined by the size of the organisation you end up working for.

So the message is: don't panic if you don't know where you want to end up, but if you do know where you want to end up, take full advantage of your clarity and do everything you can to work towards it.

There are many areas you can specialise in, and the degree to which your role is narrowed down is partly determined by the size of the organisation you end up working for. In general, the smaller the organisation the broader your role is likely to be. On these few pages are some of the more common areas you might be drawn to.

Sportswear designer

This might include both performance-enhancing sports clothing and the kind of sportswear worn as ordinary leisurewear. You might therefore find yourself working closely with garment and fabric technologists to achieve fabric that makes the body more streamlined and aerodynamic, or that absorbs sweat without getting wet, while also looking at catwalk trends. Different sports areas have their own clear identities, and the styles you would produce for surfwear would be quite distinct from cycling garments and skating apparel.

Mood board showing inspiration for sportswear by Julie Armstrong.

Bridalwear designer

A wedding dress is usually the most significant item of clothing a woman will ever own. It's got to embody childhood dreams along with hopes for the future. Wedding dresses are expensive, luxurious, sumptuous and beautiful. They are also almost always white or ivory (this might be frustrating if you love colour!), and it's usually the bride who is in charge ('I want more frills. . .'). There's a requirement for constant fittings, rather like couture. You can work for a design house producing dresses for the mass market, or you may work on one-of-a-kind dresses made for the individual. Bridalwear encompasses a tremendous range, from Alexander McQueen to Berkertex – both highly successful but at opposite ends of the market spectrum.

ABOVE A sketch for a wedding dress design by Anita Massarella.
BELOW Sources of inspiration pinned to the studio wall.

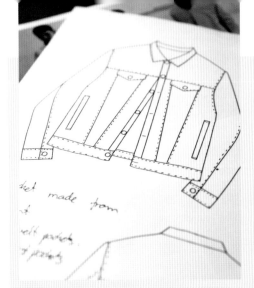

Technical flat drawings for a denim jacket design.

Denim designer

As a denim designer you work with only one fabric, so you need to know everything about it, and because you are dealing with only one fabric, you need to be extremely creative with your ideas and designs. As a denim designer you will also need to experiment with washes, finishes, prints and trimmings, and must apply the season's trends to the cuts and silhouettes that will work in denim.

Denim has evolved a lot in the relatively short time it has been a fashion staple. Lightweight construction is one of the biggest recent developments, and the 'jeggings' that hit the high street a few years ago are still bestsellers. One of the key ways to innovate is through the use of new denim blends and finishes.

Uniform designer

Uniforms are not seen as the most glamorous element of the fashion design industry, but as a design challenge they can be really interesting. Uniforms, whether for a fast-food chain, a building site or the military, need to be extremely functional and absolutely fit for purpose, and although following trends is not the first priority, the garments still need to be relatively in line with current fashions.

Childrenswear designer

Childrenswear is increasingly similar to grown-up wear. Little girls want to look like their mothers and little boys want to wear just what their dads are wearing, so focus on trends and short timelines are becoming issues. But the real challenge here is incorporating all the other things that children need such as expandable waists, stain-resistant fabrics, glow-in-the-dark features and character motifs, while ensuring that you understand the legislation around children's clothing and that you appeal to the mums as well as the children. Safety is always an important consideration.

Technical illustrations for children's outerwear by Julie Armstrong.

Eveningwear designer

Designing eveningwear is quite a specialism. First of all the fabrics that tend to be used for eveningwear are different from those commonly used in the rest of womenswear, so designers need to become familiar with the properties and behaviour of fabrics such as silk and organza. Trimmings are often a key part of eveningwear designs, so designers need to learn about such techniques as beading, lace making and applying corsages – even if you won't be making these elements yourself, you need to know about them and be able to brief others in making them to your specifications. Finally, the structure of the garments is crucial to the success of many eveningwear dresses, so designers need to become familiar with skills such as boning. Eveningwear designers are often drawn to this field because of the joy of working with such luxurious materials and designing garments that are very special to the wearer.

Designer Antonia Pugh-Thomas at work in her studio.

Knitwear designer

Knitwear is a design specialism that can take you beyond garment design to accessories, soft furnishings and interiors. In addition to the understanding of silhouettes, colours and trends that is needed for all areas of garment design, knitwear designers need to know their yarns (types of yarn, weights of yarn, durability of the fabric produced) and need to have specialist knowledge of knit constructions, stitch structures and the technical capabilities of a knitting machine.

A sketch design for a knit garment by Kitty Dong.

Technologists use their understanding of the science of fabric to ensure quality, and they work to produce new kinds of fabrics and garments that can improve the look, feel, fit or durability of our clothes.

garment technologist

Technologists can have quite different kinds of jobs depending on where they work and which products they work on. Some are drawn to the technical engineering required in the areas of tailoring and lingerie, others like the variety and breadth that you get in womenswear. Some jobs are very quality-assurance based, whereas others are more creative and innovation-led. Technicians work within the fields of fabrics or garments, and may work for a production company, a designer or a retailer.

Quality

The technologist (or quality assurance manager) is responsible for making sure that all garments are fit for purpose. A customer will expect that all size 12 dresses are the same size, and all longer length trousers are the same length; they will demand that the garments are well made and don't fall apart within a few weeks; they don't want the colour to fade or run, and they will expect that the garments won't shrink after a wash.

The quality assurance manager will be involved in the garment production process from beginning to end. You might be asked to advise on the suitability of fabrics for particular designs, be integral in developing measurements, be involved in fittings, and invited to check that the colours are right. When that's all done, the whole process of checking that the garments are fit for the purpose is up to you. You need to wash them and stretch them and get people to wear them for a while; you need to check for pilling and seams splitting, colours fading or stitches puckering, and you need to carry out spot checks on garments before they are packed up and sent to the stores. In some fields, such as home furnishings or childrenswear, you also need to ensure legal compliance.

Finally, it is the responsibility of the technologist to deal with any feedback on any of the issues mentioned, so if complaints are made and items returned as a result of any technical problems it is the job of the quality team to identify what went wrong and to ensure it doesn't happen again!

Innovation

Innovation will look very different in different product areas, but essentially the technologists are trying to identify or create new kinds of fabric or new ways to make garments that will make their company more competitive, either through the garments selling better or costing less.

The technologist will need to be aware of the customers, the competition and the emerging technologies and will put the three together to produce new ideas. For example,

Study

- Garment quality control
- Textiles science
- Pattern making and garment construction
- Textile testing

Links

The Association of Suppliers to the British Clothing Industry have a student membership association, which is a great place to network. They sponsor a graduate dissertation prize each year. www.asbci.co.uk
Lots of **news and information** and 'emerging talent award' for recent graduates. www.interiortextiles.co.uk

Rating

Average salary: ● ● ●
Entrance difficulty: ● ● ●

Stand out from the crowd

Learn a language. English is the *lingua franca* of the fashion industry, but if you can speak a little Mandarin, Cantonese, Spanish or Hindi, then you will be all the more welcome abroad.

A technologist checks a consignment of jackets. It is vital to ensure that each garment reaches the required standard.

developments in the production of elastane in Japan have led to ladder-resistant tights; memory foam developed in the Far East has led to bras that permanently mould to the shape of your body on the inside of the garment to give perfect fit and support while retaining a smooth outline; and scuff-resistant leather has become a bestseller in children's shoes.

Many garment technologists work closely with design teams to research and source new fabrics for the collections. In search of the newest textiles and yarns, the technologists travel widely, going to European and domestic fabric shows and continually exploring the latest offerings from all of their local fabric vendors.

Two emerging trends have had a huge impact on the role of the product developer: ethics and the environment. The press coverage and rising strength of public feeling about health and safety, and the wages and conditions provided by factories overseas, has meant that retailers and suppliers need to monitor their production companies very closely. As they often have some of the closest relationships with the

factories, this role often falls to the technologist, who needs to make spot checks to ensure that the factories are safe, the workers are over 16 and that they are paid a living wage.

The second area is the environment. This has had an influence on the technologist's priorities, as they are now expected to provide garments that are made from responsibly sourced materials and that are as carbon neutral as possible while still remaining competitively priced.

Routes in

The old-fashioned apprenticeship has more or less disappeared and these days technologists need to have a degree in textiles technology or something similar. The wholesale shift of manufacturing to plants overseas means that most technologists will spend at least some part of their career working abroad, close to the production companies.

Best bits

- ▲ Seeing things sell in stores and seeing a positive press reaction
- ▲ Being creative in order to get the commercial advantage from the technologies
- ▲ Travel overseas
- ▲ Discovering innovative fabrics and yarns

Worst bits

- ▼ When things go wrong and items either don't sell well or need to be withdrawn from the sales floor

Skills needed

- • Technical knowledge
- • Good communication skills
- • Creativity

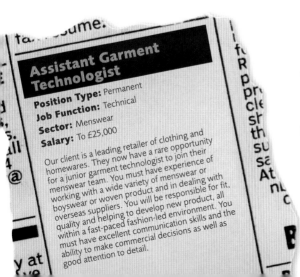

Assistant Garment Technologist

Position Type: Permanent
Job Function: Technical
Sector: Menswear
Salary: To £25,000

Our client is a leading retailer of clothing and homewares. They now have a rare opportunity for a junior garment technologist to join their menswear team. You must have experience of working with a wide variety of menswear or boyswear or woven product and in dealing with overseas suppliers. You will be responsible for fit, quality and helping to develop new product, all within a fast-paced fashion-led environment. You must have excellent communication skills and the ability to make commercial decisions as well as good attention to detail.

Forecasters make predictions about trends that will be big for the next season. They suggest to designers how different groups of customers will want to wear each new trend.

fashion forecaster

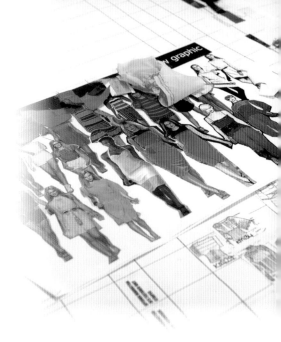

Forecasting can be short-term or long-term. For short-term trend-spotting, forecasters will look at key celebrities and artists to see what ideas are emerging, and they will visit the major exhibitions and the most cutting-edge shops and markets to see what is new. At the moment fine art is probably the most influential source of inspiration for designers, so forecasters spend a lot of time going to exhibitions and seeing what the up-and-coming artists are producing, but they will also look at trends in the music business, album and DVD covers and video and film. 'Short term' can mean anything from a few weeks to one or two seasons. Turnaround time within high street fashion has become incredibly quick, and a version of a PVC cape as worn by Lady Gaga can find its way into chain stores within a month.

Longer-term trend-spotting is more influenced by society, economic changes and social trends, so a forecaster might, for example, note that home working is becoming more widespread and will think about the implications for the kinds of clothes that people will want to buy.

A forecaster might be asked to produce something fairly broad (trends for swimwear for the next season) or might be asked to contribute to a report for a particular client. In this instance, they would be required to interpret the trends and think not only about what's coming in the next season, but how a particular customer might want to see this interpreted.

Forecasters say that they do their jobs mostly on instinct, and there is always some talk about the zeitgeist, but it seems that designers are in general responding to the same influences. Forecasters tend to be people who live and breathe fashion, so looking out for trends is something that comes very naturally to them. There are a few sort-of-tricks-of-the-trade that you can learn (next season's trend is often the exact opposite of this season's: stripes follow plains, bright colours follow black, etc), but it's really about looking in the right places, having a strong visual sense and being able to analyse the information you are seeing. You need to have a pretty open mind about aesthetics – this is not a job about what you think ought to be the next trend, or what you'd like to see people wearing, so if you are very focused on your own fashion likes and dislikes you might find it difficult.

Study
- Fashion trends – where they come from and how they influence
- Market intelligence – trade fairs, magazines, trend agencies
- Observe social and cultural influences
- Develop your fashion 'instinct' and 'intuition'
- Research methods
- Fashion history
- Illustration, CAD

Links
London's fashion week is a showcase for top designers.
www.londonfashionweek.co.uk
WGSN, a fashion trend provider.
www.wgsn.com
New Designers – a great place to see what and who is up and coming.
www.newdesigners.com

Rating
Average salary:
Entrance difficulty: ● ● ●

Stand out from the crowd
Get some design experience first – this will give you a great understanding of the process and the customers.

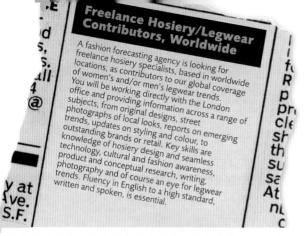

It's useful to have been a designer yourself before you start to work as a forecaster, and although you may often work in a particular specialism (such as womenswear, interiors or footwear), design today is all very connected: boyswear is based on menswear, wallpaper is influenced by fashion, and lingerie uses womenswear prints. The skills of observation and analysis are also very transferable so it can be quite easy to move from one area to another.

Having a background in design is a really useful path towards forecasting. It's difficult to identify and predict trends without a clear and detailed knowledge of the current designs and the trends of the recent past, so forecasting companies are keen to have a mixture of in-house

> *Forecasters tend to be people who live and breathe fashion, so looking out for trends is something that comes very naturally to them.*

forecasters and freelancers who also work as designers. Major retailers and suppliers will also have their own teams of forecasters.

It is also useful to be a strong illustrator, and skilled in CAD. Forecasting services put together seasonal books, showing their predicted trends, silhouettes and colours. Although they do hire illustrators, your artistic skills could give you an advantage.

Routes in
It's useful to have spent a few years working as a designer, both to learn about the field and to make some contacts – networking is the usual route to a job in this area. Where jobs are advertised it would usually be in *Drapers* or on companies' own websites.

Best bits
▲ Getting paid to do something that you do anyway

IN HER OWN WORDS:

Deepa is a freelance designer and consultant.

'My background is in multimedia design and textiles, but I have designed womenswear, menswear, jewellery, footwear, wallpaper and car interiors. What I'm good at is knowing my customer, seeing what's on trend, and creating beautiful designs, and those skills can be applied to any aspect of design.'

Deepa has worked for a range of designers covering everything from ready-to-wear designer to high street, and she has always enjoyed the mix: 'The high street work is what pays the bills, but the high-end designer work is what I really love – my creativity can go wild and I can really express my own personality.'

She has recently started to work for WGSN, the fashion forecasting website. Her particular area of specialism is print, but she finds that her knowledge of the whole field of fashion and design really helps her. Deepa puts her success as a trend-spotter down to passion and a good eye.

'I absolutely love it. I do it all the time and it's just the way I think about the world. You need to do a lot of research – I spend a lot of time at street markets, and travel abroad is really valuable, but then it's down to instinct and a good eye.'

Her advice to anyone thinking about this field is to first work with some designers, particularly in womenswear where you need to follow trends not only every season, but sometimes every week.

'Then make sure that you network, network, network. Be nice to everyone.'

Worst bits
▼ Because you're getting paid to do something that you do anyway, you never really switch off

Skills needed
• A good eye for aesthetics
• An open mind
• An ability to analyse information
• An excellent understanding of customers
• Versatility
• Cultural awareness
• Understanding of the interconnectivity of happenings
• Research skills
• Both global and regional awareness
• Good communication skills

CHAPTER TWO

accessories design

The term 'accessories' covers a large and diverse range of products. The obvious ones are footwear, handbags, hats and jewellery, but it also includes 'soft' accessories such as gloves and scarves, ties, socks and handkerchiefs. Accessory designers are often asked to design 'other' items – novelty key rings, hair clips or giveaways, for example.

The process for getting accessories from concept to store is fairly similar to the process for clothes. Some companies, such as Furla or Radley, focus purely on accessories. However, in many others, accessories need to complement the garment collections for the season, while also needing to stand on their own, as they are often displayed in different parts of the shop. The links can usually be seen in the colour palettes used and in the way that both garments and accessories are designed to fit the brand and appeal to the same customers. Accessories tend to work at a slower pace than clothing, with the time from concept to store being longer and the number of seasons and drops within each season far fewer; an accessory department might work on two seasons each year with one collection per season, whereas a garment department might work on four seasons with two drops for each season, (ie, one collection delivered every six weeks – for example, early summer and midsummer collections). In that case, the colour palette for the accessories would need to coordinate with both apparel collections.

Depending on the kind of company, an accessory designer might get a brief from either the creative director or the buying team. The brief will tend to be quite conceptual and will link in with the themes for clothing that season. They might, for example, be asked to produce accessories along an African safari theme or with a nautical feel. The designer will then produce a mood board with some ideas for the accessories collection. The mood board

A mood board for a Pringle Autumn accessories collection.

might include a colour palette, some images of accessories from other designers that they want to base their designs on and some swatches of fabric and other textiles. Once the ideas are approved by the buyers or creative directors, the accessories designers will sketch some ideas for the key items for each category, laying out the details of the collections, how many items in each category, the price points, the colour palette and the materials.

FAR LEFT Tartan shoe-boot design by Jerome Rousseau.

LEFT Sketch for a handbag by Kitty Dong.

The next stage is the production development. This is where the designers work with technologists and product managers to make sure that the designs for each item can be effectively produced as drawn. They might work together to work out which materials would need to be used in order to meet the right price points, or decide which trims are most suitable for the design.

The last stage is the production. The factories that produce the accessories are nearly all overseas. Jewellery is usually produced in India, scarves in the Far East and premium leather goods in Italy. Accessories can be manufactured in India and the Far East at a fraction of the cost they would be in the UK. In terms of the leather goods, the raw materials are purchased from Italy, so it's cheaper to manufacture the goods in the same country rather than transporting the materials to the UK and then on somewhere else. Factories produce samples of the accessories, and if these are accepted, then they go into mass production for the shops.

As with other areas within fashion design, companies structure their accessory departments in different ways, so as an accessories designer you can choose the extent to which you specialise both in terms of the kind of product and in the production process. High-end design companies such as Burberry tend to have highly specialised accessory teams. They will have teams who specialise in the product category – bags, scarves, belts, footwear, etc – and

As an accessories designer you can choose the extent to which you specialise, both in terms of the kind of product and in the production process.

will have teams who focus on the different stages of the production process, with teams of designers, teams of product developers and teams who look after the actual production.

Within accessories, more than other areas in the fashion industry, skills are seen as genuinely transferable. Employers are looking for an understanding of colour, textiles, aesthetic, brand and customers, but beyond that are often happy to take someone from a jewellery background and put them onto soft accessories, say, and it's not unusual for people to transfer from more dramatically different spheres such as the sales side, or packaging design, to accessories.

A concept sketch for an extravagant headpiece by milliner Philip Treacy.

Jewellery can encompass all sorts of things and jewellers are limited only by their imaginations! All kinds of materials are used: leather, paper, plastic, fabric, cork and rubber, as well as metals and stones.

jewellery designer

To start with, jewellers need to learn about drawing and develop rendering skills. Rendering is the process of making a very detailed and specific drawing of what the finished item is going to look like. Some roles will demand hand-rendering skills, whereas others will require you to use CAD (computer-aided design). As a jeweller you will need to learn about the different materials that are used and what the properties of those materials are – and you will also learn skills and techniques such as how to set stones and how to hammer the metal into the shape you want it. Finally you will develop the skills needed to clean and polish finished items.

There is no very clear career path for jewellers, and although this means that it may be tricky to work out what steps to take, it also means that you can decide what kind of jeweller you would like to be.

There are lots of different specialisms for a jeweller to choose from. One of the most secure routes is to get a job as a designer or production manager for a design company or jewellery company. Companies can range from the big international names like Tiffany or DeBeers, to smaller, often family-run, businesses, for example in Hatton Gardens.

Fashion companies might employ jewellers, either to work on their accessories ranges, or to work on jewelled garments such as dresses with beading.

High street retailers, either specialist jewellery and accessories stores such as Accessorize or general fashion stores who sell jewellery such as Marks & Spencer or Kew, will employ jewellery designers to design and create ranges, but the actual production is usually carried out oversees in places such as India, where the raw materials can be easily sourced and the labour costs are low.

Many jewellers make their living as designer-makers. This is a field that can be quite suited to creating your own products as machinery is relatively cheap and compact, so turning a garage or a bedroom into a studio isn't impractical. Designer-makers can join associations such as Cockpit Arts and the Crafts Council who provide business support, an opportunity to market your work and a network of colleagues in the same field. A lot of sole trader jewellers will sell their work through their own websites and can also exhibit their work on Etsy or at shows such as Dazzle. Some jewellers categorise their products as works of art and show their work at exhibitions and galleries.

Study

- Metalwork/casting
- Silver soldering
- Cutting, piercing and fabricating in silver or non-precious metals
- Working with wire
- Imprinting designs in sheet metals
- Working with resins through mould making and casting
- Safe workshop practice
- Development of hand skills: forming, fabricating and finishing
- Explorations of 3D form
- Surface treatment
- Combining materials

Links

Hatton Gardens newsletter: for jobs, opportunities and news. www.benchpeg.co.uk
News, information and opportunities with a fine art slant. www.a-n.co.uk
Crafts Council: the national development agency for crafts. www.craftscouncil.org.uk
International **resource for jewellery**. Kilmt02.net
Cockpit Arts: a creative incubator for designer-makers. www.cockpitarts.com

Rating

Average salary: ● ● ●
Entrance difficulty: ● ● ○

Stand out from the crowd

Jewellery is an art form with limitless possibilities. Truly explore form and innovative use of materials. Work hard to perfect your skills and push yourself creatively. Consumers are often willing to be extravagant for a piece of unique jewellery that speaks to them, but it must be well executed.

'Spiral Rings' by Daniela
Dobesova. Manipulating
silver is a key skill for a
jeweller to develop.

CASE STUDY:

Caroline originally trained and worked as a jewellery designer but would now describe herself as working in 'textiles art'.

After her degree in jewellery design, Caroline set up a jewellery studio, trying to balance – as many jewellery artists do – her creativity and her need to make money. This worked relatively well for a while, but after a while she found it tricky to satisfy both needs, so she split her practice in two, spending half of her time producing items that would sell commercially, and half her time working on her own pieces, which were more about textiles and fine art. This split is not uncommon among jewellers who have a leaning towards fine art, and plenty of artists and designers find themselves doing paid work that is less fulfilling in order to fund their practice.

Caroline exhibited her own collections in galleries and shows, and started to get some great feedback and press. Eventually she got enough exposure to devote herself to her own practice full-time, and she also won a textiles competition, which gave her some financial help and a lot of recognition for her work. Since then she has received international acclaim for her work, but continues to subsidise it, although these days with teaching.

Within the jewellery industry there are people who specialise in all sorts of different things. It is a very skilled field and mistakes are costly so it is common to find jewellers who have a developed real specialism in a particular niche, such as diamond setting, metalwork, finishing or plating.

Routes in

Most jewellers start with a degree in jewellery or jewellery and silversmithing. There are a few specialist colleges for this (such as the Holt jewellery academy) or you can study at a more generalist college such as Central.Saint Martins. There are very many specialist short courses that you can take to develop your skills in any direction.

Jewellers then need to decide which route they want to pursue and start to get some unpaid work experience or a junior role, for example, as a jewellery cleaner or polisher, to start to learn the business.

There is no very clear career path for jewellers... this means that you can decide what kind of jeweller you would like to be.

Best bits

▲ You're dealing with small and very tangible items
▲ Jewellery fulfils a very special function for many wearers; it can be a pleasure to work on something so significant
▲ You can carve out your niche

Worst bits

▼ Life as a designer-maker can be quite solitary
▼ There might be times in your career when the work is a bit repetitive; for example, cleaning up castings

Skills needed

• Ability to communicate ideas through drawing/making
• Curiosity about materials
• An eye for detail
• Precision

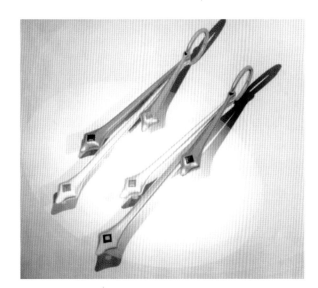

CAD pieces designed and
drawn by Leonard of London
for a private commission.

The usual accessories associated with the term 'soft' are scarves and gloves, but the soft accessories designer may also end up working on bags, soft hats, belts, socks, hosiery, hair clips and many other diverse products.

soft accessories designer

ABOVE A cable fur scarf from a Pringle Autumn collection.

One of the unusual things about being an accessories designer is how transferable your skills are. The degree to which your job is a specialist one will depend on who you work for and the diversity and size of their accessories ranges. A retailer such as Accessorize who makes only accessories or one such as Burberry where their accessory ranges are key to their brand might have designers who focus solely on one particular product, whereas the accessories designer for a clothing retail chain such as Boden or Kew might need to design everything that is sold, including scarves, hats, gloves, bags, handbags and jewellery and even some footwear.

As with all design within the fashion industry, the designer needs to balance the sometimes competing demands of trend, functionality and customer needs. Within accessories the balance between these changes is dependent on the particular item. For some accessories, the emphasis is on functionality as much as fashion. A hair clip, for example, that doesn't actually hold your hair in place, or a wallet that doesn't hold your coins safely is never going to become a bestseller. Customers buy these products with their heads, not with their hearts, so designers need to focus their attention on the practical a little more than on the psychological. Other products within the accessories portfolio are more emotional purchases: scarves and hats are on show whenever they are being worn so they will always be a key part of an outfit, and their practical function is fairly straightforward and not too complicated to achieve. These products are more about shape, style, fabric and fashion.

Soft accessories designers will usually work to fewer seasons than garment designers, but this makes their relationship with fashion trends a little complex. As well as using all the usual techniques to identify trends within accessories (analysing the catwalks, seeing what's on sale across the world and using forecasting websites such as

Study

- Range planning
- Design
- Realisation
- Pattern development
- Manufacturing and construction techniques for each specialist area
- Textile and materials technology
- Illustration

Links

Skillfast UK: The sector skills council for fashion and textiles, helping graduates find out about careers in in the clothing, footwear and textiles industry. Click on 'Careers' for information and advice. www.skillfast-uk.org

Can U Cut It? includes profiles of people working in all areas of fashion, tips for securing work experience in the industry, and an overview of the range of qualifications available www.canucutit.co.uk

Rating

Average salary: ● ● ○
Entrance difficulty: ● ● ○

Stand out from the crowd

This is a design field that allows you to be intensely creative and requires an abundance of fresh ideas! Collect everything – colours, prints, cultural artefacts, fabric swatches, postcards, magazine clippings – and organise them in files for future inspiration. Watch trends, but also people on the street. Sketch continuously.

A mood board for a Pringle Summer accessories collection.

CASE STUDY:

Emma now works as a senior menswear accessories designer for a high-end luxury brand.

This is the job Emma had always wanted as she loves working with expensive materials ('cashmere is so much nicer to work with than lambswool'), but she's had to take a circuitous route to get there.

Her first degree was in printed textiles. She loved working with textiles, the feel of the fabrics, and got a real pleasure from the surface decoration and manipulation of the products. Although Emma graduated with a first-class degree, she still found it hard to get her first job. 'I applied for every job I saw – using agencies, websites and newspapers – and eventually got a placement in childrenswear design.'

Emma's first paid job was as a design assistant for a small group of perfume and luxury goods retailers. She had no packaging or perfume experience, but the design manager saw that she had an eye for detail and colour. Emma worked hard and was asked to do all the menial and administrative tasks, but she loved the products. After two years, she was offered a job with one of their suppliers, designing accessories.

Although she had a lot to learn about the product area, she still relied on her eye for detail and a sense of colour and aesthetics. With some accessories experience under her belt, Emma got a maternity leave cover as the head of accessories for a growing high street womenswear chain, designing all the accessories in their stores, including footwear, leather goods, jewellery, scarves, hats and gloves.

Finally Emma's career dream came true when she landed her current role designing ties, cufflinks, scarves and gloves for a very well-respected luxury brand.

WGSN), the accessories designer needs to fit in with the fashion trends as well as the accessories trends and must come up with designs that span more than one season so that their scarves and gloves will complement the clothes on sale for the autumn and winter seasons, for example.

Routes in

A relevant degree is useful, but that could be in fashion, textiles or accessories. Then it's unpaid internships, networking and looking for opportunities, even if they seem a bit removed from your ultimate goal.

Best bits

- ▲ So varied – both within one role, and across a career
- ▲ Getting to work with so many different materials
- ▲ The accessories market is booming so this is a dynamic area of the industry to work in

Worst bits

- ▼ Being the repository for anything that doesn't quite fit in elsewhere – some may love the unexpected challenges, but for others, learning how to make a key ring or a cuddly toy isn't quite what they joined the business for!

Skills needed

- • Exceptional 3D skills
- • An understanding of ergonomics
- • Good people skills
- • Developing relationships
- • Adaptability
- • Strong design and drawing skills
- • Good colour sense

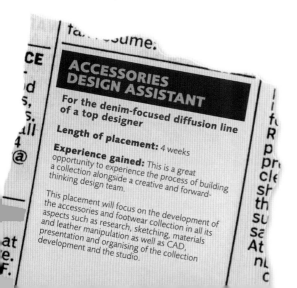

ACCESSORIES DESIGN ASSISTANT

For the denim-focused diffusion line of a top designer

Length of placement: 4 weeks

Experience gained: This is a great opportunity to experience the process of building a collection alongside a creative and forward-thinking design team.

This placement will focus on the development of the accessories and footwear collection in all its aspects such as research, sketching, materials and leather manipulation as well as CAD, presentation and organising of the collection development and the studio.

Getting a shoe from concept to sales floor is extraordinarily complicated. A typical shoe design might involve a sole, insole, buckle, heel, top piece, sock, toe puff, stiffener, shank and steel pins, as well as a last for each size.

footwear designer

Each individual piece for a shoe will usually be made by a different company or individual and requires expensive equipment. The process is complex, time-consuming and expensive. New technology introduced in the last few years means that the processes are becoming far more streamlined and prototypes can be developed far quicker than before, but shoes remain complex.

Footwear designers can work for fashion design houses, retail chains or suppliers (companies who design footwear to the specifications of a retail buyer). Nearly all of the shoes sold in the UK are also designed there, but the production of footwear has moved more or less entirely overseas. There are very few footwear manufacturers left in the UK, and they tend to be the very exclusive brands such as Lobbs, who make bespoke shoes and jobs with them are few and far between. Manufacturing for the most part occurs either in Spain and Italy – where the leather is produced – or in China and the Far East, where production costs are far lower.

Graduates can choose to work in design, manufacture or product development and can specialise in sports shoes, bridal shoes, outdoor and hiking, men's, women's or children's. It is rare to set up on your own as a footwear designer-maker as the equipment is so expensive and the processes so complex, but you can work freelance.

The design process for footwear is broadly similar to other areas of fashion design. The designers will get a brief from the buyers or design managers and then will create some initial sketches for a range. When these are approved they will start to come up with more specific designs for the footwear, working either by hand (more likely with higher-end designers) or with CAD packages such as Illustrator or Photoshop (more usual with mass manufacturing). They need to consider materials, trims, durability and fit. In some contexts, the shoes need to be made to fit in with particular garments or ranges, or for specialist shoe shops the footwear needs to be on trend and suitable for the season's colours, shapes and styles in clothing.

Routes in

Because designing footwear is so complex and so technical, having a degree is pretty essential. Graduates need to get

Study

- Footwear materials and processes
- Footwear design and industrial studies
- Footwear consolidation studies
- Footwear design development and range planning
- Footwear portfolio and skills development
- Footwear design and realisation

Links

Drapers Footwear Awards
Yearly retailer awards includes 'Student Footwear Designer of the Year' and 'Student Accessories Designer of the Year'. www.drapersfootwearawards.co.uk
British Footwear Association: the representative body of UK suppliers of footwear.
www.britfoot.com
Cordwainers www.lcf.arts.ac.uk
DeMontfort University
www.dmu.ac.uk

Rating

Average salary: ● ● ○
Entrance difficulty: ● ● ●

Stand out from the crowd

Do lots of three-dimensional thinking. Draw 3D objects and think about them from top, bottom, back, and front, and inside and out.

ABOVE A shoe designer works on a last (the shoe mould) for a new design. As well as being highly creative, shoe design is still an incredibly technical process.

some relevant work experience, and then start as a junior designer, before progressing to a senior designer, creative director and then design manager.

Best bits
▲ Travelling the world to visit retailers, suppliers and manufacturers
▲ The joy of getting such a complicated process exactly right

Worst bits
▼ Working with clothing designers who don't always understand the complexities of the process or the time it takes
▼ Being reliant on a wide range of different suppliers and manufacturers

Skills needed
• Precision and an eye for detail – costs are high and mistakes are very exposed and very expensive
• Hand skills and computer skills
• 3D design skills are essential – footwear is sculpture
• Passion – if you don't love it, you won't make it

CASE STUDY:

Sue works as a designer for a large footwear company.

Sue knew from a young age that she wanted to be a dressmaker. But at university her course included modules on fashion and textiles and she chose to focus on footwear for her final project. That decided her: footwear design was the career for her. A specialist degree followed, and Sue learned about the complex process of making the shoes as well as the aesthetics of the design. She did two placements while she was at college with high-end made-to-order shoe manufacturers, and loved them.

She decided that she was really keen to work for the high-end market rather than the mass manufacturing side of the industry, but this limited her choice of job opportunities. After a seemingly endless round of sending off CVs and approaching companies with her portfolio, Sue managed to get herself a job as an unpaid intern, customising shoes for the catwalk for a designer, and this was the break that she needed. She got some great experience, some brilliant images for her portfolio and made some good contacts.

She had a few other short spells as an intern for fashion designers, before managing to land a design job. She now works on two collections each year and these are on sale in department stores across the country. She relishes the fact that she can focus exclusively on design but knows that it was the knowledge of production that she gained from university plus her early work experience placement that makes her good at what she does.

The finished articles: Yellow ostrich shoe and canvas and tan leather shoe-boot, both by Jerome Rousseau.

Trainee Designer

For ladies' high-fashion footwear importers

Duties: Design, from concept to range-building with an eye for trend and commerciality. Work with factories for sourcing and with sales team for direction.

Requirements: Motivation, creativity and an eye for spotting trends; good communication dynamic to follow design from concept to sample.

Salary: £20,000 to £25,000 p.a. depending on qualification and experience.

To apply: Please email CV and covering letter.

Hat designers, or milliners, are people who design or make hats. Hats may be one-of-a-kind pieces, part of a designer's ready-to-wear collection (with a limited number produced), or mass produced for chain stores.

hat designer/ milliner

There are basically only four styles of hat: brimmed, brimless, hat or cap. Milliners use colour, fabric, shape and trimmings to create an endless number of variations around these four starting points.

It's not easy to make a career for yourself as a hat maker, and there is no single path to millinery success. Most milliners work freelance or are self-employed. Some major retailers will employ one or two to work year-round on their hat collections, but most retailers wouldn't stock a broad enough range of hats to make it worth their while to employ someone full-time, so they are more likely to contract a freelancer to do some work each season. Some milliners will develop skills in retail and work for a hat store (or open their own), allowing them to earn an income both from designing and producing the hats and from selling other people's designs. Others might work as sole-trader designer-makers, creating and producing their own one-of-a-kind designs and selling them in a variety of ways through websites, at market stalls and at trade fairs. They might find that they can make a better living if they broaden their skills and develop a range of accessories to complement their hats.

The design process of the milliner is similar to that of any other fashion designer. They will be involved in forecasting and analysing trends in hats, fabrics and colours; working closely with buyers, suppliers, clients and customers;

ABOVE Sketch for a hat design by Philip Treacy, a haute couture and ready-to-wear milliner. **BELOW** Philip Treacy at work in his studio.

producing designs by hand or using CAD; making decisions about fabrics and trims; and making up samples. The techniques they use, however, will tend to be quite different, with hat designers getting involved in blocking (actually making the hat shape from a wooden or metal block), using hydraulic machinery to shape hats for mass production and applying special chemicals.

ta... ...ume.

Intern wanted

We are a small company who create both bespoke headwear and ready-to-wear collections. This is a rare opportunity for a talented and enthusiastic individual to become immersed in a budding fashion company as it prepares for its Autumn collection launch.

Experience gained: The student could gain experience of an independent fashion designer and retailer and of working as part of a small team. Initiative and a desire to learn are essential. You will have the opportunity to use your Photoshop skills and build mood boards and put your fashion PR/marketing knowledge into action.

If you have some experience of fashion marketing, promotion, and ha... is the placement f...

Sketch and finished
hat design by
Stephen Jones.

Best bits
▲ People who succeed as hat makers are almost invariably
   passionate about hats, so for almost everyone, the best
   thing is being able to work with hats for a living
▲ There are a lot of interesting, talented, kind people
   working in the hat industry

Worst bits
▼ It's not the most lucrative part of the fashion industry
▼ Not only is it hard to get into the profession, it's also
   really hard to make a living long-term

Routes in
You need to learn as many skills and techniques as you can,
so you should research millinery courses. There are many
short courses that will allow you to learn specific techniques.
Getting some work experience with an established milliner
or in a hat store is important, and then it's a case of starting
to get your name known through selling your hat designs at
small boutiques, through a website or supplying to a hat
shop. Any press coverage that you can generate will boost
your reputation and will help you to make sales.

Skills needed
• A good eye for shapes
• Manual dexterity and practicality
• Determination
• A passion for hats
• A knowledge of materials

Study
• Blocking
• Working with and shaping straw and felt
• Pattern cutting for fabric hats
• Decorative finishing and trims

Links
British Hat Guild www.britishhatguild.co.uk
Skillfast UK: the UK's sector skills council
for the fashion industry; for news, information
and advice about working in the industry.
www.skillfast-uk.org
The Hat Magazine: The trade magazine for the
trade; also has some job vacancies.
www.thehatmagazine.com
Kensington and Chelsea College: A range of
millinery courses including the UK's only remaining
BA in millinery. www.kcc.ac.uk

Rating
Average salary: ● ● ●
Entrance difficulty: ● ● ●

Stand out from the crowd
Persistence and adaptability are
essential in this difficult-to-break-
into area.

Everyone has a bag. Or two. Or actually, on average, six. Men's, women's, children's, shopping bags, evening bags, laptop bags, beach bags, man bags… Designing and producing bags is really varied with huge potential for creativity.

bag designer

Bags are not as trend sensitive as other areas of fashion, which makes the process a bit less stressful and demanding than for garments, but a bag designer will still be expected to produce a line for each season and sometimes two lines per season, so that can be up to ten different ranges each year. Lead-in times vary but tend to be quite similar to those for garments, so for the high street it can be anything from six weeks to 18 months.

The process for designing a bag, or a range of bags, is quite similar to designing garments. The designer or buyer (depending on the kind of store) will do some research into the bag trends for the season, in terms of colours, shapes and materials. They will see what bags have been shown on the ready-to-wear catwalk collections, see what bags are in the shops around the world (it's a tough job. . .) and may consult with some trend-spotting companies to check that their analysis and instincts are right. They might also look at other products such as jewellery and clothing to see if there are any trends that could be reflected in bags. If the bags are made by a supplier there might then be some discussions and consultations before the concept for the range is finalised. Suppliers will usually be working for more

than one retailer so can be a really useful source of information about trends and ideas.

Designers may have the artistic freedom to create original concepts and innovative shapes, or may be asked to model their designs around photographs of 'designer' bags. Either way, they are always thinking of the consumer profile and the kinds of things a customer might want from a bag.

Many bag professionals are designer-makers. Depending on what kind of bag you are making, it may be relatively easy to start to make your own collection, using a room in your house or sharing some studio space. You might then sell your bags on the Internet, show them at craft fairs and markets or take a stand at a fair to get some exposure.

Study

- Trend research
- Preparing design/ mood boards
- Developing design ideas
- Creating costumer profiles
- Working drawings, spec sheets and material specifications
- Pattern cutting techniques
- Working on industrial machines
- Pockets, handles and closures
- Leather work

Links

Skillfast UK: The sector skills council for fashion and textiles, helping graduates find out about careers in in the clothing, footwear and textiles industry. Click on 'Careers' for information and advice. www.skillfast-uk.org
Can U Cut It? includes profiles of people working in all areas of fashion, tips for securing work experience in the industry, and an overview of the range of qualifications available www.canucutit.co.uk

Rating

Average salary:
Entrance difficulty:

Stand out from the crowd

Start thinking in three dimensions – and demonstrate this ability in your portfolio. Think about and draw objects from the back, the front, the top, the bottom, the inside and the outside.

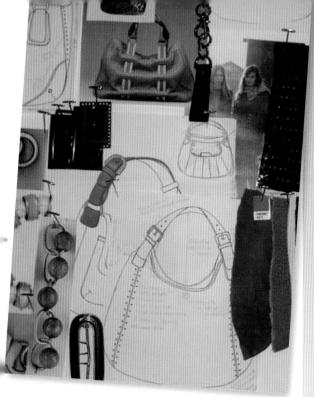

ABOVE Like apparel designers, bag designers use mood boards to generate ideas at the beginning of the design process.

Routes in
A relevant degree is more or less a prerequisite, but it's not essential that the degree should be in accessory or bag design. Bag designers will come from fashion or textiles degrees, and it's not uncommon to go from one area of the fashion industry into bag design later in your career.

Best bits
▲ The utter pleasure of seeing someone carrying one of your bags

Worst bits
▼ The process, especially if you are working for a supplier or retailer, can be annoyingly tedious, with revisions and more revisions before everyone has signed the range off

Skills needed
- An understanding of textiles and materials
- The ability to adapt catwalk designs for your customers
- Practicality
- An eye for detail
- Strong three-dimensional skills
- Creativity and innovation

DAY IN THE LIFE:
Bag designer

Andrea designs innovative bags for her company, Andrea Valenti. Although no two days are alike, Andrea's days are intensely creative.

9.00AM TRIP TO A MANUFACTURING PLANT TO EXPLORE MATERIALS
Finding unique materials, often industrial or recycled, is the first step in Andrea's design process, along with imagining unique ways the materials can be used. Andrea looks for texture, colour, pliability and potential for unexpected uses in her materials.

11.00AM BACK TO THE STUDIO
Experimenting with the materials, creating inventive shapes and exploring construction methods, Andrea discovers what the new materials can do. Combining them with components recycled from a previous year, Andrea sketches a design for a new satchel and mocks it up in cardboard to test the shape.

2.00PM OFF TO THE FACTORY
Andrea reviews her cardboard proto with the technical team. They will make a sample of the new design in the selected materials she has brought. Together they discuss construction issues, trimmings and closures.

3.30PM MEETING WITH HER MARKETING MANAGER
Andrea plans out the number of styles, SKUs, pricing and delivery schedules for the upcoming season's collection. Computer flat sketches of the bags are edited to reflect the final collection, and the styles are adopted.

4.30PM PR MEETING
Andrea meets with her public relations team to discuss the upcoming charity fashion show and press release. Andrea's bags will be featured with clothing designer David Yoo in the runway show.

5.00PM BACK TO THE FACTORY
Andrea checks progress on the new satchel prototype. Andrea works with the pattern cutter on proportion corrections, and she approves the use of materials. A final sample is requested. Andrea visualises additional designs to create a group from the successful concept and puts the ideas into motion with the technical team.

6.00PM HOME
Home to dress for an event to benefit the American Heart Association, where Andrea's bags will be displayed and raffled in a silent auction. She will be interviewed by the press and network with potential buyers, while contributing to a good cause.

CHAPTER THREE

textiles

The textiles industry is quite a different place from ten years ago. The companies that are left have survived by changing and adapting to market needs. The UK industry is now more about distribution than manufacturing, and more about high-end luxury and niche products than the mass market.

The decline in the textiles industry was all about costs; mostly labour costs, but this led to other savings in costs of premises, raw materials and shipping. In essence, the world realised that in the Far East and South Asia, wages were far lower than in the UK or Europe. They worked out that even with the increased costs of shipping the goods, they could produce high volumes of clothing far cheaper than they ever had before, and with the increasing competition in the shops, this was a huge advantage. Given that the garments were being manufactured overseas, the retailers then looked to see if they could find raw materials locally, which produced savings both because of the lower labour costs associated with producing the materials, and because of the lower transport costs. So the textiles industry, along with the garment manufacturing industry in the UK and Europe, declined. Many companies folded, and the industry now is a fraction of the size it was in the 1970s and 1980s.

But things seem to be looking up. First, the difference between the cost of producing in the developing world and in the UK is decreasing, as wages have increased and the costs of raw materials abroad have gone up due to increasing scarcity of resources. There is also currently quite an interest in the provenance of goods. High-end luxury brands pride themselves on their UK suppliers, and customers are more likely to have confidence in the quality of the product and the quality of the factories where the garments are made if it's all UK-based.

Companies are pleased to see this increase in the demand, but are responding cautiously. In the first place, there is no longer the infrastructure within the UK to support a wholesale return to the way things were. Machinery and factories are not big enough or modern enough to cope with mass manufacture, and after years and years of redundancies, employers are going to be slow to take on large numbers of new staff.

The roles within the textiles industry are quite diverse, and range from the mainstream to the very niche. With woven and knitted fabrics the designs are part of the process of manufacture – colours and patterns are designed and chosen before the fabric is made up and the fabric and design are created as a single process. With other textiles, the two processes are separated – the fabric is first made up

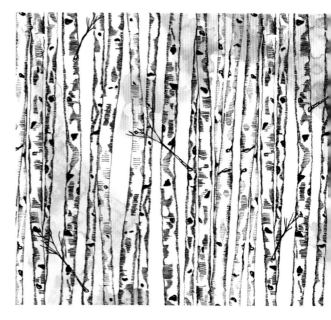

BELOW A knitted
textile designer
at work.
RIGHT Print design for
cotton fabric by
Jessica Stuart Crump.

and then the textiles designer creates the pattern, which is printed or stitched onto the fabric. There is still a strong movement of hand designers within the textiles industry, but the mainstream designers are moving towards computer-aided design to save time and money.

Textiles conservation and restoration are all about working with existing textiles and either putting measures in place to keep the textiles in their current state, in the case of conservation, or trying to restore the textiles to the state that they were once in, in the case of restoration.

Routes in
Most of the areas mentioned above would expect you to have a relevant degree. You are likely to have to work unpaid for some time before you earn any money.

Best bits
▲ Often very creative
▲ Can be satisfying working so early in the process
▲ It's often thought of as a more gentle side of the fashion industry

Worst bits
▼ The work is very often freelance, which may not suit everyone

▼ It's competitive and usually involves unpaid work experience

Skills needed
• A great passion for textiles
• A good eye and sense of colour
• Creativity
• Ability to market yourself (when working freelance)
• Some financial skills
• Ability to adapt to a work pattern that is ever-changing and often not secure

Links
The Crafts Council provides all sorts of support for designer-makers in the UK. www.craftscouncil.org
www.surfacedesign.org.uk
Première Vision: details of the leading international textiles and fabric show in Paris.
Charity supporting new textiles designers in the UK.
www.texprint.org.uk

Print designers may be employed by fashion retailers, fabric manufacturers and printers, or interior design and production companies. The industry is beginning to acknowledge that the print can 'make' the garment.

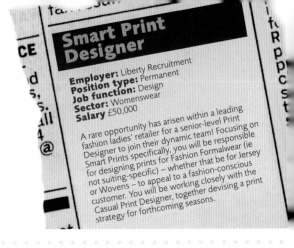

Smart Print Designer

Employer: Liberty Recruitment
Position type: Permanent
Job function: Design
Sector: Womenswear
Salary £50,000

A rare opportunity has arisen within a leading fashion ladies' retailer for a senior-level Print Designer to join their dynamic team! Focusing on Smart Prints specifically, you will be responsible for designing prints for Fashion Formalwear (ie not suiting-specific) – whether that be for Jersey or Wovens – to appeal to a fashion-conscious customer. You will be working closely with the Casual Print Designer, together devising a print strategy for forthcoming seasons.

print designer

The print designer will usually be given a brief by the buyer, but will then be expected to interpret that in their own way and with their own style. The brief from the buyers might be quite broad. They might, for example, ask for something that fits with a vintage 1950s trend, and the designer might be given a colour palette and some swatches of fabric. The designer will then go and do some of their own research, in markets or even overseas. The designer then sketches out some ideas and brings them back to the buyer, and when they reach agreement the designer works up the designs in more detail, usually using Illustrator or Photoshop.

Once the designs are signed off, the artwork for the designs needs to be prepared, ready for production. This can be quite an involved process and the designer needs to be technically capable as well as artistic. Artwork needs to be different depending on whether it is a repeat design, half drop, placement print or a border design.

Production of fabric now mostly happens overseas, in China and Bangladesh, and the print designer may be involved in travelling to the factories, or may do all the work via email.

Not every design house, manufacturer or retailer has an in-house art staff. Freelance artists and print designers often sell their artwork to independent art studios. These art studios represent a large number of artists, marketing their original work to designers, manufacturers and retailers who value the fact that the prints will be unique to them. When a piece of artwork is sold, the artist and art studio will divide the profit. Print designers are contracted by the art studio to do this print preparation, or they may actually work in-house for the studio. Most of the preparation work is done in CAD, which makes adjusting the artwork more efficient. Numerous art studios also show their collections of artwork at large print shows.

Routes in

Print designers can have diverse backgrounds, and your training may be in graphics, surface design, fine art, illustration or fashion design. Unpaid experience during or following your degree course will usually lead to a paid job.

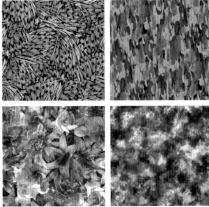

LEFT Davina Nathan's print studio.
ABOVE Prints by Ana Romero.

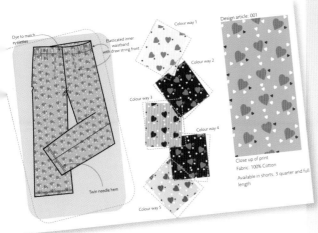

Illustration for a print design showing different colourways and examples of how it might be used.

Best bits
- ▲ You can be very creative; you can inject your own style and personality into your designs
- ▲ Seeing people wearing your designs

Worst bits
- ▼ As an artist you want to work on your designs until they are perfect. But as a print designer you don't have the time; it's easy to end up working very long hours

Skills needed
- A love of fashion
- A good eye for colour
- An understanding of garments and their construction
- Good artistic skills

CASE STUDY:

Janine is a print designer for a UK chain store.

Janine did a degree in multimedia textiles that focused on designs for all different sorts of surfaces including fabric, wood and leather. Janine then applied for a job doing graphic design – for a fashion supplier, providing graphic design for prints for Top Shop and other mass-market retailers. She didn't particularly enjoy working for the company, but the job was interesting.

After a couple of years she decided to do another degree, in textile futures, in London. This was a hard course but really interesting, and it allowed her to develop a different perspective of textiles; London was also the best place to be for the fashion industry. During her course, Janine did a lot of work experience with a whole range of different designers. She networked all she could during this time and had some brilliant experiences.

Eventually she got herself a paid job working for Nissan – designing interiors for cars. This proved to be much slower paced, and Janine soon realised that she missed the fashion world, so eventually, after applying, applying and applying, she got a job with the design team at Alexander McQueen. This was a tough environment to work in, but she found it inspirational and did some of her best work there, a real highlight being when some of her designs went onto the catwalk in Milan.

She then got a job as a print designer for New Look and has been there now for two years. Her advice to anyone looking to work in the fashion industry: 'Network, network, network.'

Study
- Print design
- CAD, Photoshop, Illustrator, U4ia
- Colour, different media
- Art history
- Drawing, painting and illustration

Links
Association of Suppliers to the British Clothing Industry (ASBCI): for industry news and making contacts. www.asbci.co.uk
British Interior Textiles Association: includes directory of manufacturers. www.interiortextiles.co.uk
Can U Cut It? Careers information and case studies. www.canucutit.co.uk
Drapers The industry magazine. www.drapersonline.com

Rating
Average salary: ● ● ○
Entrance difficulty: ● ● ○

Stand out from the crowd
Draw, draw, draw! Some production and design jobs do not place an emphasis on drawing, but this is one area where an artistic capability will really set you apart.

The craft of embroidery has been around for hundreds of years. These days, much hand embroidery is carried out in India, and there are also computer-aided design software and machines that can stitch for you.

embroidery designer

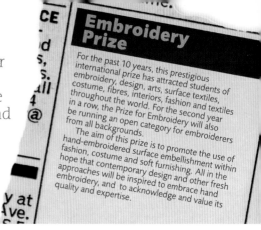

Embroiderers are nearly all freelancers, working on specific commissions. Some might have close links with particular fashion designers or fashion houses, and provide the designs for their garments and accessories. Others work as sole-trader designer-makers, selling their wares at craft markets and on websites. In addition to the fashion industry, embroiderers can produce work for a range of items including soft furnishings and decorative pieces.

The process

The traditional method of embroidery is known as 'prick and pounce' and is still the way that many embroiderers produce

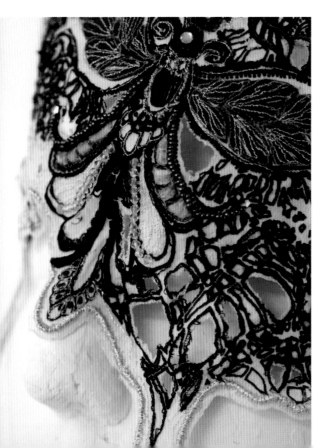

their work. An outline of the embroidery design is produced on the fabric in fine talc, through tiny holes in a piece of paper. These days, most embroiderers use quicker and more efficient methods, with designs being created in CAD software and drawn straight onto the fabric and highly technical sewing machines able to produce really fine embroidery.

Many fashion designers use embroidery and embellishment in their collections without actually stitching the embroidery. Artists or designers, who have a thorough knowledge of embroidery stitches and a good eye for motifs and placement, develop beautiful embroidery designs in sketch form with meticulous drawings depicting the stitches, techniques and colours to be used. These are usually included with the spec packages to be sent to India or China, where the embroidered samples are made.

There is a resurgence of respect for embellishment crafts. Many of the finest examples of embroidery and beading are done by the renowned House of Lesage, where exquisite and extensive embroidery is seen on the haute couture gowns of Chanel, Lanvin and Dior. Select students have studied under the tutelage of Jean Francois Lesage to carry on his long history of decorative art, assuring that the House of Lesage will remain at the pinnacle of this art form.

Techniques

Embroidery is a highly skilled craft and there are many different techniques you can specialise in. The basic stitches include chain stitch, cross stitch and blanket stitch, and the more complex stitches include Jacobean couching and laced herringbone. You can learn about ribbonwork, cutwork, shadowwork and smocking, or specialise in skills such as appliqué, paints and beading.

Routes in

Ideally you need a degree or some other higher-level qualification in embroidery, and then you can start making contacts and getting your name known.

Hand embroidery is very skilled, painstaking work, so it is increasingly mass-produced by machine overseas.

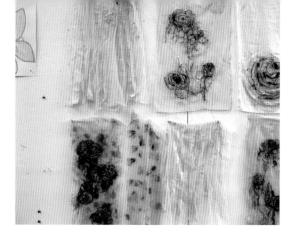

ABOVE Embroidery samples arranged for comparison.

Best bits
- ▲ Embroiderers talk with great pleasure about the process of stitching and working with the fabric
- ▲ It's rewarding to see the results of your labour so clearly

Worst bits
- ▼ Some of the work can be repetitive, either producing a number of identical items, or a repeated pattern on a single item
- ▼ Demand for this craft is reliant on fashion trends – some seasons it is everywhere, others it disappears
- ▼ Almost all embroidery is outsourced, usually to India

Skills needed
- Patience is essential – it's slow and painstaking work, and if it's not right the first time you have to unpick it and start again
- Great precision
- Manual dexterity
- Attention to detail
- Meticulous standards

CASE STUDY:

Annette is an embroiderer who also works as a teacher.

Annette was originally taught to do embroidery by her mother and her grandmother who were both keen amateur enthusiasts. It didn't occur to Annette that embroidery could be anything other than a hobby, so she went to university to study biology and then did a teacher training course and worked as a high school science teacher for years. But embroidery continued to be her first love. Her particular speciality was jewellery, and friends soon asked if she would make them bracelets or brooches, and then she would be asked to make something for a friend of a friend, or somebody's colleague, and she gradually built up quite a sideline.

As the work was trickling in, she found herself very busy but also frustrated that she didn't have time to promote herself as much as she would have liked, so after a while, she decided to take the plunge and reduce her teaching hours to two days a week. 'I wasn't quite ready to rely solely on my income from embroidery, but I knew that if I continued full time at school, I wouldn't have the motivation to grow my business, so working part time was the perfect answer.'

With some extra time on her hands, Annette started to think about ways to promote herself more widely. She developed a website and sells a bit through that and, also, particularly in the run-up to Christmas, will take a stall at local craft fairs. 'It's never going to make me rich, but I get such a pleasure from creating my designs that I could never give it up.'

Study
- Gold embroidery
- Beading
- Crewel work
- Embroidery stitch techniques
- Fashion history
- Drawing and rendering
- Fabric manipulation

Links
The Royal School of Needlework runs a range of courses in embroidery. www.royal-needlework.org.uk
Embroiderers Guild: for information, news and opportunities to network with other embroiderers, and includes a Young Embroiderers group. www.embroderersguild.com
Hand and Lock Embroidery: this firm incorporates an embroidery school and runs an annual embroidery prize. www.handembroidery.com

Rating
Average salary: ● ● ●
Entrance difficulty: ● ● ●

Stand out from the crowd
Make sure you've got another skill or sideline to rely on. You'll likely be working sporadically, and the work is not well paid.

Weavers in the UK are almost all self-employed. Some weavers use software, but some prefer weaving a prototype. This allows them to experiment with variations and see subtle differences in colour, yarn or weave more closely.

weaver

When the weaver is happy with a design, they would then give the instructions and technical notes to a mill, together with the yarn. When the mill has completed their part of the process, the woven fabric needs to be sent away for finishing. This involves washing and pressing it and making sure the tension is even. The fabric is then usually sent back to the mill where it is cut up and returned to the designer.

Designers can work as designer-makers, doing commissions and selling their work from their studios or online, under their own name. Alternatively (or often concurrently) they can produce weave designs for a design house or retailer. Weavers can also work with more of a fine-art sensibility, producing works of art that are shown in galleries or displayed on walls. There is a very large community of artists who use the medium in this way.

There are some opportunities for those who want the security of an employment contract, but many of those who originally trained as weavers end up doing a related job, where an understanding of weave is important, such as working as a textiles buyer or overseeing weave production.

Routes in
A degree in textiles is the usual place to start, and then it's great to get some work experience before looking for a paid job or going it alone.

CASE STUDY:

Eleanor is a weaver with two quite different strands to her practice.

Eleanor works as a self-employed weave designer, making blankets and other pieces sold both under her own name and as part of other designers' collections. She also undertakes commissioned work.

Eleanor originally did a degree in history. After a few years, she decided to go back to college and do a degree in textiles. She learned a lot technically, and about the processes, but perhaps more significantly, she developed her own voice. She was able to show her final-year collection at Première Vision. Here she was spotted by Christian Lacroix and asked to make outerwear fabrics for their winter collection.

After this amazing start, she got involved with two organisations who provide support and practical help for designer-makers, and she started to make her own designs while continuing to make money from work with ready-to-wear collections.

Best bits
▲ One of the things that differentiates weaving from print design is that the design, pattern, colour and fabric are all created simultaneously – a magical process

Worst bits
▼ The hand-to-mouth existence of being self-employed

Skills needed
- A flair for colour and pattern
- The ability to manage your time
- A knowledge of accounts, pricing and self-marketing

Study
- Traditional craft processes
- New technological advances
- Ideas and concepts
- Colour interaction
- Yarn capabilities

Links
The Crafts Council provides all sorts of support for designer-makers in the UK. www.craftscouncil.org
www.surfacedesign.org.uk
Première Vision: details of the leading international textiles and fabric show in Paris.
Charity supporting new textiles designers in the UK.
www.texprint.org.uk

Rating
Average salary:
Entrance difficulty:

Stand out from the crowd
Go to Milan (a centre for textiles) and get some work experience there. Be experimental and unique in your weaving, and present innovative examples of your creativity.

The impact of the cheap wages in the Far East has been significant within the yarn industry. The companies that have survived tend to produce for particular niche markets, or focus on yarn distribution; almost all are smaller than they once were.

yarn supplier

Sweater YARN – Senior Purchaser / Purchaser

A Garment Manufactory & Exporter is urgently inviting high-calibre candidates to fill the following vacancies: Sweater YARN – Senior Purchaser / Purchaser (Garment Trims). Min 2–5 years purchasing experience in SWEATER YARN. Must be able to handle yarn purchasing and sourcing and price negotiation.

Role based in Hong Kong.

Knitting is one of the few areas of production that is still relatively buoyant in the UK as it is not particularly labour intensive.

A lot of the business of yarn is about colour, and the process would usually start about 18 months before the season, with the designer coming up with a new collection of colours. The new collection will be based on intelligence from forecasters ('brown is the new black') and analysis of sales history ('that shade of pink does not sell'). The designers then get their factories overseas to make up some samples in the new colourways.

The factories will import the desired wool and start by scouring it to remove the impurities. The next step is to add the colour, blending different colours together to get the right shades. The wool then undergoes a process of 'carding' where it is fed through wire-covered rollers to remove any vegetable matter, and then it is ready for spinning. Once spun, the yarn is put on a 'cone' and sent over to the distributors.

Samples of the new yarns are made into a sample card, and the new range is launched at trade shows. The two most prestigious ones are both in Italy: in Milan and Florence. Manufacturers, retailers and design houses will come along to the trade shows and order yarns, and the suppliers will also send their sample cards to their mailing list of smaller organisations and sole traders who work within knitting and weaving.

Routes in
Take a relevant degree – this could be in textiles, marketing, manufacture or design. Lots of work experience in a range of areas helps, and then take any job you can find to get your foot in the door.

Best bits
▲ Working as a yarn supplier is very exciting – every day is different because you are selling to such a wide variety of end users
▲ You are working with many small businesses and individual freelancers, and so relationships are usually very personal

Bad bits
▼ The textiles industry has had a great deal of bad press over the last decade, so dealing with the media's attitude can be demoralising
▼ You may need to work overseas to get your career started

Skills needed
• A flair for colour and design
• Ability to build relationships with people
• Adaptability

Study
• Raw materials
• Design development
• Production
• 2D and 3D design
• Colour
• Commercial knowledge

Links
International **textiles news and events**. www.textileindustry.org
For **information on textiles markets internationally**. www.emergingtextiles.com
Trend forecasting website including information about colours and textiles. www.wgsn.com
East Midlands Textiles Association www.emtex.org.uk

Rating
Average salary:
Entrance difficulty: ● ○ ○

Stand out from the crowd
Be prepared to travel to where the opportunities are, whether that's in Milan, Turkey or the outer reaches of Scotland. Learn to knit or weave so that you can gain knowledge of the creative capabilities of yarn and demonstrate your passion for the range of textures and colours yarns provide.

The role of the fashion and textiles conservator is to conserve or preserve fabrics. Conservators usually work in museums that have textiles collections.

textiles conservator

There are a few private companies that provide expertise in textiles conservation, and some professionals work in a freelance capacity. Others may be employed by organisations who hold collections, such as museums. Depending on the organisation they work for this might include clothing collections from 500 years ago to the present day, as well as tapestries, furniture and other textile pieces.

The process would usually start with a meeting with the curators to find out about a particular object and how it is going to be displayed. The conservators then need to make a decision about what needs to be done and what kind of treatments the fabric can withstand. The item may well need to be cleaned, so the conservator needs to analyse the fabric and make a judgement on the most

It's a fairly scientific job, where you need to have a reasonable understanding of how different fabrics react in different conditions.

suitable cleaning process, be that wet cleaning, vacuuming or cleaning with solvents. The next stage would usually be to think about what kind of mending or support the item needs, identifying any rips, holes or areas of weakness that need to be looked at. Then the conservator needs to work out the best process for each piece, considering whether the item might need to be stuck together, sewn together or attached to a backing.

This work all needs to be done within a critical time frame. The conservators might start working on an exhibition up to three years in advance, but there might be up to 100 items that they would need to look at for that exhibition, while keeping on top of all the other ongoing requirements of the museum, so decisions about restoration are often pragmatic ones, based on what can be achieved in the time available.

Other tasks that a conservator might be involved with could include packing garments that are no longer being displayed into storage, and working on items to be loaned to other museums. It's a fairly scientific job, where you need to have an understanding of how different fabrics react in different conditions, as well as dyeing processes. It's also important to know about the characteristics of different kinds of fabrics, and how they behave in the long term – you need to be able to identify a compound weave, and know your linens from your jutes, for example.

Routes in

You'd need a relevant postgraduate degree in actual textiles conservation, or one of the more general courses in surface conservation, followed by an internship with one of the museums. There are occasionally opportunities to train on the job. A background in chemistry is also really useful.

LEFT Textile conservation at the V&A Museum, London.

CASE STUDY:

Wendy has been working at the Victoria and Albert Museum in London as a textiles conservator for 12 years.

Wendy's route into this field was quite an unusual one. She left school at 16 and started her career as a graphic designer. She enjoyed the work to an extent, but it soon became clear to her that this wasn't how she wanted to spend her working life. She decided that she was interested in restoration and conservation and then managed to find the details of someone who worked at the V&A. She contacted them and eventually got a three-year apprenticeship.

Since then Wendy has worked as a conservator in all sorts of different fields, before coming back to the V&A. She has been at the V&A for a while now, and although she keeps thinking that it ought to be time for a change, she can't really imagine working anywhere else. The thing she most loves about her work there is the expertise that exists within the museum. She works closely with some of the best technicians and curators in the world and gets to work with some amazing objects and garments within their fashion and textiles collections.

Her advice to anyone trying to get into this field is to get the relevant qualifications and then get as much work experience as you can.

Best bits
▲ There's great variety – you might be working on a pair of Coptic socks one day and a spacesuit the next, and on garments from the fifteenth century to this season's catwalk masterpieces

Worst bits
▼ There can be a fair bit of tedium – you can be stitching the same tapestry day in, day out for weeks on end
▼ There is a great feeling of responsibility, as you may be dealing with objects that have been around for hundreds of years

Skills needed
• Manual dexterity
• The ability to colour match
• Practical problem-solving and the ability to apply logic
• Patience
• Quick thinking to avert potential disasters
• Meticulous craftsmanship

Study
• Historical pattern cutting and construction
• Tailoring
• Corsetry and frames
• Millinery
• Surface and textile decoration
• Print and dyeing

Links
The Institute of Conservation (Icon), the professional body for conservators, has jobs, information and news and a magazine for members. www.icon.org.uk
Museums Association
www.museumsassociation.org
National Trust
www.nationaltrust.org.uk

Rating
Average salary: ● ● ●
Entrance difficulty: ● ● ●

Stand out from the crowd
Learn how to handle valuable objects; they're precious, but you need to feel confident with them.

CHAPTER FOUR

production

'Fashion production' covers the processes and techniques that convert the raw materials to the finished garments. The processes can be enormously complex as there are so many different materials that are used and so many different things that can be done to them.

Research and development within production is significant here, as competition within the fashion industry is so fierce and profit margins are so slight that any advances that will make the process quicker or cheaper, and anything that might make the garments better or stronger or more attractive, will be worth a lot of money.

Sourcing

Sourcing plays an essential role in the production process. The UK manufacturer or retailer's production team must assess each garment, and based upon their knowledge of the capabilities of factories around the world, make decisions about what country to manufacture that garment in. For example, if there is a 'lot of needle' (a lot of stitching detail) they might go to Hong Kong or China. If there is a lot of hand embellishment, they may place it in India. Production teams travel to factories around the world negotiating prices and delivery timing, as well as checking on the quality of the work in the factories. In some cases, companies will use a production agent in the country they are considering, who will do the negotiating and overseeing of product when the UK production team has left. The whole process is a team effort with the objective of supplying the best possible product for the best price, at the right delivery time.

The process

Raw materials can be natural, such as cotton from plants or wool from animals, or may be man-made, for example nylon and elastane. Some, such as leather, will just need to be treated and then cut to size, but most will need to be made into yarn or thread before being woven or knitted into fabric. Man-made fibres are produced as a continuous thread that is simply cut to size, while natural fibres come as short strands and are then spun into yarn.

If they come from a natural source, the fibres or yarns will need to be washed and chemically treated to get rid of any vegetable or other matter in them.

Colour can be added to the yarn or fabric at more or less any stage of the process: the fibres, yarn or fabric itself could be naturally coloured or dyed, and patterns can be added either during the weaving process or printed or sewn onto the fabric at a later stage. There are pros and cons to each method of adding colour, and decisions are made based on the cost and quality of the resulting fabric.

The processes of spinning, weaving, knitting and dyeing may all be carried out by the same company or might be

Yarns ready
for shipping.

carried out by different organisations. The part of the process described so far constitutes the textile production industry: converting fibres to cloth. This part of the industry is usually quite capital-investment heavy, in that these processes all require machines, and usually quite hefty, expensive ones.

Any advances that might make garments better or stronger or more attractive, will be worth a lot of money.

Garment production

The second part of the process is the garment production. Once the designers have created their designs for the garments, the pattern cutters need to get to work. Pattern cutting and grading are roles that span both design and production, so professionals might be employed by manufacturing companies, design houses or retailers. The fabric then needs to be cut, the pieces

sewn together and the trims and finishes added. The garment production side of the industry is increasingly automated, but is still, in general, pretty labour intensive, and this is one of the reasons for the large-scale move of manufacturing to countries overseas, in particular the Far East and the Indian subcontinent.

The context

In the UK, the textiles and clothing manufacturing industry was very important in the eighteenth and nineteenth centuries and the early part of the twentieth century.

Much of the textile manufacturing process involves working with heavy machinery.

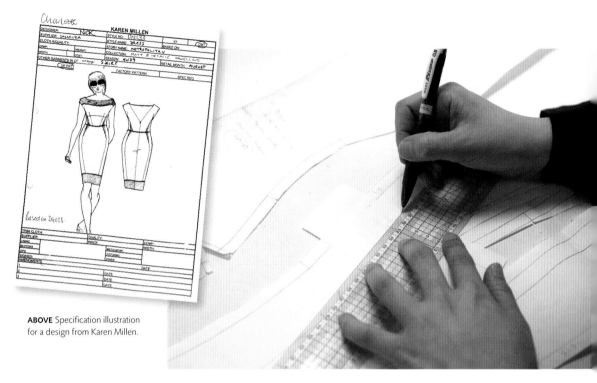

ABOVE Specification illustration for a design from Karen Millen.

However, the UK's involvement in the two world wars, and competition from newly industrialising countries began to take its toll on the sector, and the rise of the service sector and a whole host of other factors (political, economic and social) increased the rate of decline throughout the twentieth century. In the mid 1980s, the industry discovered that it was possible to have garments made up overseas for a fraction of the cost of production on the UK, as wages in developing countries were so much lower. From 1995 to 2002 the UK lost over half of its jobs in the clothing industry, and prices of clothing and footwear declined by 35 per cent.

Current trends

There is a hint of a reversal of this trend at the moment. There has been a significant amount of publicity around the conditions in factories overseas, in particular, around child labour, health and safety and campaigns for a living wage. The other interesting trend emerging is a focus on the environmental impacts of the production, with retailers being encouraged to buy their raw materials locally to reduce air miles.

Roles

Job roles in this field are clustered around the different parts of the process. You can be employed making yarn, adding colour or making up garments. Technologists and research and development specialists are employed at every stage of the process, and each stage will need project managers, technologists and sales managers.

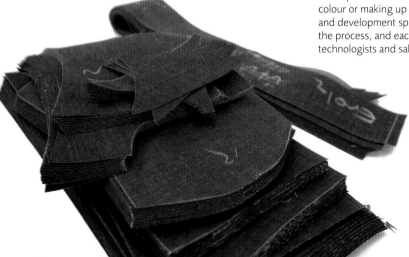

Lay planners use software to ensure that the fabric is cut efficiently and with minimal wastage.

LEFT Pattern cutting requires great attention to detail.

RIGHT Computer-aided design (CAD) is increasingly vital in the industry.

Routes in

There are still some apprenticeships, which will be advertised either online or in local papers. You can also approach factories directly or use recruitment agencies to see what entry-level posts there are.

Best bits

- ▲ The almost alchemic magic of making some cloth out of some fibres, or a garment out of fabric
- ▲ The results are very tangible
- ▲ Opportunity for lots of travel and living and working abroad
- ▲ It's less competitive than many other areas within the industry

Worst bits

- ▼ The opportunities within the UK are limited and many people will spend some part of their careers working overseas. This will not suit all people and all lifestyles
- ▼ These are very practical roles, and your opportunities to use your creative skills are limited

Skills needed

- Practicality
- Manual dexterity
- An ability to work quickly and carefully
- A relevant degree is needed for some of the positions
- For others, the skills are learned on the job
- Attention to detail
- Good people skills

Links

Drapers Online: the industry trade magazine, with news, information and job vacancies. www.drapersonline.com
The Association of Suppliers to the British Clothing Industry have a student membership association which is a great place to network. They sponsor a graduate dissertation prize each year. www.asbci.co.uk

The production manager oversees all aspects of the production of the garments, from beginning to end. This involves estimating fabric yardage and ordering it along with all trims, and ensuring that garments are made on time and to the required standards, and that they are shipped correctly.

production manager

The process of actually making a garment for someone to wear is complicated, but creating a real product from a drawing can feel quite magical. The production process works to the same annual cycle as the fashion design process.

The time frames for those working in production will vary tremendously depending on what kinds of garments they are producing and who they are producing them for, but on average the process might start around a year in advance. The client would start with a design brief, giving a broad overview as to what they are looking for this season and the kinds of trends they want to see in the garments. The production manager would then work with a team to put a strategy together to present to the client. The production team would want to respond to the client's brief but try to build on it and offer something extra. They would research the market themselves, using information gleaned from shopping trips and other clients, and in their strategy would offer a whole range of options that the client could choose from.

If the client likes what they see, then the factory can go straight into sample production, but the client may well be hearing strategies from a few different production companies, so the production managers might end up in a competitive negotiation with the client playing one factory against the other to get the best ideas for the best prices.

Once they've been given the go-ahead, the production manager would send a product brief to the factory to get some samples produced to the specifications that have been set. Fabrics or yarns might be supplied by the clients or the suppliers will be given a clear brief and asked to source them themselves.

The production manager would work with the packaging design team to decide what kind of packaging to use and to write the words that would go on the labels (this might sometimes be outsourced to a specific packaging company).

When the samples come back from the factories, the production manager would present them to the client, and the client might make some changes and then make a final decision about whether to start production.

If the order goes ahead, the production manager then commissions the factory to make a dozen or so garments, which are then sent out to garment testers – a group of people who wear the products and feed back on their fit and comfort – and if that stage all goes to plan, the production manager and technical director would set up a contract seal meeting with the client and get mass production in motion.

Many manufacturers and retailers who design their own product have production managers and a whole production team. These production managers function in much the

Study
- Garment construction
- Business courses
- Textile management
- Production processes

Links

Drapers Online: the industry trade magazine, with news, information and job vacancies. www.drapersonline.com
Creativepool: for vacancies and opportunities. www.creativepool.co.uk

Rating

Average salary: ● ● ○
Entrance difficulty: ● ● ○

Stand out from the crowd

Learn a language: the bulk of clothes and accessories are produced overseas, and if you can speak Hindi, Turkish or Mandarin, you are going to really open up your options.

CASE STUDY:

Jane is a production manager.

Jane graduated in textiles technology, but at that point there was a recession, and the use of computers was revolutionising the technology side of the industry, so there were very few jobs available – those that were advertised were hugely oversubscribed.

As an interim measure, Jane decided to go into sales but used her knowledge and understanding of textiles, selling fabrics to the industry. She really enjoyed working with the fabrics and developing good relationships with some of her clients but never thoroughly embraced the straightforward sales side of the role. She began to specialise and went into selling lace to lingerie designers, and gradually worked her way up to a sales director role.

At this stage she decided to take a leap of faith and changed direction, returning to the technology side of the industry that she had first trained in. Because of her experience in senior management and her expertise in textiles, as well as her aptitude for organisation, she was able to enter the technology side of the business at a fairly senior level and after two years became a production manager.

Making a career for yourself entirely within production is tricky at the moment, but Jane's advice is: 'Don't rule it out as an option. Lots of companies have their manufacturing plants offshore but have design and development at home. There are still a lot of design, production teams and technical teams connected with factories overseas, so don't give up on the idea altogether!'

same way as factory production managers, analysing and pricing garments, but they negotiate with factory managers to find the best placement for the specific garments. They work closely with the designers, merchandisers and buyers on the details and the embellishments of the garments and with the production managers in the factories to make sure that the spec packages are followed exactly.

Routes in

A relevant degree is needed, and the industry is more interested in a graduate of a technical subject such as textiles management rather than design. Many production manager jobs are overseas, so if you are prepared to spend some time overseas you will have more opportunities. This is a much less fiercely competitive area than fashion design and there are fewer people going for each advertised vacancy, so unpaid work experience, while still useful, is often not needed.

Best bits

- ▲ If you enjoy creating things, it's fascinating to take something from 2D to 3D – or from yarn to garment
- ▲ Production managers get a real buzz out of working in the actual factories – right at the heart of the industry

Worst bits

- ▼ Currently the production industry in the UK is fragile, and although there are signs of a return to mass production, the future is very uncertain
- ▼ The industry is also fickle. New value retailers have swept into the market with their very low price points undercutting all the established producers, and the focus in the industry is now on high fashion and speed to market. These are tough times for factories

Skills needed

- Practicality
- Project management skills
- Problem-solving abilities

Production Manager

For a leading and well-established fashion jewellery design company.

Duties: Will include maintenance of components and beads, production of outwork orders and assisting the jewellery designer in streamlining production samples.

Requirements: Attitude and ability will shine over previous experience. A display of good organisational skills, an eye for detail and practical ability.

Salary: £30,000

There are two sides to the role of the fabric technician. In some organisations, one technician will fulfil both functions, but in others the roles will be split. Fabric technicians usually work for fabric manufacturers or retailers, and although it is possible to work freelance, they are usually employed by a particular organisation.

fabric technician

Quality

The first, and most common, function of the fabric technician is to ensure that the fabric or yarn that a firm is producing is of good quality, fit for purpose and meets the criteria set out. The fabric technician would run a series of tests to check a range of properties in the fabric, which might include spot checks on a small proportion of the finished products, checking every single product at some point in the production and ensuring that systems and procedures are effective and working well. The technician will check for the consistency of colour – making sure that the dyeing process has left all parts of the fabric exactly the same shade – and colourfastness (ensuring that when you wash the fabric the colour doesn't run or fade too quickly). They will look at the weave and check that there are no imperfections or parts of the fabric where the tension of the thread is inconsistent.

> *The fabric technician ensures that the fabric or yarn is of good quality, fit for purpose and meets the criteria set out.*

Development

The second part of the technician's role is to work on research and development of fabric. The technician will make sure that they are aware of the technological advances in yarns, fabrics and techniques to be certain that their firm can take advantage of new developments in the industry and maintain a competitive edge.

In addition to this technical understanding, the technician needs to be able to develop and maintain good working relationships. They will be working closely with teams of designers and manufacturers and will get involved in the sales and price negotiations, so need to have a good commercial understanding.

As with most jobs in the production sector, a lot of the work involves travelling or relocating overseas.

Some fabric technicians are also responsible for researching new fabrics for the design team, buyers or merchandisers. This can be a fun component of the job, as they travel widely to explore the latest fabric trends and work closely with the designers on the development of new textiles. Cataloguing and documenting the fabrics is essential, as well as maintaining relationships with mills and fabric suppliers.

Study

- Textile management
- Production processes

Links

Drapers Online: the industry trade magazine, with news, information and job vacancies. www.drapersonline.com

Association of Suppliers to the British Clothing Industry (ASBCI): for industry news and making contacts. www.asbci.co.uk

Lots of **news and information** and 'emerging talent award' for recent graduates. www.interiortextiles.co.uk

Rating

Average salary: ● ● ○
Entrance difficulty: ● ○ ○

Stand out from the crowd

Any technician who can speak another language, such as Mandarin or Hindi, is usually in great demand.

DAY IN THE LIFE:
Fabric specialist

Nicole is a fabric specialist for a sportswear manufacturer. She works closely with the design team and the factories.

8.30AM NICOLE JUST RETURNED FROM ITALY
She brought back swatches of recycled textiles and cut-and-sew fabrics that she is eager to show the designers.

9.00AM FABRICATION MEETING
Nicole shares swatches of the fabrics, with information: price, content, width, minimums, lead times. The designers ask Nicole to order sample yardage of the Italian fabrics and request additional fabric research. Nicole loves the challenge of finding new textiles and working with the designers.

11.00AM A STRIKE-OFF (A PRINTED TEST) OF A FLORAL PRINT HAS ARRIVED FROM JAPAN
Nicole examines the strike-off in a lightbox (to test colour accuracy). She emails the mill with corrections.

12.45PM A CUTTER TEXTS NICOLE TO RUSH TO THE FACTORY
The linen has arrived with streaks. Nicole grabs a bagel and a cab. At the factory, a huge bolt of the linen is put onto the roller for examination. Definitely seconds! Nicole calls the fabric supplier and negotiates a settlement.

3.00PM NICOLE STOPS TO LOOK AT YARN-DYE STRIPES AT A FABRIC IMPORTER
She pegs new colours with the Pantone chips from the designer's palette, and asks for a computer rendering to show the designer.

4.00PM FABRIC LIBRARY
At Cotton Incorporated (a library of cotton fabrics), Nicole searches for twill for one of the designers.

5.00PM WRAPPING UP
Nicole returns to check on her assistant's documentation of new fabrics for their fabric library. They share a latte and review the day.

Routes in
A degree in textiles or fabric technology and then an entry-level job or internship with a manufacturing firm.

Best bits
▲ The combination of people and technical skills
▲ The product development side of things can be exciting
▲ Opportunities for travel

Worst bits
▼ Quality control can be less stimulating
▼ You may need to relocate overseas

Skills needed
• Technical interest and understanding
• A good knowledge of fabrics and how they behave
• Excellent people skills
• Commercial acumen

Here the process moves on from the ideas of the designer to the point where the fabric is ready to be cut. These jobs are the link between the designers and the manufacturers, and professionals in these roles need to have a good understanding of both sides of the process. Though practical roles, sympathy towards the creative process is very helpful.

pattern cutter, grader and lay planner

The pattern cutter needs to translate the designer's ideas and images into actual patterns that can be used to make garments, with minimal fabric waste. The designer, sometimes working with the technical designer, will create a pattern specification sheet, which is a list of measurements for the finished garment. The pattern cutter will then have to work out what shape and size of fabric is needed for each of the different pieces that will be sewn together to make the garment. Pattern cutters can do this either by hand, using flat pattern cutting techniques, or using computer-aided design (CAD). The layout of pattern pieces is known as a 'marker'. A sample is made in fabric and the pattern is revised if necessary.

The pattern grader will then do the calculations to get the right measurements for each different size: the original garments might be made up in a size 10, for example, but the grader will then need to make patterns for sizes 8–16.

The lay planner will then work out, either manually or using CAD, the best way to lay the pattern pieces onto the fabric to use the fabric most efficiently.

Pattern cutters, graders and lay planners can work for designers or manufacturers, or for specialist pattern-cutting agencies who provide these services on a consultancy basis to others in the industry. It is also possible to work freelance in this field once you have built up some contacts. In some small organisations the roles are performed by one person, but in larger organisations it is common to have three different people in the different roles. Often, pattern cutters have an area of specialism, such as knitwear. Designers also sometimes cut and grade their own patterns.

Routes in

Cutters, graders and lay planners can learn their trade either through a degree course such as fashion technology or fashion design, or they may take an apprenticeship and learn their skills on the job.

Best bits

▲ For some, being on the fringes of the design process is a great place to be. You don't have the responsibility of coming up with the ideas yourself
▲ Pattern cutters do have enormous creative input, though, and can make or break a design through the quality of fit they achieve
▲ Jobs tend to be relatively stable and secure

Pattern Cutter Assistant/Intern
Emerging high-end womenswear brand.

Length of placement: 4 weeks

Experience gained: The student could gain experience of pattern cutting and sampling. The successful candidate will be assisting the pattern cutter in everyday duties: tracing patterns, toiling and daily studio organisation. This placement would benefit a flexible, organised Fashion/Pattern Cutting student/graduate.

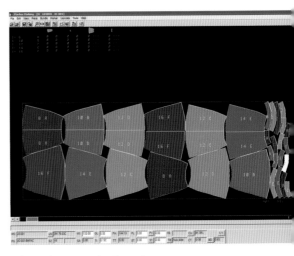

Software demonstrates how best to lay the pattern pieces on the fabric to minimise wastage.

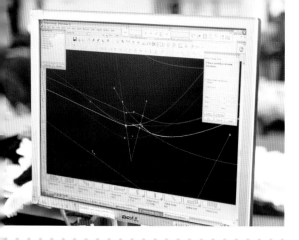

Worst bits

▼ That feeling of being on the fringes of the design process might not be satisfying if you are a frustrated designer

▼ The need for accuracy can sometimes create quite a stressful environment

Skills needed

- Accuracy. Patterns need to be cut to very precise sizes. Mistakes can add up to thousands of wasted dollars if the size 10 doesn't turn out to be significantly bigger than the size 8

You are working with designers but don't have the responsibility of coming up with the ideas yourself.

- Attention to detail
- An excellent understanding of the design process and how garments are actually made
- Exceptional understanding of fabric behavior
- The ability to collaborate with the designer to realise a vision

📁 CASE STUDY:

Louise is a pattern cutter for a pattern-cutting agency.

Louise was born into the world of fashion, as her father was a salesman for a fabric company. As she got older her passion for clothes and fashion grew and she started a degree in fashion design.

Louise enjoyed the course, but it gradually became clear that although she loved the industry and being surrounded by creative people making fabulous clothes, she wasn't one of the leading lights in the class, and she started to doubt that her chosen career path was the right one for her. 'I did really enjoy creating and making garments, but I found it all really stressful. The fashion industry is tough and I wasn't sure that I was prepared to put myself through all that unpaid work experience and those long tough hours, if I wasn't that likely to make it to the top.' So she started thinking about what else she could do. She had really enjoyed the pattern cutting that they had done at college and her tutor was very encouraging: 'When I started the course I don't think I even knew that there was a job called "pattern cutting" but the more I found out about it, the more I realised that this was just right for me.'

Louise did a work placement with a pattern-cutting agency and loved it. She really excelled and enjoyed the precision of it and the certainty of knowing that there were right and wrong answers. She kept in touch with the company and went back during each holiday. When she graduated they offered her a job there, and three years later she has moved up to be senior pattern cutter and is thriving.

Study

- Techniques such as slashing and pivoting of darts
- Drafts and sample patterns
- Varying silhouettes for bodices, skirts, sleeves and collars
- Provisions for fastenings
- Basic draping techniques
- Interpreting flat drawings into patterns
- Grading principles

Links

Drapers Online: the industry trade magazine, with news, information and job vacancies. www.drapersonline.com
Association of Suppliers to the British Clothing Industry (ASBCI): for industry news and making contacts. www.asbci.co.uk
Lots of **news and information** and 'emerging talent award' for recent graduates. www.interiortextiles.co.uk

Rating

Average salary: ● ● ●
Entrance difficulty: ● ● ●

Stand out from the crowd

Some experience of the design process is helpful.

The job of a tailor is to create commissioned suits made to the exact measurements and the specific design requirements of each individual client.

Luxury Tailor

Role Details To display a high degree of ability in the measuring, fitting and skillful marking of finished garments for alteration.

Administer and organise customer orders, alteration documentation and workroom returns.

Communicate internally between the department, main factories and local adjustment workrooms as and when required.

Deal with customers in a professional and friendly manner, ensuring that they receive a first-class service at all times.

To work with colleagues in the Tailoring Department.

tailor

A traditional tailor will hand make and hand finish every part of a suit and will create a pattern for the suit based on the exact measurements of the client, but the industry is now seeing the rise of the semi-made-to-order suit. Here tailors will take the client's measurements but will make their pattern from existing 'blocks', which are cut to size by an automated computer system.

A tailor might be involved in every part of the process, from meeting and greeting clients, taking measurements and helping the clients to choose fabrics and styles, through to actually cutting the fabric and sewing the garments. An individual would more likely specialise in either the front-of-house role or the production side, and it is often the case that tailors start their careers making the suits and then move into the front-of-house work as they get more experienced.

The front-of-house tailor will talk to the clients about the cloth, the lining, the style, what's going to suit their body shape and what kind of finishings they might like. They will also take the clients' measurements and deal with fittings and any alterations that might be needed.

The actual suit makers will then take these measurements and make up the pattern, cut the cloth, sew the pieces together and finish the garment off.

Tailors' clients are more varied than you might imagine. There still are a good number of very wealthy men and women who can simply afford the luxury, but it is very common for people who have an unusual body shape to have clothes specially made as they can't find a good fit in regular shops. And the wedding market is a big one – many grooms and best men will have suits specially made for their big day.

Routes in

A qualification in something relevant – textiles or fashion design or pattern cutting – can be helpful but is not always necessary. Jobs are advertised in *Drapers*, or you can get in touch with individual tailors speculatively. Apprenticeship with a tailor is the best preparation.

Best bits

▲ Satisfied customers – seeing how pleased a client is with a suit that you've made for them
▲ Being involved in the fashion industry, but not quite at the (sometimes) cut-throat cutting edge of it
▲ Meeting and working with so many different people

A tailored lace jacket design by Karen Millen is pressed on a mannequin.

Worst bits

▼ Although most clients are a real pleasure to work with there can be one or two who have unrealistic expectations or who are rude or difficult

▼ It's a great job, but a tailor is not a designer. Very creative designers might find it frustrating to be limited to suits

Skills needed

• You need to be a good people person
• Good with detail and careful with your hands
• An interest in the clothes that you will be making
• Knowledge of fabrics, sewing in general and techniques other than tailoring – often learned on the job
• An exceptional eye for minute detail in the fitting process – tailoring is a very, very specific world (not unlike denim), and an understanding of the minutiae of types and weights of fabrics make its possibilities almost limitless

> *It's a great job, but a tailor is not a designer. Very creative designers might find it frustrating to be limited to suits.*

CASE STUDY:

Neil works for a firm of tailors and travels around for meetings with clients, fittings and alterations.

Neil started his career straight from school as an apprentice in a mill. This was great training for his current role as he learned all about fabrics: how they feel, how they look, what you can do with them, how they wear and wash and how they behave in different conditions.

After about five years he moved on to train as a tailor. The firm he works with now outsources the actual making of the suits to a supplier, but although Neil doesn't work as a suit manufacturer, he spent the first three months at his current job seconded to one of their suppliers to really learn the process inside out.

For Neil the best part of the job is the clients. He loves the variety: 'One day you'll be working with a TV celebrity and the next it's a guy who's spent the last two years saving to buy a suit.' And for Neil the best days are the days when he sees a happy customer: 'You hand over the suit and you see the guy strutting around the fitting room like a peacock. It's magic.' Neil's advice to anyone thinking about a career in tailoring is simple: 'If you love suits and you love people, it's the best job you could get.'

Study

• Fabrics and textiles
• Hand stitching
• Machine sewing
• Techniques such as collars, sleeves and pockets
• Cut
• Construction
• CAD
• Tailoring techniques

Links

Univeristy of the Arts London, London College of Fashion: for a BA in tailoring. www.fashion.arts.ac.uk

Drapers Online: the industry trade magazine, with news, information and job vacancies. www.drapersonline.com

Rating

Average salary: ● ● ○
Entrance difficulty: ● ● ○

Stand out from the crowd

Take your portfolio to Savile Row and knock on some doors. Your proactive attitude may go down very well. Be willing to start at the bottom and learn.

The machinist is the person who makes up the garments. They may sew by hand, use sewing machines for individual garments or computerised machinery.

machinist

As production has moved overseas, the number of machinists in the UK has dropped dramatically; now most jobs are based in the Midlands and the north, or in the East End of London, where there are still a few factories left.

Increasingly the production of garments is becoming more computerised and the machinist is now likely to get involved in programming a computerised sewing machine and feeding in parts of garments, such as collars and cuffs, to the machine.

In a smaller factory the machinist might be required to do all the sewing to make up the finished garment, whereas in a larger factory, the machinist might work as part of a larger team and might specialise in one particular type of sewing or one particular element of the finished garment, such as the sleeves. This is called piece work.

In addition to the factory work, machinists are used by design houses to make up samples. They prefer getting these made up in the UK, as what they have to pay out in the UK's higher wages is more than made up for by the convenience and control of having the samples made locally. Being a sample machinist is a role that a machinist might go into after gaining some experience in factories first, and the designers might expect a good understanding of fashion and design as well as sewing skills.

Routes in

This is one area within the industry that doesn't demand a degree or unpaid work experience, but completing a basic sewing course will stand you in good stead. Some

CASE STUDY:

Claire works for a factory that produces knitwear for a number of high street retailers.

Claire wasn't particularly strong at the academic subjects at school but had a fantastic art and design teacher who really encouraged her. She went to college and did a short course in sewing and then got an apprenticeship at a local factory, where she had flexitime each week to go to college and learn more about the techniques she was using in her daily work.

For Claire, the best things about her job are her colleagues and the fact that she is doing something practical. Claire feels that being neat and having a really good eye for detail are the things that make a good machinist. For now she is quite happy with the job, but hopes in the future to be a sample machinist, and in the future she'd love to open her own business making clothes for children.

organisations offer apprenticeships or you can apply for entry-level jobs and work your way up.

Best bits
- ▲ Working environments are often relaxed and informal
- ▲ It can be very satisfying to see the results of your work so clearly and swiftly

Worst bits
- ▼ Working environments can often get very hot and noisy
- ▼ The work can be repetitive
- ▼ It's not well paid

Skills needed
- Care and attention to detail
- Patience and an ability to follow instructions to the letter
- Good sewing skills

Study
- Fashion
- Textiles
- Sewing
- Apparel manufacturing technology
- Garment technology
- Sample production techniques

Links
The ABC Awards for information about courses and qualifications.
www.abcawards.co.uk
Apprenticeships
www.apprenticeships.org.uk
The Textile Institute: For information about the industry.
www.texi.org

Rating
Average salary: ● ● ●
Entrance difficulty: ● ● ●

Stand out from the crowd
A really good eye for detail will stand you in good stead.

Many fabrics can be bought in a great variety of colours, but some come in only a limited range. Designers and directors sometimes have a very specific shade in mind and must ask a dyer to produce this for them.

dyer and colourist

Most designers get their bulk orders of fabric dyed and coloured near the factories that are producing the garments, and as so many of these are in the Far East and other overseas locations, the career of the colourist or dyer in the UK ends up being quite specialised. They will tend to produce one-off garments rather than fabric for mass production. They may work with couture collections or with more mainstream manufacturers to produce samples. Dyers also work with theatres, operas, movies and TV to produce exactly the shade of fabric a director is looking for, as well as for interior design firms, wedding dress designers and manufacturers and on all sorts of other projects. There are also a few companies who specialise in dyeing individual pieces for private clients.

Dyeing is a much broader arena than it might sound. To dye fabrics effectively you need to know how different fabrics respond to different chemicals or what shade of dye you need to use on a satin trim to make it the same shade as the cotton dress it goes with. You need to know about techniques such as ombreying (making fabric darker at one end and lighter at the other), or how to make a shirt look worn (known as breakdown).

Another role that has colour at its heart is that of a colourist. Colourists might work for yarn or fabric manufacturers, creating new colourways for each season, and might be employed by forecasting companies to make predictions about the colours that will be popular for the next season. They may also be employed on the more technical side of the business, ensuring colourfastness or consistent quality of colour.

Dyers and colourists are often freelance, but some are employed by major retailers and performance companies or by specialist dyeing firms.

Routes in
Take a degree in something relevant – textiles, fashion or costume; then it's lots of networking and unpaid work experience.

Best bits
▲ A freelance dyer and colourist can have an enormous amount of variety in their work

Worst bits
▼ Things go wrong and fabric and dyes don't always behave as they should
▼ It can be quite pressurised as you are often working for other people who have very tight deadlines

Skills needed
• Patience
• Your work needs to be extremely precise
• You need a good eye for colour

CASE STUDY:

Sheila works as a freelance dyer for couture designers, high street retailers and other clients.

Sheila's degree was in fashion and textiles. She had a year in industry as part of her course and worked with a firm of converters (people who convert designs to prints) and a designer. From then on she worked on making fabrics and in her degree show was spotted by a designer who used all of Sheila's fabrics for her collection. For a while she did some freelance textiles design work, but then she heard that the dyeing department at the Royal Opera House in London wanted to recruit a dyer who knew something about print and textiles, and Sheila got the job. Nearly 20 years later she still works for the opera house, but now as a freelancer, alongside other projects.

Study
• Chemistry of colourants
• Polymers: properties and production
• Organisation and management
• Preparation, dyeing and finishing
• Textile printing technology

Links
News and information about the textiles dyeing industry. www.textiledyer.com
The Society of Dyers and Colourists for news and information. www.sdc.org.uk

Rating
Average salary: ● ● ○
Entrance difficulty: ● ● ●

Stand out from the crowd
Experiment with creative dyeing techniques and build a portfolio.

CHAPTER FIVE

costume design

The entertainment industry is in the throes of a thriving and seemingly endless boom. We are increasingly a leisure society, and during our leisure time we love nothing more than a trip to the cinema or the theatre, or a night in, in front of the TV. And every character on every screen, stage or channel needs to be dressed...

This, you can imagine, is quite a feat! In some cases, the greatest compliment you can pay the costume team is that you didn't notice the clothes: the extras in a sitcom would be an example of this. For some shows, the goal is historical accuracy (zips weren't introduced until 1891, you know. . .), while for others, your goal might be to elicit a particular emotion – whether the 'Wow!' of the transformation of Julia Roberts from prostitute to operagoer in *Pretty Woman*, or a 'yuck' for the aliens in a sci-fi flick. But what the costume teams are all doing is trying to support and enhance their director's ideas. This might be done by reflecting the look and feel of the production, the time and place of the narrative or the plot itself, but is most often achieved through the characters. The costume team needs to make sure that every element of a character's appearance reflects the viewer's perceptions of their personality, circumstances and

A Michael Kaplan design from *Fight Club.*

history so that the viewer has a clear idea of the character before they even speak.

So the concepts are complex, and so too is the implementation. Once the designers have decided what they are looking for, the outfits need to be found: bought, hired, made or sometimes all three. And then the cast needs to be fitted and dressed. Now, finding costumes for an intimate conversation between two characters in a contemporary setting might not feel too challenging, but try getting your head around how you would get hold of and lace up 200 corsets and put on 200 hairpieces for a Victorian ball scene!

Working with live performances has its own particular set of challenges and rewards. The costume team get to watch the actors rehearse so have quite some time to see how the outfits work on stage, and the time to change things if they need to. On the other hand, the logistics of making sure that all the outfits for the whole cast are always clean and ironed, and are always in the right place at the right time, can be tough. And with some long-running shows, the principal characters might only be in the cast for a short time (even

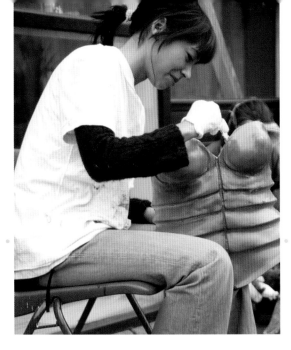

LEFT The work of the costume department is often practical and very detailed.

RIGHT Costume design for Britney Spears' 'The Circus Starring Britney Spears' tour.

just a few performances in the case of opera) so the costumes need to be made and re-made regularly.

As with so many of the jobs in this book, the roles of those who work with costumes have, at their core, creativity and teamwork. And 'creativity' here means something quite broad. It's not just a case of the visual creativity of creating a particular garment or outfit, although that is important. It's also about problem solving. How to get 150 gladiators clothed when there are only 40 gladiator outfits in London? How to evoke fabulous, sumptuous wealth on a shoestring budget?

The people side is equally important. The costume team need to be able to understand what their colleagues mean, be that the designer interpreting the director, or writers or set designer, or the wardrobe mistresses having a clear sense of exactly what needs to be laundered and when; and mistakes are costly. The costume team also need to develop good rapport with the actors they are working with. The dressing part of a production can take hours and involves a lot of waiting around for the actors, so the dressers do not always get to see them at their most charming! Tact, empathy and sensitivity are all important.

Routes in
You need a relevant degree and then plenty of unpaid work experience. You have to be passionate about costumes. Costume design or wardrobe work in small theatre productions, college performances or independent films are all ways to build your CV and level of experience. Build contacts as you build your portfolio and stay connected.

Best bits
- ▲ A combination of psychology and creativity
- ▲ It's great for people who love the idea of working on productions but don't want to be in the limelight
- ▲ A real variety of colleagues

Worst bits
- ▼ Long hours and sometimes long periods away from home
- ▼ Work can be insecure
- ▼ Actors aren't always the easiest people to work with

Skills needed
- Creativity
- People skills
- The ability to work effectively in teams
- An interest in semiotics is important: what messages do different clothes send out?
- A good grasp of detail and an aptitude for research

Links
BECTU is the trade union for the entertainment business and offers support and advice.
www.bectu.org.uk
Information about the **BBC's costume trainee scheme**.
http://www.bbc.co.uk/jobs/design/costume.shtml
The Costume Designers Guild: for working in the US.
www.costumedesignersguild.com

The costume designer develops the visual identity of the characters in a script. This involves understanding how to convey a personality, character and background in an instant.

costume designer

Costume
Department Intern

Location: NYC

I am looking for young, enthusiastic spirits who would like to get some hands-on experience in the costume department in exchange for their time and help. Since we are a small team, you will get the chance to be incorporated into all aspects of costuming. It would be great if you had some clothing background but your willingness to learn is sufficient. I look forward to hearing from you.

As a costume designer you are an integral part of a team. It is your job to decide how the characters should be expressed visually, but to do this you need to work closely and effectively with a number of colleagues. The production designer will always be key: they design the world and you build the people, but you also need to work with make-up artists, the writers, the actors, tailors, assistants, costumiers, and of course the director.

You would usually start the process with the script and talk to the director in more detail about the characters, gradually building up a clear picture of who they all are. For each one, you need to think about a whole range of factors: their socioeconomic status, their salary, their job, whether they went to college, their hobbies, family set-up and aspirations. You might need to think about the action in the film and whether the costume can be used to help the drama (for example, a sweeping cloak as a character rushes down a street), and you would need to know a bit about where the drama is all taking place – era, country, season and location.

Your first task would be to produce a book. This is a sort of mood board for the main characters. In this you would put anything that will help to explain your ideas. You might sketch some outfits and include some swatches of fabric, some ideas for the colour palette, some photographs of your influences and you might use words to supplement these images.

Once your basic concepts are agreed by the director, your next task might be to have a meeting with the main actors and talk through your ideas with them. You might bring some outfits with you to illustrate your ideas – whether these are hired from an agency, or bought from nearby shops. Depending on the size of the production, you might be expected to come up with outfits for everyone, or you might have an assistant designer who would take on your concepts and dress the minor characters and the crowd scenes.

Once filming has started the focus of your role may change a bit. You will be in charge of the costume supervisors and wardrobe mistresses and masters who make sure that the clothes are properly laundered and protected. As the filming takes place you may need to respond to changes: a new bedroom scene might require different outfits or a change in the background wallpaper might mean that the black outfit that you had selected no longer looks as dramatic.

As a designer you can work on television, film and video, adverts or in theatre. You are likely to work freelance and will have an agent who helps find you work and get the best deals for you. The process of costume design is broadly

Study

- Historical pattern cutting and construction
- Tailoring
- Corsetry and frames
- Millinery
- Surface and textile decoration
- Print and dyeing

Links

Creative and Cultural Skills: the sector skills council for design, with news, information and careers support for designers. www.ccskills.org.uk
Skillset: the sector skills council for the media, with information about careers within all aspects of the media. www.skillset.org
Society of British Theatre Designers (SBTD): for news and information. www.theatredesign.org.uk

Rating

Average salary: ● ● ●
Entrance difficulty: ● ● ●

Stand out from the crowd

To climb to costume designer, your CV as an assistant costume designer should list a range of shows where you contributed to the success of the production through your creativity. Build a brilliant portfolio.

ABOVE As a costume designer you work with an amazing array of garments. Some may be quite unconventional, such as this feathered headdress.

similar wherever you work, but the particular stresses and strains will vary depending on the context. When working on adverts, the agencies have usually done an enormous amount of research before they hire the designer, so may already have a clear idea of the look they want for their characters, whereas in film and TV drama the costume designer is brought in quite early in the creative process and is likely to have a bit more creative freedom. In a theatre the actors will rehearse in their costumes, so you are more able to try things out and change them as rehearsals progress. Within opera, your might need to create costumes that can be easily altered as one singer replaces another, and with live performances, the audience is seeing the characters from further away so this might lead to a different emphasis on the clothes. Timescales and budgets will also impact on the experience.

Routes in
Get as much experience as you can. Write to designers you like and ask to meet them and do some work experience with them.

Best bits
▲ It's great fun. It's physically, mentally and emotionally consuming
▲ You get to see amazing places and work with amazing people

Worst bits
▼ Long hours
▼ You'll spend most of your career freelancing, and with that come certain constraints such as having no job security, paid holidays or pension

 **IN HER OWN WORDS:**

Liz is a freelance costume designer.

'I graduated with a degree in fashion textiles. I had sold my designs throughout my degree course so when I graduated I continued to do this freelance for a while, but soon became a bit isolated.

'I got a job at the Royal Opera House at Covent Garden, doing a maternity leave cover as a dyer. Although I like to flatter myself that it was my sparkling personality and brilliant sense of colour that got me the job, I was told that I had been hired because I had a very clear speaking voice and my closest colleague was a little deaf! I spent two years there dyeing fabrics for cloaks, and then went to work as a technician while I did a masters. I got a few freelance jobs while I was studying, mostly working on dyeing and breakdown, but after a while became a bit despondent about whether I was ever going to move forward at all.

'Then my moment of serendipity came by chance one day when I started chatting to someone in a café who turned out to be a producer who was looking for an assistant costume designer. He asked me to come and see him at work the next day and I was hired to work on his series of 24 short films. There is no doubt that this was a great bit of luck, and making it in this field is often down to luck, but it's also about being in the right situation to take advantage of the opportunity. This director would have had no interest in me had I not spent the previous five years getting qualified and experienced. So yes, it was down to chance, but hard graft and the right skills played their part too.'

Skills needed
• You need to know clothes backwards, forwards, inside out and upside down. How they're made, where to get them and who can create them for you
• You need to have a real interest in and instinct for identifying the kinds of clothes that different kinds of people wear (how would you make someone look American? Or 30 rather than 40? Or a graduate rather than a non-graduate?)
• You need a strong visual sense and good vision
• You will probably spend your career working freelance so this means you have to work when the work is there and often means working 16-hour days and six-day weeks, away from home for weeks on end. If you are not prepared or able to do this, you might need to think again
• It's a very team-based job, and you need to be able to get along with all kinds of people, and to make good judgements around your negotiations

The role of assistant costume designer is to work with the costume designer to provide outfits for the cast.

assistant costume designer

Following the instructions of the costume designer, the assistant costume designer helps to design, source, purchase, hire and/or make all costumes for a production. They may work with a costume hire agency who will have hundreds or even thousands of garments to select from. The costume designer will give the assistant a brief to work from such as 'I need 200 costumes for French peasant women in the 18th century', or 'I need an outfit for someone on jury duty: he is 34, married with two small children, university-educated, smokes and enjoys playing football'. The assistant costume designer will then have a look at their stock and see what is available. They might need to alter existing stock with trimmings, source some clothes or fabrics from shops or arrange for new garments to be made up. They would also be present at fittings with actors, and work with extras to ensure that they are appropriately costumed.

Assistant costume designers can become specialists in areas such as fabric dyeing and 'breakdown' (making a shirt look as though the actor has rolled around in the mud or been mauled by a tiger). The assistant communicates with the costume shop and wardrobe supervisor to ensure that the costume designer's vision is carried out. This position requires costume designers' union certification for professional productions in the US (see page 108).

ABOVE An assistant costume designer helps an actor with her period costume.

Routes in

There are some excellent courses that you can study in costume. Having a degree is important, but having the right skill set is essential. You would need to know about the history of fashion and how garments are – and were – constructed, how to illustrate your costume concepts and how to work effectively with a range of people. Some of the technical side of things you will learn on the job.

One of the best ways to start in the field of costume design is to offer assistance in small theatre productions. You may be able to assist the designers or costume makers and get some real experience in the process, as well as

Study

- History of fashion
- Illustration
- Garment construction
- Textiles
- Fashion design
- Fashion for production

Links

Creative and Cultural Skills: the sector skills council for design, with news, information and careers support for designers. www.ccskills.org.uk
Skillset: the sector skills council for the media, with information about careers within all aspects of the media. www.skillset.org
Society of British Theatre Designers (SBTD): for news and information. www.theatredesign.org.uk

Rating

Average salary:
Entrance difficulty:

Stand out from the crowd

Build an exciting portfolio of costume design work, with colour sketches of costumes and photographs of three-dimensional creations. Show your ability to work in unconventional materials. Highlight your research abilities and knowledge of fashion history.

being able to list the production on your CV. Work experience is the way that most people start, and paid jobs are rarely advertised. It's worth checking mandy.com for the occasional costume posting, but you might be better off reading trade magazines to find out what shows or films are in pre-production and then get in touch with their costume designer to see if you could work as an intern, production assistant or to see if there are any openings for a dresser role. A dresser would be paid by the day to come along and help get the cast ready for filming – particularly called for if there is a large crowd scene. No specialist skills are needed for this, but it can be a great way to learn more about the costume industry and make some contacts. Dressers may progress to being production assistants, assistant costume designers and then costume designers.

> *The costume designer will give the assistant a brief to work from, such as 'I need 200 costumes for French peasant women in the 18th century'.*

Best bits

▲ One of the best aspects of the role of costume assistant is the exposure to the costume design process, as well as the resources used in costume design

▲ The costume assistant is part of a creative team and has the opportunity to absorb information, make contacts and contribute to the success of the production

Worst bits

▼ Working away from home on film sets for extended periods of location-shooting (although some students will see this as a best bit!)

CASE STUDY:

Deborah worked her way up from costume assistant and is now a designer for film, television, adverts and live theatre.

Deborah graduated from Rhode Island School of Design in the US with a BFA, majoring in Illustration. Coming from a family involved in performance, she gravitated towards costume and enjoyed the creative process of building things. She secured an internship with Trinity Repertory Theater as a costume assistant, while taking additional courses in costume design. After two years of working on various theatre projects, she decided to return to school to earn her masters degree in costume design at the University of North Carolina at Chapel Hill. While designing costumes for Playmakers, Theater by the Sea, varied summer productions, and diverse freelance projects, Deborah was building her portfolio to gain admission into the costume designers' union, which is essential for a professional costume designer in the US. Since acquiring her union card, Deborah has designed for a diverse range of projects including film, television, adverts and live theatre, including work on the Broadway production of *Wicked*.

Skills needed

- Organisational skills
- Resourcefulness
- Eagerness to assist in whatever task is assigned by the designer or wardrobe supervisor
- You need to recognise that you are part of a team and you should provide support proactively while absorbing all of the design processes of the team
- You need to be willing to work very hard without complaint

The role of the costume supervisor is to take an overview of the whole costume process from the big-picture concepts right through to the laundry and make sure it all happens in the right way, at the right time and at the right cost.

costume supervisor

The costume supervisor works closely with the costume designer and costume design assistant to make sure that the designer's vision gets realised. Exactly who does what will vary depending on the size of the costume team, the number of actors they need to get clothes for and the particular preferences of the individuals within the team, but broadly speaking the designer will come up with the concepts, and the supervisor will actually have to get hold of the clothes. This can be achieved in many different ways, but it will usually be some combination of buying them, hiring them and having them made.

In addition to getting the clothes, the costume supervisor is also usually in charge of the budgets, and is also in charge of the wardrobe staff, who look after the costumes and help to get the actors dressed.

The logistics of costumes on set can be complex. The supervisor would be in charge of making sure that each actor has an appropriate outfit, which fits them, for each scene, and might need to be involved with ordering costume trucks and hangers and getting the costumes transported to the different locations for different scenes. Your systems need to be infallible!

Supervisors can work for television and film, or for theatre and opera houses, but in each arena the role is more or less the same. There are a few employed roles for costume supervisors, mostly within theatres and opera houses, but most people spend their careers working freelance.

Routes in
It's a small world, and jobs nearly always go to people who know people, so you do need to start to get to know the right people. A relevant degree is very useful, and then some unpaid work experience is usually the way in.

Best bits
- ▲ The results of your work are very tangible, and it's satisfying to see a complex production coming together
- ▲ It's a great combination of fashion, film and history

The costume team will often need to carry out research to ensure historical and cultural accuracy.

Worst bits

▼ The hours are long – you need to have pretty good stamina

▼ As it's mostly freelance, you need to be comfortable with the lack of security and stability in your career, and need to be reasonably good at self-marketing

Skills needed

- Organisational skills
- Teamwork is very important, and you need to be working together with the designers and wardrobe people
- Creative problem-solving skills. It's not quite such an aesthetically creative job as that of a designer, but you do need to have the kind of mind that can think of different solutions to the many problems that will arise

The costume supervisor makes sure that the designer's vision gets realised.

CASE STUDY:

Marion is a costume supervisor for theatre, film and television.

Marion grew up in a family where everyone sewed. Her mother, her grandmother and her sister were all excellent seamstresses and her father worked in garment production. She loved clothes, but when she left school she decided to do a degree in fine art. She enjoyed her time at art school but decided that she didn't want the kind of life that usually goes with a career in fine art, so she got herself a job as an alterations assistant for a theatre.

Marion absolutely loved the environment of the theatre but after a few months decided that she couldn't bear to sew another hem, so she left and started doing some costume work for fringe theatres. It didn't pay well – sometimes not at all – but she learned loads and made some very important contacts.

Her next step was a job at the Royal Court theatre as a wardrobe mistress, which she did for a few years. She did really enjoy this, but started to feel that she was never going to be able to go any higher, until she was asked if she would like to work as a costume supervisor on a film.

Marion was torn, as she had always thought that she would spend her career in the theatre that she loved so much, but it was such a good opportunity for her that she took the job. She was very soon seduced by the big costume budgets – it was such a pleasure to be able to have the time and money to make really beautiful costumes. Of course not all films have substantial budgets, but Marion is now quite happy to swap between theatre, film and television as the jobs come up.

Study

- History of fashion
- Textiles
- Fashion design
- Fashion for production

Links

BECTU is the trade union for the entertainment business and offers support and advice. www.bectu.org.uk

Creative and Cultural Skills: the sector skills council for design, with news, information and careers support for designers. www.ccskills.org.uk

Job opportunities. www.mandy.com

Rating

Average salary: ● ● ○
Entrance difficulty: ● ● ○

Stand out from the crowd

Build a strong CV of costume work from past productions, showing that you have knowledge of every part of the costume process, as well as leadership experience.

These roles involve looking after the costumes, making sure that they are ready to wear and getting the actors dressed and ready to perform.

wardrobe master/mistress and wardrobe assistant

Wardrobe master/mistress

The wardrobe masters (men) and mistresses (women) are responsible for looking after the costumes. It's their job to make sure that the costumes are clean and ironed before the actors get dressed, and to ensure continuity if the director breaks the filming of a scene partway through – making sure that if a character is wearing a yellow tie at the beginning of a conversation, he is also wearing it at the end of the conversation. Within a theatre, the actors will be wearing the same costumes night after night, so the wardrobe master or mistress will have to do the laundry each day and the role might involve repairing any tears or re-dyeing the shoes, for example.

Wardrobe assistant

Wardrobe assistants used to be called 'dressers', and although their titles have been changed to reflect the greater breadth of their roles, their original name is still a good indication of what they spend most of their time doing. Their job is to help the actors get into their costumes for each scene. Within film and television, the challenges can be with large crowd scenes or with historical costumes. Lacing 100 actors into corsets for a ball scene can take some time! At the theatre the challenges are usually connected with timing. If an actor needs to change costumes quickly,

the dresser will be waiting in the wings for a cue, ready to leap into action to get the actor changed in time for the next scene.

In order to facilitate getting the actors dressed efficiently, the assistants have to make sure that the right costumes are ready and waiting for the actors and will be involved in making minor alterations and repairs.

Wardrobe assistants and wardrobe masters/mistresses would usually work freelance, but there are a few opportunities for permanent employed staff in theatres and opera companies. Assistants can be employed for a single day, here and there (for example, a film that has one battle scene might need extra assistants on the day they are filming that scene), or on longer-term contracts.

It's the job of the wardrobe masters or mistresses to look after the costumes and ensure that they are ready to wear.

Study

- History of fashion
- Textiles
- Fashion design
- Fashion for production

Links

BECTU is the trade union for the entertainment business and offers support and advice. www.bectu.org.uk
Job opportunities. www.mandy.com
The Knowledge is a comprehensive list of contacts within the broadcasting industry. www.theknowledgeonline.com

Rating

Average salary:
Entrance difficulty:

Stand out from the crowd

Excellent construction skills are a real asset in this job. Bring a small sample of your work that showcases your attention to detail.

Routes in

Take a relevant college course (anything fashion- or textiles-based) and then get some work experience. Jobs tend to come through word of mouth.

Best bits

▲ These roles are a great foot in the door for costume work; they are the best way to learn more about the work and make some contacts

▲ It's a really exciting environment to work in

Worst bits

▼ In theatre the timing for costume changes can be really tight and mistakes can be very exposed; while this can make for an exciting job, it can also be quite stressful

▼ Actors are usually very professional and supportive and understanding of the job that you are trying to do. Sometimes, however, they are not. . .

Skills needed

• Attention to detail – mistakes are very exposed and if a costume is not well laundered, or a button not replaced, then you are likely to hold the whole crew up while the problem is solved

• Teamwork and people skills – you will be working together with your costume and wardrobe colleagues, the rest of the crew and the actors

• You need to be well organised – you're responsible for ensuring that the costumes are all set out and ready to wear when the actors need them

CASE STUDY:

Gwendolyn is a costume assistant for television.

As a child, Gwendolyn always wanted to be on TV. She and her friends were always putting on shows for their parents, and Gwendolyn would make them all dress up and insist on being the presenter herself. As she grew older, the desire to be in front of the camera diminished, but the interest in getting people to dress up grew and grew. She was amazed to discover that there was a degree course in Costume for Performance, which to her mind seemed to tick every one of her boxes, and she was delighted to get a place.

She had a great time at college and got involved in the costumes for the drama students' productions and the media students' film and TV productions, but although she had loads of very relevant and interesting experience, none of it enabled her to make the contacts that she needed to get her first job.

After graduating she went to her college careers service and spent days perfecting her CV, reading all the trade journals to try to get some information about what was going on in the industry. 'I must have sent over 50 CVs off. I did my research really really well and tailored each one to the particular costume designer, supervisor or producer that I was writing to; and I really think it paid off.' Out of the 50 CVs that she sent off, Gwendolyn got over 30 responses. Mostly rejections, but supportive and positive and along the lines of: 'We've got nothing now, but get back to us in the New Year. . .' Two, however, invited her for interview, and one of them gave her a job as a costume assistant, working on a series for Channel 4.

CHAPTER SIX

retail

The retail business is the largest private sector employer, with nearly 3 million employees and an annual turnover of over £300bn. Fashion retail accounts for about 10 per cent of the total, with 18,000 shops, half a million employees and an annual turnover of around £30 million.

Styles of store

Fashion retailing incorporates many different kinds of store, and the job roles and day-to-day duties will vary tremendously, depending on where you end up working. In a typical shopping centre you might be able to buy clothes from a department store (John Lewis or Debenhams), chain stores (Top Shop, Marks & Spencer), independent boutiques, and a charity shop or two. Out of town you might find a hypermarket (Tesco Extra), a retail warehouse (Mothercare World) and a factory outlet (such as Bicester Village), and then there are mail-order catalogue that either supplement sales from stores (such as Next Directory) or that stand alone as mail-order businesses (such as Boden), and of course, the Internet. There are also smaller specialist shops who cater to a loyal clientele with unique merchandise and independent designer lines.

Trends

There are a number of trends that are influencing the way that we shop and these will impact on the kinds of jobs available within the industry.

Ethical retail

Despite our voracious appetite for cheap, fast fashion, we are also, paradoxically, showing an increasing interest in ethical shopping. Major retailers are having to be very careful about the conditions and wages in their overseas production houses, and need to source their raw materials responsibly, with care for the employees and the environment. Many companies have policies in place to discourage the use of plastic bags and there are some signs that, at the high end of the market, at least, there is a renewed enthusiasm for garments produced locally.

Striking shop windows are at the heart of good retail, which is why big stores employ teams of people just to ensure the windows look good.

Harvey Nichols, Dublin. A great deal of care is taken to make sure the window displays are perfect.

Occupations: what do people actually do within fashion retail?

Perhaps not surprisingly, the majority of people employed in the sector are frontline sales staff. Sales assistants and customer services roles account for about half of the employees, with sales managers accounting for a further 18 per cent, and then what is known as 'elementary occupations', which include non-skilled roles such as trolley collection and shelf stacking, make up another 13 per cent. So the people you actually see in the shops make up 80 per cent of the total number employed. The remaining fifth of employees are mostly head-office staff. These will include designers (designers might work for the retailer, a supplier, or the production company – see the chapter on Fashion Design for more details); buyers and merchandisers, who together are in charge of what goes into the stores; security and stock checkers, who make sure that the right things stay in the right places; and all the back-office functions that you would find in any major organisation such as finance, HR, marketing and administration.

Workforce

The workforce is young, diverse, and flexible. Under 25s account for a third of the total workforce, and if you are aged between 16 and 19 you are four times as likely to work in retail as anywhere else. The industry is relatively ethnically diverse and employs a large proportion of the migrant population, and more than half of the employees are women. Nearly half the

Internet and value retailing

The major retailing revolution of a generation, the Internet has had a huge impact on shoppers and store owners over the last ten years. Almost every major chain store is now using the Internet as an additional way to attract customers, and there are also some major Internet retail success stories that don't have a physical presence at all, such as ASOS and eBay. The Internet is also a great tool for those who want to promote their own labels but don't have the capital to set up a store.

Value retailers such as Primark, and grocery stores that have diversified into value fashion such as Asda and Tesco, have taken the fashion retail world by storm. The prices are eye-wateringly small, and the turnover of clothes is incredibly fast. We might suspect that somewhere along the chain someone hasn't been very well paid for their efforts, but such is our love of low-cost, on-trend garments that we are turning a collective blind eye to this and snapping up bargains everywhere.

ABOVE A behind-the-scenes view at Selfridges in London, showing mood boards and garments being prepared for display.

BELOW Engaging displays and good service draw shoppers to the tills.

workforce is part-time and this results in a flexible workforce that can easily and efficiently respond to the changing climate. Predictions are that the workforce within retail will increase by 6 per cent by 2017.

Differences in markets

Retail markets vary enormously. For example, at Chanel boutiques, staff are expected to keep customer files and

Job roles and day-to-day duties will vary tremendously, depending on where you end up working.

to interact on an individual level with each shopper. At the other end of the spectrum, typical branches of H&M would expect 1,000 or so customers every Saturday, so the interaction between staff and shoppers would be very different there.

Routes in

Sales assistant jobs are probably the most straightforward jobs to get within the whole fashion industry. Get a few copies of your CV printed out and then go down to your local shopping centre, either looking for adverts in shop windows or just pop into the stores you'd like to work in and

Good window displays are a vital part of attracting customers.

ask them if there are vacancies and how they would like you to apply. The more genuine enthusiasm you can show for the retailer, the more likely you are to get the job, so pick stores whose collections you admire, and places you like to shop yourself.

Recruitment agencies are good options for management and head-office roles, and it's worth looking in local papers as well as checking websites for opportunities.

Best bits

▲ Retail is all about providing a real product that a real person will use. Whether you're putting lines together as a buyer, thinking about which colours will sell or actually talking to someone in a store, this part of the fashion industry is all about the end product and how it's used. If you like the idea of connecting the product and the people, then this might be the right area for you

▲ It's a great starting point for a career in the fashion industry. Whatever your ultimate goal, it will always stand you in good stead to get some exposure to the customers, the stock and the selling process

Worst bits

▼ It's not the glamorous side of the business, so if you're attracted by catwalk shows and trendy parties, then you should look elsewhere

▼ The hours can be quite unsociable, as evening hours, Sunday work and even 24-hour stores are becoming more common

Skills needed

• Commercial sense
• An interest in selling
• People skills

Links

The **sector skills council for retail**, with information, news and research on the sector. www.skillsmartretail.com
The British Retail Consortium has news and information and access to *Retailer* magazine. www.brc.org.uk
Drapers Online is the key industry magazine for the fashion world. Includes information and job vacancies across the industry. www.drapersonline.com

The job of a sales assistant is not thought of as glamorous, it's not particularly well paid and it's certainly not the ultimate goal for many aspiring fashionistas, but it is the bedrock of the entire industry.

sales assistant

As a sales assistant, it's your job to make sure that the sales floor looks as appealing as it can and that the customers are as happy as possible. You need to look after the stock, making sure that everything is in the right place, that the garments are on the correct hangers and the floor is well stocked with all sizes and colours. You might need to work with your managers to move stock around as new lines come in, and check that everything looks neat, tidy and attractive.

You will spend some time on the tills. For some, this might not be the most exciting part of the job, but others really enjoy the interaction with customers it brings.

Dealing with customers will make up a substantial proportion of your working day.

Dealing with customers will make up a substantial proportion of your working day. They come in all shapes and sizes and backgrounds and nationalities, and all different temperaments and moods. You need to be warm, welcoming and empathetic, and will need to try to meet their needs and respond to their particular situations. You must get the balance right between giving them all the help they need, and not making them feel pressurised or closely watched. A really good knowledge of the stock is very helpful, as you can find your customers exactly what they want and make helpful suggestions about alternatives. Some customers will want you to be actively involved and help them to pick out outfits that might work, while others will simply want a brief answer to a question. Another side of the job is dealing with customer complaints, and you will have to listen to people's issues and then use your judgement to decide what to do. If you like people and are good at interacting with people you haven't met before, you are likely to do well.

It's a job that is fairly demanding physically – you will find that you're on your feet almost all day, and because you're in front of customers so much, you need to be polite and professional at all times – however you're feeling inside!

For some this is a job with enough variety and stimulation to keep them satisfied for years, but for others it can be a really useful stepping-stone towards another goal within the industry. Experience on the sales floor will stand you in good stead if you are interested in buying, merchandising

Study

- Retail trends and structures
- Retail management tools
- Product management
- Store presentation
- Retail maths

Links

The **sector skills council for retail**, with information, news and research on the sector. www.skillsmartretail.com
Retail Careers: an online source for vacancies. www.retailcareers.co.uk
Retail Week: a website with news, information and vacancies in the sector. www.retail-week.com
The Appointment: a careers magazine for the fashion retail sector. www.theappointment.co.uk

Rating

Average salary:
Entrance difficulty:

Stand out from the crowd

Before an interview spend some time on the sales floor. Get to know the stock and see what the customers are like and what they are looking at; being able to talk about this in an interview will be a huge help.

and designing and is essential if you are interested in store management.

Routes in

This is one area within the industry where you don't need a degree and you can get into a paid job without any previous experience. You can look on websites and use recruitment agencies, but the best way is to get a few copies of your CV printed out and just walk into the shops you want to work for and ask to speak to a manager.

Best bits
- ▲ Working with the clothes, seeing new lines come in
- ▲ Helping customers to get exactly what they want
- ▲ Learning firsthand what sells and why

Worst bits
- ▼ It's tiring and the hours are long
- ▼ Unreasonable customers who are supposed to be 'always right'!

Skills needed
- • Enjoyment of interacting with different people
- • An interest in the clothes you are selling

DAY IN THE LIFE: Sales associate

Jeanne is a sales associate at a shop selling European designer fashions. Customer service is the first priority and the store's high price points require a refined retail presentation.

9.00AM PREPARATION
Jeanne arrives early to preview the inventory, checking that all garments are properly hanging in consecutive sizes by style, evenly spaced on the rack. She replaces missing pieces from stock, straightens the garments and dusts the accessory shelves.

10.00AM STORE OPENS
Jeanne greets Gina, a frequent customer, asking if there is anything special for today. Gina is going on a cruise and needs pieces that travel well. Jeanne knows her style and suggests several options.

10.20AM A NEW CUSTOMER COMES IN
After welcoming her, Jeanne explains the layout of the store, the sizing and the location of various designers. Showing her the items on sale, Jeanne also highlights the new spring merchandise.

10.30AM CHECKING
Jeanne checks on Gina in the changing room and retrieves a smaller size for her.

11.30AM PURCHASE
Gina makes final selections and Jeanne takes them to the desk for purchase.

12.00PM BREAK
During her break, Jeanne begins unpacking new spring designs, checking them against the purchase order, hang-tagging them and switching them to the store's signature hangers.

1.00PM SERVING CUSTOMERS
The afternoon passes quickly with numerous customers coming in to shop.

5.00PM WINDING DOWN
Jeanne assists the store manager in styling mannequins with new spring merchandise, then she gives the shop a final assessment, reorganising and fine-tuning the racks.

Your job as the manager of a shop, department or concession in a department store is to manage the stock, people and processes to maximise sales and minimise costs.

Assistant Manager

Footwear retailer

We currently have opportunities for a 37.5 hr Assistant Manager (fully flexible Sunday to Saturday) in our new store.

Salary: £20,000–£28,000 per annum plus

Benefits: Would you like to work for a business where the passion is shoes?

Our client is the number one footwear provider in the UK and trades in over 50 countries worldwide and the key to our success is our people and the high levels of customer service that they deliver.

You will be responsible for driving the sales team on the shop floor.

as

store manager

As a store manager you will spend a surprising amount of time managing people, and that is often both the stimulation and the challenge of the job. Your staff team is likely to be made up of a real mix of people: those for whom it is the first step on a retail career ladder, those who are working their way through university and those who need a job quickly and don't care what it is – people who love it and people who really don't. Dealing with this range of people, and trying to make sure that everyone knows what they are doing, has the skills and knowledge to do it well and is motivated, is a daily challenge. You will be drawing up schedules, training and monitoring staff (there is usually a high turnover of staff in retail sales, so training new staff is often a big part of the job) and making sure that someone is on the tills, someone has put the stock on the shelves and someone is available to speak to the customers, while ensuring that all staff get a lunch break, tea break and the early-shift staff get to leave at four.

The stock on the sales floor is your responsibility, and you need to manage deliveries, making sure that the right garments are on the sales floor, and do regular stock inventory to monitor stock loss and theft. You will be involved in floor reorganisation, shifting merchandise to make space for new stock, highlight particular lines or lay things out for a sale.

As a rule, the more senior you are within store management the less contact you would have with customers on a daily basis, but as a manager you would tend to get involved in customer complaints so your good judgement, negotiation capabilities and customer service skills are important.

Trying to make sure that everyone knows what they are doing and are motivated is a daily challenge.

You can work within a department store, a chain store or an independent store. Department stores and other larger stores can sometimes be more sociable and have perks such as an in-store lounge, but you would have more responsibility

Study

- Retail trends and structures
- Retail management tools
- Product management
- Store presentation
- Public speaking
- Communications
- Consumer psychology

Links

One of the UK's leading **recruitment agencies** for retail. www.retailhumanresources.com **The British Retail Consortium**, great for up-to-date news on the sector. www.brc.org.uk For **graduate vacancies**. www.prospects.ac.uk **The Appointment**: a careers magazine for the fashion retail sector. www.theappointment.co.uk

Rating

Average salary: ● ● ●
Entrance difficulty: ● ● ●

Stand out from the crowd

Think commercial: what motivates people to buy? Research the company, and the competitors, too. You need to be able to discuss these topics when interviewed, specifically relating to the shop you hope to work for.

Managerial roles in retail vary enormously depending on the customer base. It's all about understanding what your particular customer expects and what will make them feel comfortable.

working for a smaller independent store – you are expected to behave as though it were your own business and make a wider range of decisions on your own.

Routes in

Most major department stores and chains have management training programmes. These programmes identify the skills needed to be a future senior manager and fast-track the trainees through a range of sales roles in the expectation that they will become senior managers within five or so years. This only accounts for a small proportion of retail managers. The other route is to work your way up from the shop floor, gaining responsibility, perhaps as a Saturday supervisor, and then an assistant manager. A degree is essential for the graduate training schemes but not for the other routes. Degrees in retail management can be a great help, but stores will take graduates from any discipline.

There is a clear hierarchy of career progression within retail. From a departmental manager you can work up to store manager and regional manager. It is quite common to take a sideways shift and work in head-office roles such as buyer or merchandiser.

Best bits

- ▲ Working with fashion – if you love clothes, it's a real pleasure to work with them all day
- ▲ Working with people – staff, managers, head-office colleagues and customers

Worst bits

- ▼ Customers can be difficult
- ▼ Hours are long and can be unpredictable, and it's physically hard work – you're on your feet all day
- ▼ The 'holidays' are your busiest and most stressful time
- ▼ No weekends

Skills needed

- A love for the clothes you're working with
- Confidence with customers
- Lots of energy
- An eye for detail
- Commercial acumen
- Multi-tasking

The second-floor 'Superbrands' area at Selfridges in London. Shown here is the Balenciaga concession.

The buyer is the link between the designer and the retailer. It's a very team-based role; you work closely with the designers, the manufacturers and the merchandisers, who work out how much to buy and decide where it goes.

buyer

The role of the buyer varies greatly from store to store, depending on the size and scope of the retailer. A buyer for a smaller store will usually purchase branded merchandise from numerous labels to fill the shop with product that appeals to their specific customer, while a buyer for a large chain of stores may become involved with the planning, design and development process. Buyers typically specialise in one category of product, such as casual knitwear, but in a smaller retailer, the buyer might buy a larger range of merchandise, for example, all casual wear including knitwear, shirts, trousers and skirts. Whichever role the buyer plays, the goals are the same: to supply the store with merchandise that is irresistible to their customers, well priced and well timed on the sales floor.

Research into the latest trends is an essential part of the buyer's process. They attend fashion shows in London, look at catwalk trends and consult forecasting services such as WGSN and Mudpie. They research what is being sold in the shops and the hottest items in stores around the world. Different cities are known for different areas of fashion (for example: Paris and New York for womenswear, Florence for childrenswear, Milan for menswear). Travelling to the best

cities for their category, buyers go to fashion shows, shop the stores, purchase samples, photograph people in the street and collect as much information as possible about upcoming trends.

Once they have returned from their travels, they meet together and hold a 'show and tell' of their research, looking at the prints, colour palettes, shapes, fabrics and themes, and start to narrow this down to a story. The design team is then asked to start to build up a colour palette and put together some sketches of key shapes. When this is approved, the designers will be asked to flesh out their sketches, and add ideas for trims and fabrics.

When they are happy with the designs, the buyers then start to make a decision about which suppliers to ask for costs and samples. Different suppliers might have expertise

Study

- Retail marketing management
- Supply chain management
- Product development
- Market context
- Commercial implications
- Communication
- Negotiation

Links

The Appointment: a careers magazine for the fashion retail sector. www.theappointment.co.uk
Drapers Online is the key industry magazine for the fashion world. Includes information and job vacancies across the industry. www.drapersonline.com
The **sector skills council for retail**, with information, news and research on the sector. www.skillsmartretail.com

Rating

Average salary: ● ● ●
Entrance difficulty: ● ● ●

Stand out from the crowd

Before any interview, make sure you do your research relating to the company you hope to work for. Go to the stores, look at the collections, watch the customers and think about the competition.

in different kinds of garments or different fabrics, and buyers would usually tend to get samples made up by at least two different suppliers to compare. There are still a few manufacturers left in the UK, but for the most part garments are produced overseas. As awareness has grown of the conditions in factories overseas, many retailers are very conscious of the employees used to produce their clothes, and buyers will often carry out spot checks on the factories, looking for any signs of poor conditions.

Buyers will have to send the manufacturers a great deal of detail to make sure that the sample is exactly what they are looking for. They will visit fabric fairs such as Première Vision in Paris and either actually buy the fabric needed or send swatches and sketches to the manufacturers, providing details on specifics like thread colours and stitch sizes.

CASE STUDY:

Jacky is a freelance buyer for a range of retailers.

Jacky did her degree in food, textiles and consumer studies, which was in essence a business studies degree for retail. She specialised in textiles and then got her first job as an allocator at a nationwide chain store. She hated this as she found it very mechanical and not at all creative, but it was a really useful foot in the door.

Jacky then got a job at a large fashion retail group as an assistant buyer for ladies' blouses, then tailoring and then childrenswear. She found it quite easy to move around from one area to another within this company but finally settled on menswear and worked as a buyer for seven years. She then got a bit concerned that she could end up being pigeonholed and might have to stay within menswear if she didn't move soon, so she got a job for another chain store buying childrenswear and then moved elsewhere to buy girlswear.

Jacky now works freelance, buying for a range of different retailers, as well as teaching, writing and doing some consultancy work. She has loved the variety within her career – it's been great being able to learn about so many different areas, but the best bit has been all the travelling. She gets to go to the fashion capitals of the world to see what's on sale there, and she gets to spend time in some interesting countries that are definitely off the tourists' beaten track to oversee the production process.

Assistant Buyer – childrenswear

A commercial and ambitious Assistant Kidswear Buyer is required at this top retailer.

Your responsibilities will include:
- Planning and developing future lines
- Viewing trends commercially and their relevance to the target market
- Assisting the Buyer as required

To be successful in this role you must have previous experience within buying as a BA looking to take the next step or an AB looking for a new challenge with an exciting retailer. You should possess a 'can do' attitude and look to motivate others within the team. This is a great opportunity for those looking to make the next step in their buying career.

The samples will be returned in two or three weeks' time and then the buyers start range building. They put different outfits together and decide what items work well together. At this stage the buyer will work closely with the merchandiser. The merchandiser will use the sales history to try to ensure that the collection is low risk and likely to sell well, while the buyer may be more focused on a range that is on trend, new and exciting, so there is often a lot of debate at this stage of the process!

The buyers then need to make decisions about prices, taking into account the cost to manufacture, what their customers will be prepared to pay, the mark-down at the end of season, and whether any items are going to be 'loss leaders' (they might decide to have a basic T-shirt that is so cheap that it will not make any profit, in the hope that this good, cheap T-shirt encourages customers to buy an expensive jacket to go with it). Finally, there is a series of pre-selection meetings with the senior managers, as the design teams present the themes and colours for the season, the merchandisers talk through the best and worst sellers of the previous season and the buyers present this season's lines.

The next stage is the fitting process. The manufacturers provide samples for each size, and then the buyers work with the technical design team, working either on mannequins or actual models to get the sizes right. Colours need to be checked and confirmed – the buyers will have given the manufacturers a Pantone colour, but the manufacturers will need to provide samples of different shades to choose from, and different fabrics might require different 'recipes' to look the same. These colours are then all checked to make sure they work in daylight and under the store lighting.

When the sample garments are perfect, the buyers take two identical samples, seal them, keep one and send the other back to the manufacturers for them to use in their quality control processes. The garments are then made, pressed, packed, boxed and shipped to the stores.

Buyers from stores who are purchasing merchandise from branded fashion resources meet in the manufacturers' showrooms with the sales team for that label. They review the lines and select designs that will work with the rest of the product they are buying for that season, keeping in mind the overall look of the shop within the delivery period. They negotiate price and delivery options, taking notes, before they actually place their order. If they are buying large enough quantities, buyers will often request special styles, fabrics or colours, which the wholesaler will make specifically for them. This is called 'private label'. The designs will have the manufacturer's label, but the style will be confined to their stores. Stores might have a special 'store within the store' for that particular label to give more presence to the preferred manufacturers. Buyers for large chain stores have a different role. They are intricately involved in the development of product, working in partnership with designers, merchandisers and manufacturers. They are the link between the designer and the retailer.

Routes in

These are really competitive jobs, as lots of people are drawn to the combination of creativity and commerce. A degree in something business- or fashion-related is really useful, followed by some unpaid work experience, and a job as a buyer's administrative assistant where you learn the ropes before working as a buyer's assistant, then an assistant buyer, finally working your way up to buyer.

> *As a buyer, you need an eye for fashion and colour, and a love of shopping, as well as commercial sense and a head for figures.*

Best bits
- ▲ Shopping!
- ▲ Travelling and making connections all over the world

Worst bits
- ▼ Can be very stressful, as it involves lots of different processes, and the cost implications are huge if you mess up
- ▼ You can find yourself working with some really tough people so you do need to have a thick skin

Skills needed
- An eye for fashion and colour
- A love of shopping
- Commercial sense and a head for figures
- The ability to work well with a range of people
- An ability to multi-task
- Attention to detail

The actual day-to-day job of a buyer will vary depending on the size of the company they work for, but in general a buyer will have at least one assistant, and often two tiers of support: an assistant and an administrative assistant.

buyer's assistant/
buyer's administrative assistant

In essence the jobs of the buyer's assistant (BA) and the buyer's administrative assistant (BAA) are to prevent the buyer from having to do any administrative work, while learning how to do the job themselves. The buying process is very admin-heavy. There is a lot of travel to be organised, meetings to be scheduled, notes to be taken and written up and samples to be organised, labelled and stored. And then there are the emails. The buying process works along a critical path – a standardised list of tasks to be done in a particular order and by specific deadlines. It's usually the job of the BA or BAA to ensure that everybody is crystal clear about what they need to do and when they need to do it,.

The assistants will also get involved in the more interesting and creative side of things, going to trade shows, travelling to manufacturers and suppliers and being involved in meetings where decisions are made. A supportive buyer will make sure that their assistants get a good opportunity to learn about the process and develop their skills, but the assistants may need to look for these opportunities themselves.

Routes in
This is a very competitive field so you would usually start by doing unpaid work experience, then write speculative letters or look out in the trade press for postings. A degree in a relevant subject (business or fashion) is important.

Best bits
▲ Working with clothes
▲ Learning about the process
▲ Travelling and meeting interesting people

Worst bits
▼ Lots of administration work
▼ Without you, nothing would actually happen, but you don't always get the recognition you might deserve

Skills needed
• Organisational skills
• Thick skin
• Passion for clothes
• A reasonable head for figures

Study
• Retail marketing management
• Supply chain management
• Product development
• Market context
• Commercial implications
• Communication
• Negotiation

Links
Drapers Online is the key industry magazine for the fashion world. Includes information and job vacancies across the industry. www.drapersonline.com
The **sector skills council for retail**, with information, news and research on the sector. www.skillsmartretail.com
Retail Week www.retail-week.com
Retail Human Resources: consultancy specialising in retail sales and head office roles. www.retailhumanresources.com

Rating
Average salary: ● ● ●
Entrance difficulty: ● ● ●

Stand out from the crowd
Get some work on the sales floor – make sure you understand the actual sales process and the customers.

A merchandiser who works for a retailer, usually in the head office of a chain of stores, makes the decisions about how many of each garment in each range to buy and which stores to put them in.

merchandiser

The aim of the merchandiser is to get exactly the right number of garments into every shop to enable every customer who wants to buy one to do so, and not to have any left over at the end of the season. Or at least to get as near to this as possible. It's a very business-oriented fashion role, and it is basically about maximising sales and profit.

The merchandisers do this with the help of lots of number-crunching. They will analyse last season's sales and get a clear idea of what sold well and what didn't; what made a good profit and what didn't; and how much of everything had to be discounted in the sales. They need to get to know their customers well so that they have a good sense of what is likely to sell and, if working in the head office for a chain of stores, they would need to know what is more likely to sell in different stores. This might be based on the demography of the region, the average ages and relative wealth of typical customers or on things like the weather – you're going to want to have more woolly jumpers in an Aberdeen store than in Brighton.

The job of a merchandiser is a very team-based one, but the exact nature of the role varies depending on the kind of store they work for. In smaller chains or independent retailers, a single person might fulfil both the buying and merchandising roles. In retailers who design their own lines in-house, the role of the merchandiser is very creative. They work with designers, vendors, production teams and buyers in the development of product. They are also responsible for the analytical side, working with inventory control and upper management, assessing sales projections and previous seasons' sales, and targeting gross margins to create a plan to guide the buyers and designers. For retailers who work closely with suppliers, merchandisers will work closely with the buying team. A merchandiser might be assisted by an assistant merchandiser or a merchandiser's administrative assistant, also known as an allocator.

The merchandiser will be involved in choosing the collections, but while the buyer and designers will be thinking about the catwalk influences and trends for the season ahead, the merchandiser will be more focused on thinking about what made money in the previous season and advising the buyers on which shapes, colours and fabrics are likely to sell well. The buyer, for example, might be keen to introduce some bright colours into the knitwear range, reflecting the catwalk trends, but the merchandiser might point out that black and navy have been the only colours that made any profit over the last three seasons.

The merchandiser will then get involved in the pricing of the garments. They will start with some guidelines of how much profit they want to make on a range and then work out how many individual items they are likely to sell at full price and then how many they will discount at the end of the season. They will then think about what their customers will be prepared to pay for different kinds of garments, and work out what they need to charge from there.

Study

- Retail operations
- Computers and communications – including Excel
- Commercial implications
- Communication
- Negotiation

Links

One of the UK's leading **recruitment agencies** for retail. www.retailhumanresources.com
The British Retail Consortium www.brc.org.uk
For **graduate vacancies**. www.prospects.ac.uk
The Appointment: a careers magazine for the fashion retail sector. www.theappointment.co.uk

Rating

Average salary:
Entrance difficulty: ● ● ●

Stand out from the crowd

Be up to date on what's going on in the retail world. Understand what sells, what doesn't and why.

Merchandiser

Ladies high-fashion footwear importers

Duties: Managing under Senior Sales Director allocated key accounts. Coordinating samples with factories and buyers. Providing strong administrative support to Senior Sales Director.

Requirements: Motivation, ability to work under pressure. Strong communication, IT and administration skills.

Hours: 9 am to 6 pm

Salary: £18,000 to £24,000 p.a. depending on qualification and experience

To apply: Please email CV and covering letter.

The next part of the process is working out how many particular items go into each store, based on analysis of previous seasons' sales, and liaising with the distributors and stores to make sure everyone knows what they are expecting. In some companies, the merchandisers might link in with the visual merchandisers to make sure that the garments are being displayed in the most attractive and engaging way, but elsewhere, the next task for the merchandisers is at the end of the season when they get involved in deciding on discounts. Finally, when the season has finished, the merchandisers will do in-depth analyses. This feeds into the buying decisions for the next season.

Different kinds of retailers work at very different paces, with some fashion-forward companies getting some lines into stores within two months. More typically, a merchandiser would be working nine to 12 months in advance, which means that they are looking at three or four seasons at different stages, at any one time.

Routes in
There are a few graduate training programmes around for merchandisers within retail, but the most common way to start is to do some unpaid work experience to get a foot in the door and then start in a junior role (merchandiser's administrative assistant or allocator) and learn on the job. A degree is useful, and companies are particularly interested in a numerate subject such as maths, economics or business studies.

Best bits
▲ The blend of business and creativity
▲ Being very involved in so many aspects of the business

Worst bits
▼ You can never get it exactly right

Skills needed
• A good head for figures
• Sound computer skills, especially knowledge of Excel
• Organisational abilities and the ability to multi-task
• An accurate awareness of consumer habits and trends
• An interest in fashion – not a prerequisite, but useful
• The ability to work well with people

DAY IN THE LIFE:
Merchandiser

Meredith is a senior merchandiser for a fashion retail chain that makes much of its own apparel and purchases private label product from several vendors. Her job is a fusion of analytical processes and the creative side.

9.00AM INITIAL PLANNING STAGE
This stage starts with creating a financial framework with the inventory management team, planning the sales projections for the coming Autumn season and assessing how much product is needed and how much money is available to purchase inventory.

10.30AM PLAN
Meredith translates the financial information into a plan for the designers and buyers to follow. The plan lays out the number of styles needed for each Autumn drop and the distribution of silhouettes. An assortment strategy for each store is planned based on sales history (successful trends from past seasons), growth categories and upcoming trends.

12.00PM MEETING WITH THE BUYING TEAM
Meredith presents the sales projections and the amount of product the buyers need to purchase to meet their targets. Meredith will coordinate with the buyers and vendors to develop private label product.

1.30PM MEETING WITH DESIGN TEAM
Meredith gives designers the plan for Autumn, with the number of styles for each month's drop. They discuss Autumn trends, silhouettes, colour stories and price points.

2.00PM DESIGN MEETING
After weeks of design development, the designers present their Spring line with concept boards, colour sketches, fabrics and mock-ups. After some negotiation on particular styles and the balance of silhouettes, decisions are made.

4.00PM PRODUCTION MEETING
Meredith meets with the production team to plan sourcing (where manufacturing will take place), delivery schedules and targeted pricing for each style.

6.00PM EDITING AND PLANNING
Meredith further edits the collection to meet sales goals and mark-up, based upon anticipated pricing. Visualising the store's presentation of merchandise, Meredith plans the flow of merchandise in the stores.

The career path of a merchandiser is quite clearly laid out. First, get yourself a job as a merchandiser's administrative assistant (MAA), also sometimes called an allocator, and then work up to a merchandiser's assistant (MA), junior merchandiser and then merchandiser.

merchandiser's assistant/
merchandiser's administrative assistant

Progress up to the point of being a merchandiser's assistant is usually fairly rapid, as long as you have the basic skills and are prepared to work hard, so you could reasonably expect to be in this role within five to eight years.

The role of a merchandiser's administrative assistant (or allocator) is about allocating the right garments to the right places. Once the merchandiser has decided what garments are going where, it is your job to make sure they get there. You need to liaise with the logistics and distribution teams to make sure that they know what they need to pick up and where they need to take it, and you have to link in with the stores to tell them what is coming, so that they can clear the space and make room for the new stock on the sales floor.

As an MAA you would be spending a fair amount of each day at your computer dealing with spreadsheets. You would get involved in inputting sales figures, making sure that all data is complete and up to date, and you would pull off reports for the merchandiser on any topic and answer particular queries about data (how many black polo necks were sold in the first week of December in the Birmingham store in 2009? And how does that compare to the Cardiff store in the same week in 2008?).

Routes in
Although there are a few graduate training programmes around, most MAAs will find their jobs through recruitment agencies, adverts in the trade press or via applications sent on spec. Some allocators will be lucky enough to get a job by responding to an advert. Others might have to do some unpaid work experience first to get a foot in the door. A numerate degree and an interest in fashion are important.

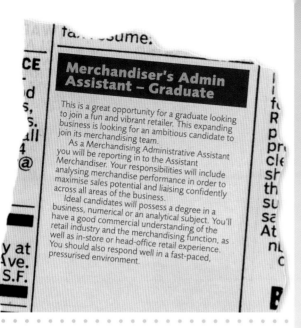

Merchandiser's Admin Assistant – Graduate

This is a great opportunity for a graduate looking to join a fun and vibrant retailer. This expanding business is looking for an ambitious candidate to join its merchandising team.

As a Merchandising Administrative Assistant you will be reporting in to the Assistant Merchandiser. Your responsibilities will include analysing merchandise performance in order to maximise sales potential and liaising confidently across all areas of the business.

Ideal candidates will possess a degree in a business, numerical or an analytical subject. You'll have a good commercial understanding of the retail industry and the merchandising function, as well as in-store or head-office retail experience. You should also respond well in a fast-paced, pressurised environment.

Best bits
- ▲ You get to learn a lot very quickly
- ▲ If you are interested in sales and business it's extremely interesting
- ▲ The potential for career growth

Worst bits
- ▼ You're often not involved with making major decisions at this stage, which can be frustrating

Skills needed
- Computer literacy – you should be very comfortable with Excel spreadsheets
- Numeracy; ability to interpret data
- Organisational skills – the logistics are complicated and it's expensive and time consuming if the stock doesn't get to the right place at the right time
- An interest in fashion

IN HER OWN WORDS:

Kerrie now works as a merchandising assistant for a department store.

'I did my degree in fashion merchandising management. I knew that I wanted to work in the fashion industry but didn't want to design. I was intending to do business studies, but while I was on work experience at a fashion design company while still at school, I was told that there were some business courses that focused on the fashion industry so I started having a look around. The course I chose included a year in industry, which sold it to me, and I would really recommend a work placement to anyone thinking about these kinds of jobs.

'You do not need to have such a directly relevant degree, but it definitely gave me an advantage, showing that I had an interest and giving me the chance to get some good work experience.

'My work experience while I was on the course was with a chain store and a department store, and I worked as a sales assistant at Top Shop to earn some money while I was studying, so by the time I left I had a pretty good grasp of the industry from both sales and head office functions. I was taken on as a merchandising administrative assistant when I graduated and spent two years with that store learning the ropes before I felt I was in a position to go for the next level up. Merchandising is not nearly as competitive as some other areas within fashion like buying and designing, so it was definitely easier for me to get my first job than for some of my friends, but it was still really important to have made some contacts and to show a genuine interest in the fashion world.'

Study
- Retail operations
- Computers and communications
  – including Excel
- Commercial implications
- Communication
- Negotiation

Links
One of the UK's leading **recruitment agencies** for retail.
www.retailhumanresources.com
The British Retail Consortium
www.brc.org.uk
For **graduate vacancies**.
www.prospects.ac.uk

Rating
Average salary: ● ○ ○
Entrance difficulty: ● ● ○

Stand out from the crowd
Be really up to date on what's going on in the retail world.

Large department stores and chains employ teams of people who make decisions on the look, feel, layout and displays for the stores. The aim is for each branch to have identical displays, to promote the garments correctly and to entice customers in.

retail designer

A typical design studio for a fashion retailer will incorporate teams who work on the packaging (such as the cardboard packet your socks come in), cardboard signage ('2 for 1 offers in swimwear'), props (baubles for Christmas or barbecues for the summer season) and displays (in windows and on the shop floor). The size of these teams will vary depending on the nature of the shop, but a large chain store will have project managers, designers, prop sourcers and visual merchandisers all working together.

Stores might have six or so different designs each year and the most important is always at Christmas. Designers start working on the Christmas displays over a year in advance. They start with lots of research. This involves having a very clear idea of the Christmas displays for the previous year both in London and New York, and finding out from forecasters what the trends for the next Christmas season are likely to be (red and velvety or silver and shimmery, for instance). The designers will then liaise with the buyers and merchandisers to make sure that the ideas link in with the clothing collections planned for that season. They will then come up with some ideas on paper – they might sketch, for example, some red draped curtains, hanging baubles and some shimmer on the floor and then present these ideas to the marketing teams.

The visual merchandisers would liaise with the buyers and merchandisers to get a good understanding of the key pieces for each collection, and then need to decide on outfits for each mannequin for each window and within each department. This could include products from any area of the store – a beach scene might include towels from the home furnishings department, a picnic hamper from the food hall and sunglasses and hats from accessories as well as the swimwear from men's, women's and children's and the flip-flops from shoes. The design teams need to ensure that the buyers and merchandisers from each department are happy with the final displays, and that they look attractive, well styled and appealing to customers.

The next step would be to mock up some actual windows and in-store displays to see what they would look like in situ, and once this has been signed off by the senior managers, the teams go into production and start sourcing the companies who can provide the red velvet curtains and make the hanging baubles.

The teams need to produce a booklet that gives detailed instructions for the individual stores on how to make the windows and in-store displays look exactly the way they want and when they need to go live.

The last part of the process then is supporting the display teams within the stores to help make sure that the displays are consistent and well styled, and to sort out any unforeseen problems (the hanging baubles are too heavy for the ceilings, the deckchairs are too large to get through the narrow windows, etc).

Retail is a fast-moving and often unpredictable world, and the window displays need to respond quickly to

Study

- Retail brands
- Information technology
- Finance
- Psychology of consumer behaviour

Links

Fashion Windows covers store windows from around the world. www. fashionwindows. com/visualmerchandising **Visual Merchandising and Store Design** is an online resource for professionals. http://vmsd.com

Rating

Average salary:
Entrance difficulty: ● ● ●

Stand out from the crowd

Be really up to date on what's going on in the retail world.

ABOVE The commercial potential of good in-store displays has become widely recognised in the last decade.

commercial changes. One wet weekend might lead to very low sales on sunglasses, so the display teams might be asked to change the displays to highlight sunglasses by the end of the following week. A key item from the display may be so popular that it sells out within a week, so the display has to be changed to foreground something else; the design teams need to be in close contact with the commercial side of the business and need to be able to respond quickly with a creative solution.

Window displays are now seen as more commercially significant than they were ten years ago. Sales managers and buyers recognise that customers will be enticed in or turned off by what they see in the windows, so the display teams have needed to become more commercial and more responsive.

Routes in
People come to these sorts of roles from lots of different backgrounds: shop floor, graphic design, agency and advertising.

Best bits
▲ Working with lots of different people both internally and externally: visual merchandisers, designers, marketing people, suppliers, printers and sales assistants

IN HER OWN WORDS:

Claire is project manager for décor at a leading retail chain in the UK.

'I did a degree in marketing and French and got my first job on a graduate training scheme in direct marketing. After a few years with that I started working for a large supermarket in the packaging department, as a freelancer. They use ad agencies to do the actual design so my role was very much liaising with the agencies and involved lots of communication about our customers and brand. I then got a job as a freelancer for a chain store, initially in their packaging team, but then moving over to the décor side. The contract was extended and extended and then finally I was made permanent.

'I really enjoy working in-house – for me it's the best of both worlds – I get the creative buzz of working with the designers, but the security and stability of an in-house role. I love my job because it's full of interesting people and it changes every day. My role now involves project managing the décor for stores up and down the country, and I love the fact that I can go into any store, wherever I happen to be and see my ideas and designs up there. My job at this level is more about coordination and liaising with people than it is about design, but I think you've got to have a good eye and an understanding of design to do it well.

'There is no very clear career path towards this kind of job, so my advice to anyone interested in it is to keep your experience broad and keep your options open. With good transferable skills you will be able to use your experience in a variety of different contexts so don't turn down a job just because it's not perfect for you.'

Worst bits
▼ Things change right up to the last minute, and although it's good to be kept on your toes, it can be very frustrating to have to deal with issues that should have been predictable

Skills needed
• Strong communication and negotiation skills
• Organisational skills
• Creativity

The visual merchandiser works for a retailer, creating and styling displays of the clothes to tempt customers into the store and to show them how they might look as a complete outfit.

visual merchandiser

The displays that the visual merchandisers (VMs) create are usually in the windows and within the store. In smaller stores the VM role is often undertaken by a sales assistant, or a regional VM who might look after the displays in five or six stores, but in larger stores there could be a whole team of VMs, specialising in different areas, on different floors or in windows or in-store displays.

In large high street chains, the head offices usually want to ensure that the windows in each shop, across the country, look the same, so will send out packs of detailed instructions and all the props that they want the VMs to use. In other kinds of shops the VMs might be given a bit more creative freedom to put their own outfits and displays together.

There has been a realisation in the retail trade over the last decade or so that visual merchandising is extremely important and that the right displays can have a significant impact on sales. VMs are increasingly key players on the commercial side of the businesses, so will be asked to feed information to senior buyers and managers.

Displays are usually trend-led, and will reflect the mood and feel of the current collection, as well as highlighting some key pieces. The VM team have to style the mannequins, incorporate all the appropriate props and arrange them in the most appealing way. It's a very practical, physical job, and although you might be working with some beautiful and exclusive garments, you will also spend a fair

ABOVE The commercial impact of a good window display is now widely recognised – but getting it right is perhaps still more of an art than a science, as this display from Selfridges in London shows.

amount of your time on your hands and knees, painting, sticking or building things.

Routes in
A degree in something fashion-related is useful, and then you need to get some work experience with a VM team. Buy plenty of magazines and go shopping a lot, and start to analyse why a store feels a particular way. Job adverts are usually placed on companies' own websites.

Study
- Retail brands
- Information technology
- Finance
- Psychology of consumer behaviour

Links
For **news and information** about training within the sector.
www.britishdisplaysociety.co.uk
Selfridges
www.selfridges .co.uk
Subtitled **The Art of Windows**, this blog regularly posts pictures of the top window displays in New York City. www.anothernormal.com
For **graduate vacancies**.
www.prospects.ac.uk

Rating
Average salary: ● ● ●
Entrance difficulty: ● ● ●

Stand out from the crowd
Get as much related creative work in your own time as you can – why not organise a fashion shoot with your friends?

Assistant Visual Merchandiser

Our store is now in its 20th season and is famous for its unique and quirky accessories, which elevate jewellery to art status through a winning combination of eccentricity, kitsch, and traditional craftsmanship. Inspirations include rock 'n' roll, fairy tales, deep-sea creatures, old horror films, flora and fauna, and circus sideshows!

Experience gained: The student will gain experience of the inner workings of our company with particular emphasis on our visual and product-merchandising department.

Students will have the opportunity to work with our central team and will experience the day-to-day reality of a successful fashion retail shop. Following interview the successful candidate will experience a wide spectrum of tasks, which could include design and construction of window displays.

Best bits
▲ It's creative but also commercial
▲ It's satisfying to see the fruits of your labour

Worst bits
▼ Although recognition of this area is improving, it's still not particularly great in terms of pay or status

Skills needed
• A good eye
• Practical problem-solving capabilities
• Loads of enthusiasm for the clothes you work with
• An interest/background in art/popular culture
• Good three-dimensional skills

IN HER OWN WORDS:

Katherine works as a visual merchandiser for Selfridges.

'Selfridges is a great place to work as a VM because we are relatively autonomous. We are given a concept brief, but are then encouraged to interpret it to suit each individual space.

'We've just opened the biggest shoe department in the world and the whole store was shouting about shoes. It's great when a single concept can work through every single department, and shoes worked really well for that because they fit with menswear, womenswear and accessories.'

One of the things she likes most about her job is feeling at the heart of the business:

'We do walk-rounds with the senior buyers and managers for each department and they are genuinely interested in feedback from us.'

The displays at Selfridges are known internationally for being very creative and the VM team collaborate a lot with artists, designers and musicians to get the look right. Katherine's tips for anyone interested in entering this field are to think very carefully about the brand – what it says and how it says it.

Window diplays for some leading department stores can be like fanciful works of art, creating a fantastic image around the idea of the store and its brand.

Personal shoppers are employed by retailers or shopping centres to encourage shoppers to buy more clothes, by helping customers to indentify clothes that look great.

personal shopper

ABOVE Top personal shoppers will be able to apply years of experience of styling men and women of all ages, shapes and sizes.

Customers seek the advice of a personal shopper for a range of reasons. Many come for a special occasion – if they are looking for something for a wedding, a significant birthday or a black tie event. Some might come because they are starting a new job and need some help putting together a capsule wardrobe, or just to treat themselves. Others come because they are just too busy to trawl the shops themselves.

The personal shopping experience is intended to make the customer feel very special. They are normally taken to a separate room, and perhaps given a cup of coffee while the personal shopper tries to find out a bit about what they are after. The personal shopper needs to find out about the occasion, the style of clothes the customer prefers and of course their budget. Having got a sense of what the customer is looking for and made some judgements about what kinds of shapes and colours are going to suit the customer, the personal shopper needs to go out to the shop floor and find some items for the customer to try on. The shopper will try to get a range of different garments that can be mixed and matched, and might bring some accessories as well to show how the finished outfit might look. Then comes the process of getting the customer to try things on to see what works and what they like.

The target of the personal shopper is to increase revenue for the store, but this is achieved in a number of ways and is not all about closing the sale on the day. If a shop has a reputation for a good personal shopping service, it is likely to attract more customers to use that service, and if the customer has a good experience they are likely to return time and again. And of course, if the personal shopper is good at their job the customer is more likely to be delighted with the outfit and how they look in it and will buy it there and then rather than shopping around.

Study

There are no particular courses that you need to study to be a personal shopper, but there are plenty of private courses out there that might teach you:
- Colour analysis
- Wardrobe planning
- Identifying clients' needs
- How to identify body shapes
- Accessorising

Links

One of the UK's leading **recruitment agencies** for retail. www.retailhumanresources.com
The British Retail Consortium www.brc.org.uk
For **graduate vacancies**. www.prospects.ac.uk

Rating

Average salary: ● ● ○
Entrance difficulty: ● ● ●

Stand out from the crowd

Get plenty of experience working with customers on the shop floor.

In the UK the majority of personal shoppers are employed by retailers in this way, but there are a few who work freelance for private clients, and their role is to go and buy whatever they are asked to. This might often be clothing, but could also be gifts, interior furnishings or indeed anything at all.

Routes in

This is not usually a first sales job, so you might start off as a sales assistant and then try to hone your skills there. Alternatively you could get some experience as a stylist and move over to retail from that starting point.

Best bits

▲ You get to shop for a living!
▲ It's great to see the customer's satisfaction as you produce the perfect outfit
▲ It can be quite lucrative

Worst bits

▼ For the most part the customers are charming, realistic and appreciative, but sometimes their expectations are unreasonably high and they can end up disappointed

Skills needed

• Excellent knowledge of the stock
• Excellent knowledge of current trends and styles
• A strong sense of style and taste
• An understanding of how to make up a good outfit
• Instincts about what is going to suit other people's shapes and colouring
• Very good people skills are vital – you need to get people to open up and feel comfortable with you

 # DAY IN THE LIFE:
Personal shopper

Mark is a personal shopper for a high-class department store. He provides a range of clients with very personal service and the ultimate shopping experience.

8.30AM SURVEY OF STOCK
Mark walks through each department familiarising himself with new styles and those on sale. He takes notes for his clients and notifies them of special pieces, especially sale items. Organisation is critical as he must be cognisant of numerous clients' needs and preferences.

10.00AM APPOINTMENT
Kate, a long-term client, needs a spectacular gown for a charity ball. Mark has selected several gowns and accessories, putting them into a changing room for Kate's appointment, along with her favourite chai tea. Kate has total confidence that Mark knows how to enhance her figure and create a glamorous vision for the event. Kate arrives and tries on four gowns, selecting two.

12.30PM INTERVIEW
A new client, Susan, has just got a new job. Mark goes to her home. They discuss her specific needs, lifestyle, preferences and price points. Mark reviews her wardrobe, documenting the labels, colours and silhouettes. This gives him a base for creating a wardrobe to suit her new position while preserving her fashion identity. He suggests new pieces to harmonise with existing garments.

2.30PM 'HUNT AND GATHER'
Mark goes back to the store to shop for pieces that will add fashionable shapes and vibrant colours to Susan's wardrobe. He partners with a sales associate to reserve several jackets, skirts and silk tops for Susan to try tomorrow.

4.30PM INTERNET SEARCH
Mark goes online to look at the latest designer collections. He makes notes of compatible pieces for several clients.

7.00PM CHARITY EVENT
In his dinner jacket, Mark mingles with guests to network and see what everyone is wearing.

CHAPTER SEVEN

communication

Informing the public about the clothes for each season is a very important part of the industry that is worth a lot of money. Designers and retailers need to let people know what they are selling and need to project the right image. The industry is competitive and customers are fickle, so people are prepared to spend considerable sums and go to considerable lengths to get their message across.

N ow, add to that the media industry: the bottom line of the press is revenue, that for the main part comes from adverts, so papers and magazines will move heaven and earth to court those who pay vast sums for advertising space. In addition to that, the journalists and editors know that their readers love coverage of fashion and the celebrities who wear it, so features on fashion boost circulation, which leads to more advertising and more revenue. You can see how these two industries need each other, thrive on each other and undermine each other.

Fashion communication is at least as big an industry as design or production.

Designers and retailers use all sorts of techniques and tricks to tell the world about their ranges. Marketers send leaflets through your door; fashion show producers link in with set designers and lighting designers to get the look and feel of a collection right; photographers take pictures of models, found through modelling agents, created by stylists and hair and make-up professionals, and their images are published by editors and written about by journalists. And so it goes on. . .

Two parts of the industry – fashion design and fashion communication – need each other, thrive on each other and undermine each other.

The communications part of the industry can be split into two broad categories: marketing and the press.

The marketing teams work on behalf of the people selling – whether it's the designers, the suppliers or the retailers. Their main aims are to make sure that customers

The catwalks are where the design process finishes and the communications process really begins.

Behind the scenes at a
fashion show is stressful
and highly pressurised.

and potential customers know what's on sale each season and that the brand is right, which basically means that the clothes are appealing to the people they're aimed at.

They create websites, catalogues and adverts, all incredibly carefully constructed to give exactly the 'right' impression about the brand. The amount of research that goes into this is astonishing. The marketers know who goes into their shops and who buys their clothes, and they also know quite a lot about the aspirations of these people. Advertising is very much about what kind of person you'd like to be as well as what kind of person you are: the campaign that is going to work for you is the one that depicts 'you' but a kind of rose-tinted version of you. So the marketing professionals need to know as much about you as they can in order to get this just right. This approach will have an impact on every detail of the campaign, from the media that is used (are the adverts shown in the middle of

X Factor, Downton Abbey or This Morning?), the models chosen (unattainably gorgeous, or girl-next-door beautiful), the celebrities that endorse your products (Victoria Beckham, Davina McCall or Prunella Scales?) and the activities they are doing (glamorous red-carpet affair or playing in the park with the kids?).

The PR teams within marketing will try every trick in the book to get the right people to endorse their products, whether it's Kate Winslet wearing your dress at a premiere, or GMTV's fashion editor raving about your latest suede boots.

BELOW The red carpet is a great opportunity for the
fashion industry, giving photographers a subject,
journalists a story and designers some publicity.

Media caricatures

This part of the industry, perhaps more than any other, is the subject of media caricatures, whether it's the ruthless bitchiness of *The Devil Wears Prada* or the comic vacuous excesses of *Ugly Betty* or even the glamour of the fashion pages of *Vogue* magazine showing a lifestyle that many of us aspire to but very few of us will ever attain.

Hair and make-up can take hours and involve a lot of sitting around.

we should all be looking out for and choose which high street versions they recommend. This really is make or break for the designers, but it is also very important for the magazine people to get it right – if they support a designer who turns out to be very unpopular or endorse a beauty product that doesn't do what it claims to do, then this does their reputation no favours.

Professionals within these fields might work in-house or for agencies, might be self-employed or on a contract and might get work for themselves or have an agent.

Routes in

You usually need a relevant degree and almost always lots of unpaid work experience, where you are invariably enthusiastic, proactive and a joy to have around; you make yourself indispensable, and you make friends with everyone you meet. Or as near to that as you can manage.

Best bits

▲ You are right at the heart of the business, and it's a very exciting environment to work in
▲ You can see the fruits of your labour very clearly, both in terms of your product (whether it's a photograph, an article or a campaign) and in terms of your bottom line, whether that is sales figures or circulation
▲ It's very creative and you'll work with lots of other creative, passionate people

Worst bits

▼ It's really hard to get your foot in the door
▼ Achieving the right work–life balance can be tricky. It's rarely a nine-to-five job, and if you're freelance you may feel a great pressure to accept every job that comes your way, regardless of whether you have a holiday planned, or haven't had a decent night's sleep for a week

Skills needed

• All roles will require excellent people skills. Relationships are extremely important, whether it's about knowing how to get the best from the people in your team, being such a consummate professional that people are always eager to

The marketing teams will also arrange fashion shows, and get collections shown at London Fashion Week. These events then involve a whole array of other professionals, including set designers, musicians, hair and make-up artists, stylists and of course, models.

The other side of communications involves the press. The main focus of this is the fashion magazines (still very big business and hugely influential), but it also includes all kinds of papers and broadcast journalism on radio and television as well as websites.

The key players here are the writers and the photographers, or at a more senior level, the editors and creative directors. They are the ones who make the decisions about what to include and what messages are going to be sent out. They review the catwalk collections, decide which designers

> *Key players are the writers, photographers, editors and creative directors. They make the decisions about the messages that are sent out.*

Journalists and editors take notes at a fashion show. They use this opportunity to pick up on key trends for the forthcoming season.

give you more work or translating contacts into friends who will do you favours. Without good people skills you are not going to make it

- Talent – talent on its own is not enough, but it is a prerequisite. Your writing, images, eye or ideas need to be creative, original and better than almost anyone else's
- You need to be efficient. If you say you're going to do something, then you need to be the kind of person who delivers, on time, on budget, something more impressive than you promised
- Persistence – this field is incredibly competitive, and you are going to suffer a whole series of setbacks before you

get your lucky break. You will probably need to work unpaid, for some time; you will possibly get treated with a fair lack of respect at some stage or other; and you will almost definitely ask yourself how long you are prepared to stick with this at some point. But essentially, the people who make it are the people who didn't give up

Links

The Chartered Institute of Marketing for information resources for sales and marketing professionals. www.cim.co.uk
The Chartered Institute of Public Relations provides news information and training on all aspects of the profession. www.cipr.co.uk
The National Union of Journalists, an influential union with news, information and training about all aspects of the profession. www.nuj.org.uk
The Association of Photographers for information, support and careers advice. www.the-aop.org.uk

PR, or public relations, is all about getting the right kind of exposure. Though it's all about selling clothes, PR tries to be a bit more subtle than advertising, focusing on image to convince the public that this is a brand they want to buy.

fashion PR

Designers and retailers might have an in-house PR team or might outsource their PR work to an agency.

There are two main thrusts to fashion PR, and depending on your product, brand and target customer, you might focus more on one than the other. The first one is all about celebrities. The celebrity culture is so strong at the moment, with journalists reporting their clothing and tastes in such minute detail, that celebrity endorsement makes an enormous difference to bottom-line sales figures.

PR teams try everything to get the right kind of celebrity to be seen wearing their clothes, so they develop relationships with the agents, stylists and PRs of the celebrities to get them to pass on the clothes. This role tends to be most prominent for the higher-end fashion designers and for fast-fashion retailers.

The other main focus of the PR team is to get journalists to write good things about their products. It is estimated that editorial cover is worth four times what paid advertising space is worth, in terms of sales; and given that a full-page advert in *Vogue* will cost upwards of £16,000, then good PR

is worth its weight in gold – almost literally. The PR team will need to develop good relationships with the fashion, beauty and celebrity journalists who write for the kinds of magazines and websites and who work on the kinds of radio and television programmes that their customers read and watch. Getting a fashion editor in a magazine to write an article on your summer

Editorial cover is worth four times what paid advertising space is worth in terms of sales.

collection or to feature your new little black dress in their 'best five party dresses' article is a surefire way to increase sales, as readers trust in the objectivity of the journalists.

In order to make this happen, the PR team needs to think of all sorts of different ways to let the journalists know

Study

- Communications/Journalism
- Public relations
- Advertising/Marketing
- Fashion merchandising
- Fashion events planning
- Fashion history

Links

Brand Republic Jobs for jobs in marketing and PR. http://jobs.brandrepublic.com
Campaign for news, information and vacancies. www.campaignlive.co.uk
The Chartered Institute of Public Relations provides news information and training on all aspects of the profession. www.cipr.co.uk

Rating

Average salary: ● ● ○
Entrance difficulty: ● ● ●

Stand out from the crowd

Build a well-organised portfolio with creative PR components. Volunteer at a charity fashion show event. It will be a great introduction to the field, a great place to network and the perfect opportunity to demonstrate your passion.

PR & Office Assistant Work Placement

A womenswear label which focuses on exclusive hand illustrated and hand printed silks, playing with feminine, flirty and wearable shapes to create wardrobe essentials for both day and night.

Length of placement: 4 weeks

Experience gained: The student/graduate could gain experience of working within a small and dynamic fashion PR team and see all aspects of a fashion label from the initial design process to PR and marketing. It will be a great opportunity to learn essential skills and gain important experience for future job opportunities.

---

about their products. Writing press releases and putting together press packs is the basic starting point for any PR campaign, but fashion journalists get so many of these landing on their desks every day that the PRs often have to work a little bit harder to get their particular product featured. Personal relationships count for a lot in this field and PRs spend time cultivating friendships with journalists and editors. They might send catalogues or look books out with details of the season's collection, send sample garments to the magazine editors for a photo shoot or run press days or other events to try to make sure that the journalists think of their products before their competitors'.

In addition to this proactive media management, PR teams also need to react to what happens in the media world. A negative story about the celebrity who endorses your product, a sweatshop exposé about the factory where your garments are made or a bad review in a major magazine could all cause a drop in sales and great damage to a hard-won reputation, and it is the PR team who would need to decide fast how to respond to the incident.

Routes in

This is a hugely competitive area of the industry and definitely one where unpaid work experience is expected. A degree is usually needed, although this could be in a fashion-, business- or literature-related field.

Best bits

▲ Reading a story you've written in the papers or seeing one of your garments actually being worn by a celebrity
▲ Mingling with fascinating people

Worst bits

▼ Not being in control of the way the press use your stories
▼ Unpredictable hours

Skills needed

- Creativity
- Great people skills
- Solid writing skills
- Organisational skills
- A great attitude
- Resilience

CASE STUDY:

Zoe works as a PR manager for a large retailer, specialising in lingerie.

Zoe did a degree in fashion promotion, and through some unpaid work experience she managed to get her first job working for a PR company who ran fashion productions and events. The company was just beginning to make it big, and as a PR assistant, Zoe had some great opportunities to work with some up-and-coming designers such as Gareth Pugh.

A lot of Zoe's early roles involved writing press releases, and she got really good at knowing how to express herself and writing about the different events they were running. Working for an agency, Zoe had lots of clients to deal with as she worked both with the agency clients and the journalists. They worked really long hours – at busy times she was starting at 5am and working through to 11pm, but she really got her hands dirty and learned the business from top to bottom. After six months the two interns there both applied for the one paid job that came up, and the other girl got the job. Zoe was really upset, but the director told her that he really valued her skills, and he asked around on her behalf.

On the strength of his recommendation, Zoe was invited to an interview for a PR assistant in-house for a wholesale lingerie company and got the job. Three years down the line she applied for the role of PR manager for an in-house team at a retailer, got the job, and has loved every minute of it. Her advice to those thinking of a career in fashion PR is not to be daunted: 'It's not just about who you know – you don't need to be friends with the right people. Believe in your own merit. Look for luck and take advantage but believe that you can do it on your own.'

Marketing is all about getting customers to buy your clothes. Marketing departments tend to have sizeable budgets and the campaigns are usually pretty direct: look at these lovely clothes and come to our shop to buy them.

marketer

ABOVE Hermès Christmas ad campaign. A successul campaign over this period can make a big difference to annual sales figures.

The marketing team will begin working with the buyers and designers to make sure that they really understand the concepts and ideas behind this season's collection and to get to know the garments. They will then decide on a marketing strategy for the season, which will include decisions about budgets, media (broadcast, print, posters, mailings or often some combination of these), themes and goals. Advertising is usually a key part of the campaign, but marketing will also encompass catalogues, direct mailings, fashion shows, packaging and special offers.

If you're working for a designer rather than a retailer, a large part of your role will involve working with the stores where your products are stocked. You would need to try and ensure that the retailers really understand the ranges and the brands to make sure that they promote the garments appropriately.

Knowing your customers is a very important part of marketing, and teams rely heavily on research to find out what customers look for and like in a product, what kinds of packaging will catch their eyes and what sort of promotion they will respond to best.

The marketing manager will usually work in a team, but depending on the size of their department, the nature of the team will vary. Large retailers will usually have a substantial in-house team that might incorporate shoot producers and designers. Small organisations might use a bank of freelancers, and many organisations will use agencies (advertising, design or event marketing) to outsource their campaigns.

Marketing professionals can work in-house or for an agency. Working for an agency will bring you more variety as you'll be working with a number of different clients, which can be very stimulating, but because you are billing your clients for the work that you've done, everything tends to be quite regimented (you need to do exactly what the client has asked for in exactly the time you've agreed). On top of that, some might prefer to be able to specialise in working for one brand that they have an affinity with, rather than having to work with whichever client the agency has made a deal with.

Knowing your customers is a very important part of marketing; teams rely on research to find out what customers look out for in a product.

Routes in
A degree in marketing or something business-related is ideal, but a background in fashion is also desirable. Work experience will stand you in good stead when applying for a

Marketing Assistant

We provide a unique environment, with exclusive womenswear, menswear, gifts and homewares. We have 21 stores offering a personalised boutique experience, with cutting-edge fashion and lifestyle products.

Duties: We currently have an opportunity for a progressive, creative and talented marketing professional to take up the post of Marketing Assistant. This role is pivotal in ensuring the brand values are maintained across the marketing mix and the wider business through visual and written communication.

Reporting directly to the Marketing Manager, a key objective is to create powerful, compelling and unique marketing campaigns that drive brand differentiation and maximum profitability.

paid job, and although not a prerequisite, this is the way that most marketers start their careers.

Best bits

▲ Seeing the campaign that you created and worked on come to life and impact on sales

▲ Marketing is a great career role. You get to be very central to the commercial business, and marketing managers will often progress to being directors

Worst bits

▼ Finding the right work–life balance is often hard; hours are long

▼ The internal politics of a commercial environment can mean that you are always having to justify your budgets and prove that your campaigns are a commercial success

Skills needed

- You need to be both creative and practical
- Excellent people skills
- Organisational abilities and the ability to stick to deadlines and budgets
- A thick skin can be helpful; learn not to take criticism personally
- An understanding of trends

CASE STUDY:

Sarah is a marketer for a major fashion retailer.

Sarah had always been really interested in fashion, but under pressure from her traditional school and even more traditional parents, she felt that she had to study what they considered to be an 'academic' subject at college. She studied history as it was her best subject, and quite enjoyed herself, but knew all along that she wouldn't want to pursue a career in anything related to that. In her final year at university, many of her friends were applying for graduate training schemes, so Sarah decided to do the same. She applied for a range of things, including retail management and sales, but found that she seemed to be much better suited to the marketing roles, as these allowed her to demonstrate her creativity, her commercial sense and her people skills.

Sarah got a job as a marketing trainee with a pharmaceutical firm, and it was a great grounding in the skills and techniques of marketing. What it wasn't, for Sarah at least, was very inspiring. She stuck it out for two years and then when the training programme had finished, started looking around for other roles. She found one in a major fashion retailer and got very excited about the idea of working within the fashion industry. Her background wasn't exactly what they wanted, but she was able to convince them of her enormous enthusiasm for the products, and she persuaded them to give her a trial. She's been there for over five years now and absolutely loves it. 'It took me quite a long time to figure out what I wanted to do, but now that I'm here, I know that I wouldn't be happy anywhere else.'

Study

- Fashion business
- Finance
- Fashion industry analysis
- Fashion management
- Public relations
- New media planning
- Communications
- Consumer behaviour/ psychology
- Sociology

Links

Brand Republic Jobs for jobs in marketing and PR. http://jobs.brandrepublic.com
Campaign for news, information and vacancies. www.campaignlive.co.uk
The Chartered Institute of Marketing for information resources for sales and marketing professionals. www.cim.co.uk

Rating

Average salary:
Entrance difficulty:

Stand out from the crowd

Bring a creative marketing project for one of the firm's clients to show your passion for the process. Research the firm and their campaigns.

As a fashion photographer you could work on editorial, advertising or catalogues. There is almost an inverse correlation between creativity and salary in this field.

fashion photographer

Catalogue work, where you are often working within very strict parameters, is often very well paid, and editorial work, where you are more likely to have a significant amount of creative input, is much less lucrative.

Photographers will often mix and match different kinds of jobs, with some giving them more creative satisfaction and others paying the bills.

The job of the fashion photographer is to show the clothes at their best. This takes a great range of skills and photographers sometimes say that the 'click' is the smallest part of their jobs. Perhaps first and foremost are people skills. The photographer needs to be able to communicate extremely effectively with the client, whether that is the designer themselves, the marketing team or the shoot or catalogue producer. They have to understand what their clients are asking them to do and make them feel confident that they are going to fulfil their brief. Then they need to communicate their own vision and directions to the people working for them, in particular the models. One of the most important skills is to be able to get the most out of the models, putting them at ease and finding ways to get them to behave and move in exactly the right way.

The photographer also needs to have a good eye and a good visual sense. They need to be able to understand what is going to look good and how to achieve it. They should have lots of their own creative ideas but should also be open to ideas from others and need to be able to translate thoughts and ideas into great images.

A love of clothes is important, too. As a photographer you could use your skills to take images of any subject, but a love of fashion will keep you motivated, allow you to understand your clients better and will probably enable you to take better images as you will instinctively know the best way to show the garments at their best.

> *The fashion photographer needs to understand what is going to look good and how to achieve it.*

Study

- Digital image production and manipulation
- Location and studio shooting
- Darkrooms
- Image construction
- Visual language
- Signature style

Links

The Association of Photographers has news and information about the industry and a student members' section to support students as they get established as photographers, including regular careers talks and a careers pack. www.the-aop.org.uk
Tips and insights into the world of fashion photography. www.fashionphotographyblog.com
A range of **courses in Fashion Photography**. www.fashion.arts.ac.uk

Rating

Average salary: varies
Entrance difficulty: ● ● ●

Stand out from the crowd

Master the art of film. Many photographers value the discipline that is needed to work with film and so look for this in an assistant.

High Fashion Photographer

A promotions company aimed at merging music together with fashion.
Duties: We need a highly skilled, highly experienced photographer who deals with high-end fashion publications. To be part of a fantastic opportunity to raise their status and brand awareness to help launch the photo shoot of an artist signed to a major record label.
Requirements: The applicant must have a proven track record in fashion, have a high level of understanding when it comes to retouching and be able to work with graphics, CGI if need be.

Fashion photographers these days almost all shoot digital images, although there are some, usually very high-end editorial jobs, that are more likely to use film. Photographers will usually need to be comfortable with both and with retouching images using Photoshop.

Most photographers are freelance, and get their work through agents and their networks. Work takes place in studios or on location, and photographers can travel the world to shoots in all sorts of exotic locations.

Routes in

There is no single foolproof method for breaking into photography, but you can bet that you'll need to be determined, resilient and passionate in order to keep yourself going through the almost inevitable setbacks. Get a great CV and a strong portfolio together and start talking to people. Try to find work as an assitant to a photographer.

Best bits

▲ The variety
▲ The creativity
▲ The people

Worst bits

▼ It's really hard to break into
▼ Most photographers are freelance and some photographers may not enjoy the lifestyle that a freelance career usually entails
▼ Some work can be repetitive

Skills needed

- Visual creativity
- Excellent people skills
- Good organisational skills
- Excellent photographic skills
- Excellent CAD knowledge

CASE STUDY:

Jamie started off his career as an assistant to a photographer.

Jamie felt as though it took him absolutely ages to get himself established as a photographer, but his story is a common one, and many successful photographers have a shaky or inconsistent start to their careers.

He was sure right from the outset that his future lay in the arena of fashion photography, so he decided to do a degree that allowed him to specialise in this. Looking back he thinks this was a really sensible move: 'It meant that by the time I graduated, my portfolio was already quite specialised, and that all the contacts I made were in my field.' Jamie was very proactive while at college and got plenty of experience working collaboratively with other students on a whole variety of projects, but it was still a very slow process getting anyone to pay him. After graduation he got himself a job on a building site to make some money. Evenings and weekends were taken up with job hunting and he thinks that he must have sent more than 100 CVs off to fashion photographers during those first few months. With hindsight he thinks he should have been more pushy: 'I was so careful not to annoy people that I think I probably missed lots of opportunities with people who were just too busy to respond.'

Eventually, he met up with one of his colleagues from his course who told him of a photographer that she had done some work for who was looking for an assistant for a two-week job overseas. Jamie contacted the photographer, went to show her some of his work and got the job. The two weeks were amazing. It was incredibly hard work physically and mentally, but he was keen to show what he could do and soon made himself indispensable to the photographer. When they returned home she asked him to work on a few jobs she had lined up and soon she started to use him whenever she could.

Digital image production and manipulation is a key part of the photographer's role.

There are three common entry-level jobs within the photography industry. You will often find that you need to start doing these jobs unpaid, but should soon start to earn some money.

photography assistants

Achieving a casual and spontaneous look on a photo shoot is a compex business involving many people and a range of specialist equipment.

Studio assistant

Photographers will often hire a studio, or a room within a studio, for a shoot. The studio managers provide a studio assistant to help make sure that all their clients' needs are met and that the studio operates smoothly. The assistant essentially works as a runner and gets involved in anything they are asked to do. Much of the work is ensuring that the clients are well treated – bringing cups of tea and coffee, organising lunches and making sure that they have everything they need. It may also involve a fair amount of physical work, either helping the clients to move their equipment around or preparing the studios beforehand or clearing up afterwards. They will usually end the day by painting the studio with white paint, ready for clients the following day. Hours are long – you will often be the first person to arrive in the morning and the last one to leave at night – but it is a great way to build your networks within the industry.

Photographer's assistant

The digitisation of photography has changed the role of the assistant quite considerably, but it is still the case that most photographers on most jobs will want an assistant with them. The role of the assistant is a combination of the physical and the technical. A photographer will often have a lot of heavy equipment – with flash lighting, bounce reflectors, umbrellas, props, laptops and monitors, and it will be the assistant who does the bulk of loading and unloading the van, and setting it all up for each location. The assistant will also get involved in the more technical and creative aspects of the shoot, doing light readings and talking through the shots with the photographer. In the days of film, the assistant would be responsible for making sure that the set was perfect, as a dustbin in the back of the scene or an

Study

- Digital image production and manipulation
- Location and studio shooting
- Darkrooms
- Image construction
- Visual language
- Signature style

Links

The Association of Photographers has news and information about the industry and a student members' section to support students as they get established as photographers, including regular careers talks and a careers pack. www.the-aop.org.uk
Tips and insights into the world of fashion photography. www.fashionphotographyblog.com A range of **courses in Fashion Photography**. www.fashion.arts.ac.uk

Rating

Average salary:
Entrance difficulty: ● ● ●

Stand out from the crowd

Learn how to be pushy without being irritating.

CASE STUDY:

Chris is a photgrapher's assistant.

Chris did a degree in photography. At this stage in his career he knew that he wanted to take pictures for a living, but hadn't yet decided what kind of photography so decided to just really enjoy his time at college and experiment with all different styles of photography. He was extremely lucky that, at his degree show, his work was spotted by a fashion photographer. She told him that she had no work at the moment, but she'd be interested in him working for her as an assistant at some point in the future.

Chris went back to living with his parents and started to contact fashion photographers, sending his CV and portfolio out to literally hundreds of fashion photographers. Most ignored him completely, some were very positive and encouraging, but none had any work for him. A few months later he went back to the photographer he had met at his degree show. She still had no work for him, but she knew that the manager of a studio she often used was looking for a studio assistant. Chris wasted no time in going down to the studio with his portfolio and finding out more. He was taken on and for a few months worked hard and enthusiastically, lugging equipment, making cups of coffee and ordering pizzas for anyone and everyone. He didn't love the job, but he loved the clients and he loved the environment.

Four months down the line he was asked by one of the regular photographers if he was interested in a job as an assistant to him and he jumped at the chance.

---

unruly bit of the model's hair might not be noticed until after the film was developed and the scene could not be reshot. These days, with digital images, the image appears up on the monitor immediately, and the photographer and client can check it thoroughly and then decide to reshoot or touch up the image afterwards. The assistant may be responsible for downloading compact flash cards and setting up the computer for digital capture.

The assistant might also get involved in the post-production of the images, using Photoshop to create exactly the look the client is after. The assistant would also be expected to do anything else that was needed for either the photographer or the client, so if someone needed to go and buy the lunches or get the coffees, it would usually be the assistant who would be asked.

> *As an assistant, hours are long and pay is low – but it's the best way to learn your craft and make contacts in the industry.*

Second assistant

On large shoots, or those requiring an unusual amount of equipment, the photographer might decide to bring two assistants along. The range of jobs that you might do as second assistant could be quite similar to those done by the first assistant, but more heavily weighted towards the fetching and carrying side of things. You would be moving lighting, wardrobe, computer equipment and props wherever they were needed, and would be expected to turn your hand to anything that was asked for.

Routes in

Network, network, network. Make loads of phone calls and send out plenty of CVs. Keep at it.

Best bits

▲ Every day is different
▲ You get to learn about the industry and the process
▲ You get to make some valuable contacts

Worst bits

▼ The assistants' jobs involve a lot of physical work and long hours
▼ It can feel a bit frustrating creatively

Skills needed

• You must be prepared to work hard, both in terms of physical effort and long hours
• A love of the process and a hunger to learn
• Reliability and loads of common sense
• The ability to get along well with colleagues and clients
• Knowledge of the photographic process and equipment

There is no single set career path for a fashion illustrator. They may be employed or freelance and can work in almost every area of the fashion industry.

illustrator

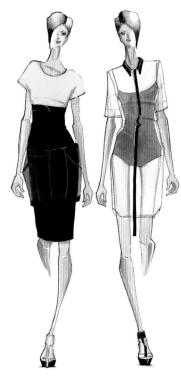

Illustrators need great drawing skills and a real understanding of how garments move on the body.

As an illustrator you might be producing illustrated displays for a high street store or a catwalk, drawing for a magazine, working for an ad agency or PR company or producing spec flat or 3D drawings for a designer's new collection. In essence a fashion illustrator creates an image from somebody else's idea. The nature of the images will depend on the product and how the drawings are to be used, but the purpose of the images would almost always be to create an interest in the garments from prospective buyers, so they must be creative, artistic and eye-catching.

In addition to producing drawings, an illustrator might have to take on a range of tasks. These could include: selecting colour, sound and animation to suit the images of a particular collection, identifying fabric patterns and designs for making the garments or producing layouts for magazines, flyers and brochures.

Drawings are usually produced both digitally and by hand, but could be produced using a variety of media, including coloured markers, charcoal, stencilling, painting or collage.

Typical employers might include: fashion designers, ad or PR agencies, magazine art directors, a direct-marketing agency or a website designer, although more often than not, the work would be freelance contracts rather than permanent employment.

Routes in

Although it's not a prerequisite for the role, most fashion illustrators have some formal qualifications in an area such as fashion design, illustration or graphics. These courses teach you the CAD skills needed, improve your skills at hand drawing and give the opportunity to draw from live models.

As an aspiring illustrator you will need an excellent portfolio, showing the depth and breadth of your work (see pages 32–35). It is also helpful to have an online portfolio or website. As with many freelance fashion roles, networking skills are paramount; start building and nurturing your networks as soon as you can.

Unpaid work experience is often the way to build your portfolio and networks, and because a lot of the work can be done from home, it can be relatively straightforward to combine this with paid part-time work.

A career as a fashion illustrator can keep you stimulated for a lifetime, but for those who get itchy feet, illustrators can either go on to other roles in the fashion design world or specialise in the fields of graphics or illustration.

Three CAD illustrations from a womenswear range.

Best bits

▲ You get to combine an interest in fashion with your art skills

▲ You're right at the heart of the industry without having the responsibility and stress of being a lone designer

Illustrator

New style and personal shopping consultancy seeks illustrator to showcase our company.

Duties: To provide illustrations for the company website, and other marketing material in the future. Illustrations will be fashion related but are not to look obviously 'fashion'. They will ideally convey images of ordinary people, not leggy, beautiful, elongated model shapes.

Requirements: Artistic skill, as well as the ability to think outside the box. The ideal candidate is someone who takes the concepts of fashion and style a step further and creates images with their own identity.

Salary: Negotiable

◆ Your career can be as varied as you want it to be

Worst bits

▼ The industry is hard to break into and you have to work hard to keep your career going

▼ Producing great illustrations is no guarantee that you'll make it: to be a success you need to know the right people and they need to know you

▼ If you're someone who craves security, it can be a challenging career for you as most work is freelance or through short contracts

Skills needed

• You need to be strong at both freehand drawing and CAD (Photoshop and Illustrator are the most widely used)

• An awareness of the fashion design and garment manufacturing processes

• An understanding of how the body moves with clothing

• A great passion for clothing trends

• Ability to work with others and grasp colleagues' ideas accurately

• A range of business skills such as self-marketing, accounts and business planning

CASE STUDY:

Jessica is a design assistant for a major international designer.

Jessica has a degree in fashion illustration. The course focused on digital graphics and traditional drawing skills. She had an internship producing some illustrated window displays for Selfridges and another internship at Burberry. After graduation, Jessica got a design assistant role for a major international designer, through contacts she had made at Burberry, where she describes her role as a mixture of illustration and graphics for clothing. She has travelled the world in the last two years in this job, working on fashion shows in New York, Milan and Paris. Alongside this, she has managed to show her portfolio and has followed her exhibition with magazine illustration work.

Study

• Illustration
• Technical specification
• CAD
• Primary research, drawing and design development

Links

The Society of Illustrators promotes the art of illustration through exhibitions, lectures, and education.
www.societyillustrators.org
Drapers Online for general fashion information and inspiration for illustrations.
www.drapersonline.com

Rating

Average salary:
Entrance difficulty:

Stand out from the crowd

Create images with their own identity; develop a style that is not too polished or perfect; be confident working in black and white as well as in a range of colour media; and finally, be reliable, efficient and able to stick to agreed schedules.

The editor has overall responsibility for and control of a magazine. They decide the features that the magazine will run, the stories it will cover and the events it will report.

magazine editor

As well as having responsibility for the text in a publication, the editor also makes decisions about images – what's going on the front cover and what photo shoots they are going to run for each edition. They will commission the journalists and photographers to produce the work and will have the final say on the look and feel of each edition. Magazines work quite far in advance of the publication date; work on the Christmas edition, for example, might start in the early summer. This means that the editor will be working on six or more editions at any one time and thinking about everything from the big picture of how the 12 editions produced within a year fit together, right down to the detail of an individual image within a single edition.

> *It's your job to produce a magazine that people want to buy and that businesses want to advertise in.*

Being a good magazine editor is all about keeping lots of plates spinning at once. You need to be very aware of the commercial side of the business: it's your job to produce a magazine that people want to buy and that businesses want to advertise in, so you have to know your readers inside and out and be very astute in predicting what they are going to want to know about and see. You also, of course, need to be extremely up to date and well connected within the fashion world (assuming the magazine is fashion-oriented). You need an excellent sense for which of the new trends are going to be big and which designers are the ones to watch.

It's also a very people-based job. The success of your magazine is usually down to the synergy of your team, and working closely with your creative director, your writers, photographers and marketing managers is crucial.

Routes in

Editors almost always start as journalists, so the classic route is a degree in journalism, unpaid work experience, a job as a junior reporter and then working your way up through the ranks.

Study

- News reporting, features, design and layout
- Media law
- Shorthand
- Research methodologies
- Business studies

Links

Vogue One of the ultimate fashion magazines, published globally. www.vogue.com
The National Union of Journalists, an influential union with news, information and training about all aspects of the profession. www.nuj.org.uk

Rating

Average salary: ● ● ●
Entrance difficulty: ● ● ●

Stand out from the crowd

It's not only about what you know (and you do need to live and breathe fashion) but it's also about who you know. You need a huge network and the talent and energy to nurture and maintain it continuously.

Best bits

▲ Being right at the heart of the industry
▲ The satisfaction of seeing the magazine that you have created appear on the shelves

Worst bits

▼ The job will take over your life, so you need to love it

Skills needed

- A passion for and sensitivity towards fashion
- Good people skills are vital
- The ability to analyse what readers want
- The ability to get the most out of people
- Drive
- Great organisational skills
- A huge number of contacts in the industry

CASE STUDY:

Anna is editor of a music and lifestyle magazine.

Anna has just got her first editorial job, working for the magazine that accompanies a major music and lifestyle TV show. Her route into journalism is quite an unusual one, in that she didn't finish her degree and she didn't start off wanting to be a writer. 'I always knew I wanted to work in the fashion business, but I don't think I had a very clear notion of what jobs there are within the industry, so applied to do a degree in fashion design without really thinking it through.'

By the end of her first year, it was becoming clear to Anna and to her tutors that design wasn't really the best route for her. She was great at analysing other people's work, but struggled when it came to coming up with the creative ideas herself. While at college she had got involved with the student newspaper and had done some work covering the end-of-year fashion shows. She decided to give up her course and went to see her careers adviser to get some ideas as to where to go next. They talked about her work with the student paper, and it seemed obvious to her that journalism was where her future lay.

Having made the decision, Anna lost no time. She continued working for the student paper, sent some of her articles to the local newspaper and eventually persuaded them to print a couple of her articles. Armed with a growing collection of published articles, she got some work experience with a teen magazine, and after a few months working unpaid, she was taken on as a junior fashion features writer. She hasn't looked back. Five years later, she has managed to get herself a job as an editor for a small publication, and although it's really busy and has been a very steep learning curve for her, she is really enjoying it.

Editor – Dubai

With more brands under one roof than any other destination in the world, ours is not only the largest mall in the world, but a central lifestyle, fashion, leisure and entertainment centre, attracting over 30 million visitors through its doors each year.

Fashion Avenue features all the top brands, including the largest Cartier boutique in the Middle East and an infinite number of names from Tom Ford to Jimmy Choo, from Louis Vuitton to Ralph Lauren.

We are now launching a dedicated lifestyle magazine with fashion at its core and are looking for an editor with experience on a recognised fashion, beauty or lifestyle title; minimum two years' experience in at least a section editor role.

Art directors work closely with copywriters or journalists. They are usually employed by retailers to promote sales or by magazines to tell stories about collections, designers and trends.

art/creative director

Art directors can come from a range of backgrounds; they might be graphic designers, fine artists, fashion designers or photographers, and may have started their careers in advertising, or gone straight into fashion. They might work freelance and get contracts through an agent or be employed on a permanent basis.

The art director will start the process by finding out what the client or editor is trying to achieve with this particular edition, catalogue or advertising campaign. They will then come up with a mood board to show their ideas. The mood board (produced on a computer but shown literally on a board) will include a range of different kinds of images, which will link together to give a particular feeling and mood. The art director may well already have a clear idea of the photographer, stylists and models they want to use so will include some images illustrating their work on the mood board.

The process needs to be a collaborative one with the clients or editor, with ideas being exchanged, concepts negotiated and battles won and lost. As an art director you need to understand the clients' ideas but use your expertise to take them further or in a slightly different direction.

The actual shoot is usually highly pressurised. Shoots are expensive – five days can easily cost £150,000 so every minute counts. You need to be very clear about what you are going to do, who needs to be where when, and where you are going with each shot, but shoots are nothing if not unpredictable. The weather can change so that your summer beach set is covered in fog for three hours; the person whose house you have arranged to film in changes her mind; the photographer gets food poisoning. . . solving problems is a big part of the art director's role on a shoot.

Routes in
Getting your foot in the door is hard. You need to get appointments with as many people as you can and show them your portfolio. If there are people in the business that

Study
There is no set path to becoming an art director, but there are some courses that you could study that would stand you in good stead:
- Photography
- Fine art
- Styling

Links
Vogue One of the ultimate fashion magazines, published globally. www.vogue.com
Drapers Online for general fashion information. www.drapersonline.com

Rating
Average salary: ● ● ●
Entrance difficulty: ● ● ●

Stand out from the crowd
Don't be afraid of criticism. Learn to be articulate about your work and to view your own and others' work critically.

IN HIS OWN WORDS:

Matt is creative director at *Elle*, and a freelance art director.

'I'd always drawn. As a teenager I started producing posters and flyers for people I knew. It was all for free, but the significant thing about it was that at 14 I was getting some good experience of client relationships and this stood me in really good stead. I did a degree in Graphic Design and then pounded the streets with my book, showing it to anyone I could find. I must have had about 50 appointments in those first couple of months and met some really helpful, inspiring people. Eventually I got some work experience with *i-D* magazine, (unpaid, of course) as an art assistant, and then was taken on as a designer. This was an amazing time for making contacts. The magazine was really social and although we worked hard, we also went out a lot together, so I developed really good friendships there which have been incredibly useful throughout my whole career – and theirs too. I then did various roles at various magazines, including *Arena*, *Elle* and *Maxim Fashion*, working in both London and New York. Throughout this time I was continuously building up my freelance work for retailers, working on catalogues and advertising campaigns. I have some really longstanding clients that I work with such as Gieves & Hawkes and Boden. It can be unusual for a retailer to stick with the same art director for some years, but I really enjoy building up the client relationships and getting to know the brands inside and out.

'The thing I love most is knowing that at any time I can get a phone call about something I've never thought about before. That is really exciting to me, and it's that that has kept me excited about the job for so long.

'Is it really as glamorous as its image? Yes. I travel the world, work with incredible people, meet celebrities, go to lots of parties and get paid well to do it. It's hard work and not without its frustrations, but I can't thing of anything else I'd like to do.'

LEFT The creative director of a magazine is an influential role within the fashion industry, and is also one of the most competitive fields.

you admire, get in touch with them. They are likely to be flattered, might even take you under their wing, will probably inspire you and the worst that they can do is say no.

Job titles vary from place to place, but you might start as an art assistant, progress to a designer, then art editor, then design director and finally reach the heady heights of art or creative director. The differences in these roles are hierarchical ones – as you progress you have more responsibility for making decisions, and get involved in more of the process – from concept to sign off.

Best bits
▲ Creative problem-solving
▲ The variety of work
▲ Meeting and working with new and amazing people
▲ It can be really glamorous
▲ Building up relationships with clients

Worst bits
▼ Long hours
▼ Hard work
▼ Having to compromise your creativity

Skills needed
• Ideas, ideas and more ideas. Art directors spend their lives outside work looking at references. They look at art, film, fashion, architecture, travel, people and anything else that might help
• Creative problem-solving skills: things go wrong, people aren't happy, the goalposts shift and it's your responsibility to come up with a new and better solution
• People skills are also essential – it's all about collaboration: you are bringing the client, photographer, models, stylists and set designers together and the relationships need to work. You should be able to keep calm under pressure
• You need to be someone who can respond well in a crisis. There is a lot riding on your work and deadlines are tight, so there can be a lot of stress

Fashion companies need photographs of their clothes for catalogues, advertising and magazines. An enormous amount of work goes into making sure that the photographs convey the right message about the garments and the brand, and it is the job of the shoot producer to make the shoot happen and to ensure it is finished on time and on budget and everyone is happy.

fashion shoot producer

The first stage is getting the brief, which is the broad outline of the concept of the shoot. The brief would usually come from the buyers, merchandisers or creative directors, and this would be based on their inspiration and vision for the range of clothes. So, for example, they might decide that if the summer range has a strong nautical feel, the shoot should take place in a harbour with some shots on a yacht.

Everything about the shoot needs to be planned, down to minute details. Shoots are expensive, so the producer needs to make sure that all bases are covered and all problems anticipated.

Shoots usually take place about six months before the season, so finding appropriate locations can be quite challenging. The images for your summer collection will be shot in the middle of winter, so if you want to do a beach shoot you are restricted to certain parts of the world, and a snow shoot for the winter collection will need to be shot at a very high altitude to get somewhere where there is still snow in July. Producers might use existing contacts or websites to identify some possible places and might go on a location scout to have a look at some of the options.

The next step is to get the right team. The producer would usually use agencies to find the right art director, photographer and hair and make-up artists. Models come through agencies and the producer might work with the buyers to make sure that they are getting models who have the right look for the product. The agency may send images of up to 400 models, from which the producer might choose 20 to work with.

The last thing to do before going on the shoot is making up the outfits and deciding what each model is going to wear, working with the stylist.

On the shoot, the producer is responsible for everything. You need to have a good grasp of all aspects of the project from the big-picture concept to the tiny details: it's up to you to ensure that everyone's got up on time, that breakfast is ready and that the models know when to come to stylists' rooms for fitting.

Back in the office the images need to be presented to the buying team, chosen and Photoshopped (they might need to get rid of a tattoo or a strange shadow), and then it's ready to go to the design team.

Shoot producers can work in-house or freelance. In-house producers would tend to be involved in the whole process, from the concept to the finished product, whereas a freelance producer would be more likely to be brought in just for the actual shoot.

> *Shoots are expensive, so the producer needs to make sure that all bases are covered and all problems anticipated.*

Shoots are complex operations, and it's the role of the producer to make them run as smoothly as possible.

Shoot Producer

RESPONSIBILITIES INCLUDE:
• Managing all production logistics of various ad campaign, catalogue, editorial, e-commerce and still life photo shoots for all brands.
• Dealing with outside agencies on sourcing talent and crew for photo shoots based on direction from creative directors and art directors, as well as negotiating competitive rates for models, hair stylists, make-up artists, wardrobe stylists, prop stylists, set designers, photographers, studios, catering and locations.
• Understanding and translating brand profile, customer profile and creative direction for specific jobs in order to recommend appropriate talent.

Routes in

Unpaid work experience as an assistant will lead to a paid job if you do it well and are prepared to do it for long enough. A degree in a related subject such as photography or fashion will help but is not necessary.

Best bits

▲ Travel
▲ Getting to work with great people
▲ Being there from the embryonic stages right through to the finished product

Worst bits

▼ Everybody thinks you know everything about everything and are there to solve any problem!

Skills needed

• Excellent organisational skills
• A strong will and a strong personality
• Capable of working with all different kinds of people

IN HER OWN WORDS:

Hayley is a fashion shoot producer for Boden.

'I think there are two really important personality traits that you need to cope in this field and to do it well. The first is to be a creative problem solver and the second is to be a bit of a psychologist. As the producer you are in a way the kind of "mother" of the shoot. You are expected to know everything that is going on, and solve every problem that comes your way, and believe me, they do come! From sorting out people's wrong coffee orders, and making sure their hotel rooms are the right temperature, right through to sorting out a beach shoot when it rains continuously for three days or coming up with an alternative plan when the venue for the entire shoot has been booked for the wrong month, it's your responsibility to make everything work. The other really helpful thing is to be able to read people well. You're dealing with such big budgets and such tight timescales that making sure that every single person is performing at their very best is enormously helpful. You have to know who to flatter, who to make a joke with and who to shout at, and anticipate and respond to people's mood changes.

'It can be tough to get your first break in this field. My advice to you is roll up your sleeves and get some experience from the bottom upwards. You can get useful experience and make useful contacts in all sort of arenas: retail head offices, production companies or photographer agencies, but wherever you are, make yourself indispensable: if you're packing clothes, then pack them well, if you're answering the phone, do it with charm and if you're photocopying, learn how to fix the copier when it goes wrong.'

Study

There are no prerequisites, but any of the following would be relevant:
• Marketing
• Advertising
• Photography
• Media studies

Links

Drapers Online for general fashion information. www.drapersonline.com
A range of **entry-level jobs** in the fashion industry. www.arts.ac.uk/student/careers/creative-opportunities.htm

Rating

Average salary: ● ● ●
Entrance difficulty: ● ● ●

Stand out from the crowd

You need to show that you're happy to get your hands dirty and will have to start right at the bottom.

Whether it's who's wearing what, what the influences for the next season are or which high street retailers are going up or down, many want to read about some element of the fashion industry.

fashion journalist

Fashion Journalist

We are an online magazine that exposes the freshest faces of fashion, music, art and culture; focusing on emerging talent and watching them climb the ladder of success.

Length of placement: 4 weeks

Experience gained: The student could gain experience of JOURNALISM, organisation, meeting deadlines, CRITICAL ANALYSIS and writing skills.

JOURNALISM/FASHION students would benefit from this placement.

Expenses: Travel expenses only

As a fashion journalist it's your job to write articles for magazines and newspapers about news, events, people and clothes in the fashion world. You might work for a magazine that has fashion at its heart, such as *Vogue* or *Elle*, a magazine that focuses on celebrities and popular culture such as *Heat* or *More* or a more traditional paper such as *The Times*. Magazines and papers will obviously have different readers who want to know about different things, but there are few publications that could claim that their readers have no interest at all in any aspect of the fashion industry.

The kinds of pieces that you'll be writing will vary from one magazine or paper to another, but it's likely that you'll be writing features, reporting news and events, providing copy to accompany editorial photo shoots and interviewing significant people. Features are longer pieces that will go into more depth about a particular issue; this could be anything from the debate around size zero models or the conditions in production factories overseas, to the lasting impact of celebrity on fashion trends. News and events stories will respond to whatever is going on in the fashion world. It might be who has worn what to the Oscars, a commentary on the new trends from the catwalks at London Fashion Week or a response to the news that M&S have broken all records with their profits this season.

Many of the major magazines will lead with images from a photo shoot, and the journalist will be asked to write some text to accompany and explain the images. These will tend to be shorter pieces, and the narrative is very much directed by the images. Finally, there are interviews. Journalists might be asked to interview designers, business leaders or celebrities about their take on the fashion industry.

Journalists can be employed by a magazine or paper, but are often freelance. Freelance journalists can spend most of their working lives writing for one or two particular publications, or can really take advantage of their freelance status and write for a whole range.

In recent years the explosion in websites and blogs has opened up another avenue to fashion writers, as they can contribute to existing websites or start their own blogs. This can be a great way for a budding journalist to get some experience of writing, or for a designer who enjoys writing to get some exposure.

The lifestyle of the fashion journalist can genuinely be pretty glamorous. Designers and retailers are always on the hunt for some good press, so they will go to great efforts to let journalists know what's going on with their collections and will try their best to make the journalists understand what makes their products special. This will often involve press releases and phone conversations but is also likely to involve invitations to fashion shows, launch parties and private views. But it's not all glamour. Much of the time the journalist is sitting by themselves at a computer trying to find some inspiring words by their 5 o'clock deadline, or trying to convince some editor, somewhere, that their great angle on the new trends for the summer season is worth commissioning.

Routes in

There are many different paths that have been taken by successful fashion journalists, but two of the most common are training as a generic journalist and then specialising in fashion, or getting experience in another role on a magazine such as a stylist or photographer and then moving over to journalism.

Journalists do not necessarily need a journalism qualification, but it can really help, both in making contacts and in teaching some of the basic skills that are useful such

as shorthand and relevant legislation. There are a lot of journalism courses out there; if you are going to do a journalism degree, make sure it's one that is accredited. Whether or not you have a qualification, you will need to start with some unpaid work experience. Often quite a lot of it. . . Your initial role on work experience will usually involve developing close relationships with the photocopier and the coffee machine, but you need to be proactive, resourceful and perhaps a little pushy to try and persuade someone to let you actually write something.

You may prefer to develop your early career in a different specialty, such as styling: if you get very involved with photo shoots and with deciding what stories you want the images to tell, then it's not considered a great leap to start writing some copy to go along with the photos.

Best bits

▲ Seeing your article appear in a paper or magazine
▲ Being paid to find out about fashion

Worst bits

▼ It's tough to break into and tough to stay in
▼ Working as a freelancer brings with it a certain lifestyle – lack of stability or certainty and no regular colleagues

▼ It can be tough being creative to a deadline or having to write about something that you're not passionate about

Skills needed

- You need to be able to write well, which means being able to communicate your ideas effectively, write in an engaging way, and adapt your style to the particular readership (the tone you use for *Heat* magazine would be quite inappropriate for the *The Times*!
- You need a great interest in, and ability to analyse, fashion – what's new, what's good and what'll last
- Being organised – you need to meet word limits and deadlines
- Good people skills. First, you need to understand your audience – what they're going to find interesting and how to talk to them. Second, you need to have good relationships with all the people in the fashion industry that you will be writing about – you need to be able to interview designers, call up PRs to get samples sent over and get exclusive stories from celebrities. Third, journalism is yet another field where careers are dominated by networking; you are much more likely to get commissioned by an editor who likes you
- The ability to be objective when reviewing fashion

Study

- News reporting, features, design and layout
- Online journalism, video for online
- Media law
- Shorthand
- Cultural trends and fashion forecasting
- Website and blog design

Links

The National Union of Journalists for information and support about journalism training and careers.
www.nuj.org.uk
Journalism UK for information about the journalism industry.
www.journalism.co.uk
Drapers Online for general fashion information.
www.drapersonline.com

Rating

Average salary: ● ● ●
Entrance difficulty: ● ● ●

Stand out from the crowd

Start a blog about some aspect of fashion that you are passionate about. It will give you a chance to showcase your writing skills and style and is a great way to network.

Twice a year designers show their collections to buyers and to the press. It's the show producer who makes this happen, and it is their job to bring the narrative of the collections to life.

fashion show producer

The starting point will always be to talk to the designer, looking at their mood boards and colour palettes, and finding out about the inspiration for the collection. This will allow you to really understand where they're coming from and what the collection means to them.

One of the important roles of the fashion show producer is to get the right team together. The producer needs to find the right set designer and lighting designer, the photographer, the film director, the sound designer and the casting director. Each of these creative professionals will need to work with the producer to a very specific brief, and it is the producer who needs to make sure that everything comes together in the right way at the right time.

It is the fashion show producer who needs to make sure that everything comes together in the right way at the right time.

The show needs to be organised down to the most minute detail with everything done to a strict budget and schedule. Costs are high and mistakes are not tolerated. One of the most important tasks is to find a venue. The producer needs to be sure that the venue is going to suit the image and style of the designer, and that not only will it be the right space for the show, but that it's also got the right ancillary spaces for the backstage and guest areas to ensure that the show is slick.

The producer might then look at the fabrics and colourways of the garments and work out what would be the best kind of lighting. They might need to think about music and what kind of soundtrack is going to be suitable.

Casting is always a significant part of the process. The producer will work with the casting director and model agents to get the right models for the show, and during Fashion Week, when there are many designers all wanting models at the same time, this can be a considerable headache to arrange.

Routes in
This job is all about passion, so demonstrating a commitment to and love for fashion is your starting point. A degree in something fashion-related is useful, but not essential; getting some work experience at a production agency is the best way to get your foot in the door.

Best bits
▲ Working with other creative people: the synergy with a team of creatives can result in an incredible process to be involved with
▲ Each show is different, and you learn something new each time – it's a very dynamic part of the industry

Clothes are arranged on racks according to the order they'll be worn in the show. Photographs attribute outfits to models.

Worst bits

▼ When things go wrong. It's all pretty high stress in the run-up to Fashion Week, and although you will try as hard as you can to anticipate the potential problems, you are often surprised by just how many unexpected problems you have to solve

Skills needed

- Creativity – you need a good eye, to be able to edit visually (see what works and what doesn't and know how to change it to make it better) and a great imagination
- People skills are absolutely critical – it's all about understanding and communicating, working with others and at the more senior level, leading a team
- Very good organisational skills are a must – if the music doesn't start at the right time or the models haven't been briefed to arrive in time for their make-up, then no amount of mind-blowing creativity is going to save you

CASE STUDY:

Charlotte is a freelance fashion show producer.

Charlotte started off her career with a degree in History of Art and Philosophy, but although that might sound like a traditionally academic background, she grew up in a very creative family so was used to being surrounded by creative people and talking about creative ideas. She worked as a stylist for Condé Nast for a few years, getting some great experience and making some brilliant contacts, and then when she was 25 she started up her own production company.

One of the best shows Charlotte has ever produced was for Emilio de la Morena at London Fashion Week 2010.

This show was all about the set design. Emilio decided that he wanted his show to take place in a 1950s car park in Soho. This was quite an unusual venue to choose and came with its own set of challenges (such as how to get power down there!), but it turned out to be the perfect venue for the show. It was a very lyrical set, inspired by Lucio Fontana, and there were pierced and stretched canvasses all around. They had white cotton voile, in translucent layers at different planes of field, and models emerged from all over the place.

One of her worst professional moments (or perhaps we should say her biggest professional challenges!) was working on a fashion show in a black tent in Milan in the height of summer, when the air-conditioning failed the day before the show. Charlotte managed to get the contact details of someone else about 200 miles away in Italy who was able to borrow a new unit and drive through the night to get it installed before the show started.

Study

- Theatre design
- TV/Theatre direction
- Fine art
- Fashion design

Links

The **British Fashion Council**, for information and news about designers in the UK.
www.britishfashioncouncil.com
Details of forthcoming **Fashion Weeks**.
www.londonfashionweek.co.uk

Rating

Average salary: ● ● ●
Entrance difficulty: ● ● ●

Stand out from the crowd

Get a range of work experience before you approach a production agency – they'll be impressed if you know about magazines, designing and merchandising.

Professionals in this arena can either specialise in make-up or hair or both. Increasingly the stylists and producers who hire the make-up and hair people are keen to find one person for both roles as that will keep their costs down.

make-up and hair professionals

Make-up and hair professionals can work for magazines, in salons or studios or for photo shoots and fashion shows. Outside the immediate world of fashion, they can also work for film, theatre and television. They often end up specialising in one particular kind of look, for example, someone might be known for their 'natural' looks, or for their vintage hairstyles. They could also specialise in prosthetics (for example, giving someone an enormous nose) or special effects such as wounds and burns.

Most hair and make-up artists work freelance and have an agent who gets work for them and negotiates good deals. Those working for salons are more likely to be employed but still would often combine the security of a regular income with the more varied work of a freelancer.

Working for a salon is quite a different experience from working for shows, shoots and film. One of the main differences is that in a salon or store you are working with ordinary people, wanting ordinary looks, whereas for shows, shoots and film you are working with designers or directors to achieve a dramatic effect that enhances their vision. You are often working with stars – whether they are actors, models or other celebrities; you need to have the confidence and sensitivity to deal with famous people, and sometimes, their famous egos. In stores and salons, part of your role is usually to sell. You may well be working directly for a make-up brand, working in a concession within a department store or a specialist shop such as MAC, or you might be working with a salon that has an exclusive deal with a brand such as Clinique or Paul Mitchell, but in all these cases you would be expected to provide not only the makeover or hairstyling service but to persuade your customers to buy some of the products that you have demonstrated. Basic salaries can be meagre, supplemented by tips and sales commission. Within these roles, you might be involved in makeovers and lessons as well as standard hair cutting, colouring, styling and make-up.

Study

- Skin and skincare
- Corrective make-up techniques
- Beauty make-up techniques
- Current beauty trends
- Preparation of hair
- Blow-drying techniques
- Ponytails and plaiting
- Hair extensions

Links

Information about and resources relating to the industry. www.makeupmag.com
An excellent source of **make-up and hair jobs**. www.gumtree.co.uk
The **sector skills council for media and fashion**. www.skillset.org.uk

Rating

Average salary: ● ● ●
Entrance difficulty: ● ● ●

Stand out from the crowd

Volunteer to do hair and make-up for a charity fashion show, or combine your efforts with a photographer, so you can both build your portfolios.

Make-up artist

Make-up artist required for Lady Gaga impersonator shoot on November 7 or 14.

This will be shot on location and in the studio. Make-up artist must be extremely creative and deliver high quality. This is not a paid position but will be an ideal portfolio and exposure piece. Please send examples of your work and contact details.

Routes in

There are lots of courses out there – degree courses, short courses, private schools and apprenticeships. Having learned your trade, either on the job, or on a formal training programme, it then takes loads of networking and unpaid work to get your name established. Registering with an agent is a good route, but usually they will only take you on after you've had a fair bit of experience in the sector. All make-up and hair professionals have a portfolio that showcases their range of work.

Best bits

▲ The actual process can be very relaxing to do

▲ You get to see the fruits of your labour very clearly and very quickly

▲ Working with such a variety of people

Make-up and hair professionals often end up specialising in one particular kind of look, for example, 'natural' make-up or vintage hairstyles.

Worst bits

▼ Some roles can involve a lot of sitting around waiting

▼ It's a tough business to break into

▼ There's a lot of discrimination in this field between the high end and the low end. The high end pays little until you make it, but if you start at the low end, it's almost impossible to break into the high end

Skills needed

• Plenty of determination
• People skills, in particular the ability to listen
• Artistic and creative ability
• The ability to work under pressure

This area of work is not just about your technical skills; developing good relationships with your clients is key to your success.

📁 ## CASE STUDY:

Laura is a freelance make-up artist and also works part-time in a beauty salon.

Laura had always loved make-up and fashion, and although she had originally wanted to become a personal shopper, decided this was a career path that she might pursue later in life. At college, she specialised in fashion make-up and learned the basics of brushes, concealers and beauty techniques, and also the differences between the styles needed for fashion, for editorial and for ordinary people.

Laura's first job after college was at a make-up store selling products, giving make-up lessons and running make-up parties! This was a great learning role for her, but the store closed down after a while and Laura struggled to get herself a new position. She eventually found one, working for a makeover studio. She had quite a mixed experience here, really enjoying the work with the public but feeling a bit as though she was a cog in a money-making wheel – always in a rush, and expected to sell the make-up to the customers.

Feeling very brave, Laura decided to go it alone. She has set herself up as a freelancer and has had quite a variety of work, through friends, contacts and responding to adverts. She's worked for television, done make-up for Lou Reed for a Reuters interview and done hair and make-up for weddings. To give herself some stability she is also now employed by a beauty salon that does hair, make-up, manicures and pedicures for girls' nights out.

Her best bit of advice? 'Don't give up. It's really tough, but you've just got to persevere.'

The modelling sector is perhaps the most glamorous part of the industry. It's filled with the über cool from all over the world – people who are paid millions just for being beautiful. And a model won't lift a finger without the say-so of their agent.

model agent

The job of the model agent is to get their models work. This involves a few different elements. The most dominant is the relationships with the clients. The agent needs to build up a really good rapport with the clients, whether they are producers, photographers or designers, to get a deep understanding about what they want from a model. Different designers have their own desired 'look' and it's the agent's job to identify exactly what this look is and put forward an appropriate shortlist of models. The casting part of any fashion production is crucial to the success of the brand so the producers will really want to take their time to get it right. The model agency might send shots of up to 400 models to the client initially, and then will arrange for a casting for the shortlist that the client has chosen (this might be around 100 models), and then spend two or three days watching the models on the catwalk, on video and in photographs. They'll also talk to the models to make sure they get the right ones for the project. The agent then needs to negotiate with the client to get the best deal they can for the work.

The agent will also work closely with the model to help them make the most of their talent and manage their careers. They will make sure that the model looks their best, and if necessary arrange for a restyling of hair and clothes. The agent will oversee test shots to ensure that the model has a great portfolio and will make all the practical arrangements needed for a casting or shoot – booking their travel and making sure they're in the right place at the right time.

Model agents can take up to 30 per cent of the model's fee so it's very much in their interests to make sure that their models have long and lucrative careers.

Model agents can specialise in men, women, children, character or plus size, and can work with established models or new faces.

The world of modelling has changed over the last ten or so years and has become more competitive and more complex. The Internet has transformed the local market into a global one and as a result agencies are competing internationally – a producer for a catalogue might very well ask agencies in London, Paris and New York to put forward some names. There are more agencies around now, but also more work – in particular the men's market has expanded hugely in the last decade.

Routes in

Many agents, bookers and scouts started their careers as models themselves – this is a good way to get to know the industry and the clients, but it's by no means essential. Formal qualifications aren't particularly relevant, but your enthusiasm, efficiency and your 'eye' are the things that will turn an unpaid work placement into a paid job.

Study
No specific courses of study

Links
Leading **recruitment agency for modelling agents** in London.
www.martinmedia.co.uk
Professional body promoting the work of agents in the UK.
www.associationofmodelagents.org
UK directory of model agencies.
www.ukmodelagencies.co.uk

Rating
Average salary: ● ● ●
Entrance difficulty: ● ● ●

Stand out from the crowd
Learn a language. The market is increasingly international, so a talent for languages can be a great asset.

Model Agency Booker Mens Division

A leading agency requires a model booker for their men's division. Ideally with previous booking experience on a men's division or experience within a men's magazine.

Please email with a copy of your CV (in Word) for further information.

Best bits

▲ Agents all say that it's the people who make it: models, colleagues and clients

Worst bits

▼ You spend quite a lot of time rejecting people – either aspiring models who just don't have what it takes or models who haven't been selected after a casting call

▼ The stress of Fashion Week

Skills needed

- Honesty is essential – the models and the clients need to know that they can trust you
- Being upbeat, enthusiastic and organised is vital; the environment can be quite stressful so a supportive team is very important
- Charm can always take you a long way

IN HER OWN WORDS:

Lonneke is a model agent.

Lonneke has worked for Select Models for 25 years and absolutely loves her job. She started as a model herself in her teenage years, but although she didn't really enjoy the actual process of modelling, she fell in love with the industry. This is her advice to anyone interested in a career as a model agent:

'The fashion industry is fiercely competitive – so if you can get work experience in an agency, go for it; if you "shine" you may well be asked to stay on. You need to be enthusiastic (embracing the mundane as well as the exciting), hardworking (we can often work until 10pm and over weekends), organised and dedicated – we also work internationally so a grasp of other languages is helpful.

'Read all the fashion magazines and blogs, get to know the names of the photographers/stylists and art directors – and get a sense of who is working for which publication.

'Scout for new models – anywhere and everywhere – if you have a "good eye" that is an ideal way to get recognition from an agency – if you can build up a reputation as someone who can spot a potential superstar then you are halfway there.'

Part of the agent's job is to create publicity materials that are representative and show the subject in his or her best light.

Of all the jobs in the glamorous world of fashion, there is perhaps none quite as desirable as that of a model. The press is full of their fabulous lifestyles, the vast sums they earn, the gorgeous clothes they wear and of course, they are all impossibly, impossibly beautiful.

model

The reality is of course a little different, and although there are a few who do reach those dizzy heights, your chances of making it are so slim that having 'supermodel' as your career goal is almost inevitably going to lead to disappointment. There are, however, many models who make at least part of their living through their modelling for a while, in a more low-key and perhaps less exciting way, so don't be put off altogether!

There are a few different kinds of work that a model could get involved with. The most well known (and also the most competitive) is working as a catwalk or editorial model. Catwalk models are hired by the designers to showcase their collections during Fashion Week and at other events. Editorial models work for magazines and papers for shoots to illustrate the garments that the magazines have chosen to write about. Beyond these two groups, there are some marginally less competitive arenas for modelling. Commercial models are those used in advertising, for television adverts and in newspaper and billboard ads. Catalogue models are employed to model the clothes for a particular retailer's catalogue. Character models are used in a range of contexts when the client is looking for plus-sized, unusual or even 'ugly' models. Life models are employed by art schools to allow the students to learn how to draw the human form.

Most modelling jobs will come through an agency so it's a really good idea to try to get yourself an agent. Different agents will specialise in different kinds of models, different kinds of work and even different kinds of looks, so it's important to do your research and find out which agency is most likely to suit you.

Routes in

Assuming that you're not spotted on your way home from school the best thing to do is get yourself an agent. You'll need to get a portfolio together so get some shots of yourself modelling; it's very common to do some trading off of skills – you model for free and in return the photographer gives you some shots for your portfolio.

Do be careful. In almost all cases you shouldn't pay out lots of money to someone promising you a glittering career, and if you're under 18 do make sure you take a parent or guardian along with you.

Modelling is a tough business, but there can be huge rewards for those who make it.

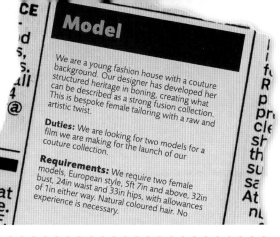

We are a young fashion house with a couture background. Our designer has developed her structured heritage in boning, creating what can be described as a strong fusion collection. This is bespoke female tailoring with a raw and artistic twist.

Duties: We are looking for two models for a film we are making for the launch of our couture collection.

Requirements: We require two female models, European style, 5ft 7in and above, 32in bust, 24in waist and 33in hips, with allowances of 1in either way. Natural coloured hair. No experience is necessary.

Best bits
▲ Travelling the world
▲ The clothes, the parties, the glamour!

Worst bits
▼ It's really hard work – long hours, sometimes in very unglamorous conditions, and there can be a lot of standing around waiting
▼ It's incredibly tough to break into, and even if you do manage to make a living from it, your career will be a short one – models are past their best by their late twenties
▼ No pay until you make it – and you will have to pay your agency for comp cards to give out at every 'go-see' you are sent to

Skills needed
• You must look right: height, weight, proportions, skin, hair, etc
• Great personality – you should be someone who is good to work with, patient and both willing and able to respond to the photographer and director
• A total lack of inhibition and the ability to act

CASE STUDY:

Jeanette is a model just starting out.

Like many little girls, Jeanette had always longed to be a model. She used to walk up and down her bedroom in her pyjamas as though she were on the catwalk at Fashion Week, and pose for hours in front of her mirror. She grew up to be a very sensible and practical teenager, did well in her studies and got a place at university to study fashion design. 'I thought that it was such a silly dream to want to be a fashion model, but at least this way I could be in the right industry.'

Jeanette enjoyed her course, but the best part for her (by far!) was when her classmates needed someone to model for their end-of-term shows; Jeanette was always eager to help. She loved it but still had no thoughts that she might make a living this way. But, while modelling her friend's collection at one end-of-year show, a model scout was in the audience and asked if she'd come to the agency for some test shoots. 'I couldn't believe it. I just couldn't believe it!' She went along, the shoots went well and she was taken on by the 'new faces' division of the agency.

The work isn't exactly flooding in, but she's been shortlisted for a few jobs, and has done two bits of paid work modelling for a catalogue, and has another audition coming up next week. Jeanette doesn't know how far she'll be able to go in the modelling world and also knows that a modelling career won't last long. She's trying to keep her feet firmly on the floor but is taking full advantage of every minute!

Study
No specific courses of study

Links
Alba Model Information, for information and tips.
www.albamodel.info
Association of Model Agents: a list of accredited and reputable modelling agencies.
www.associationofmodelagents.org
General **information and advice on modelling careers**.
www.connexions-direct.com/jobs4u

Rating
Average salary: varies
Entrance difficulty: ● ● ●

Stand out from the crowd
Trust your instinct, ask any questions that spring to mind, and if you're under 18, take a parent or guardian with you.

The stylist's job assumes good taste and an in-depth knowledge of trends (what's in stores and on the catwalks), but the most important thing about it is that you are styling for other people and for different situations.

stylist

A fashion shoot featuring Lady Gaga: 'No One Can Work Like This', by fashion stylist GK Reid (pictured on the right).

Being a stylist is not about imposing your own views on other people, but about working together with them to get the right look for the particular people and situations. Stylists usually work on shoots for magazines, catalogues or advertising, but may also work for television and for individuals. Reality television programmes and our increasing understanding of how celebrities live their lives have really raised the profile of the role of the stylist, and a stylist's career is now thought of as one of the most desirable of all fashion communication careers. If you're the kind of person who has really good style, is great at putting outfits together and, crucially, is good at identifying what would suit someone else's style, personality and figure, then this might be the area for you.

Magazine styling
The editor or creative director will brief the stylist, telling them who they need to style and what kind of look they should be aiming for. The stylist will then source the clothes that they need by contacting the PR teams working for the particular designer or retailer, or by going to the shops themselves to see what would work. The clothes will usually be lent to the stylist at no cost as it is such great publicity for the designers to have their outfits appear in a magazine. The stylist needs to put the entire outfit together so accessories and footwear must be considered, too.

The stylist will come along to the shoot, dress the models or celebrities and might work closely with the photographer and the hair and make-up artists to get the right look. An in-house stylist, actually employed by the magazine, is likely to have a much broader role than a freelancer who would tend to just get involved with the clothes and accessories and not have so much say over the overall look and the hair and make-up.

Television styling
TV shows that have 'celebrity' presenters will usually employ a stylist to work with the celebrities to get their outfits for the series. The stylist will be given a brief by the producer that will set out the kind of look they are going for and then might be given a budget to get 15 or so outfits for the whole series. The stylist will usually have a few shopping days with the presenter and will then need to present the outfits to the

producer to get the go-ahead before starting fittings. This kind of styling demands closer relationships with the people you are dressing, and the stylist needs to be supportive and reassuring. One of the challenges of this kind of role is that you need to make sure that both the production team and the presenter are pleased with your choices.

Music styling
This can be an area where stylists need to use a great deal of creativity, but this kind of styling is not without its challenges. When styling musicians for videos and concert tours, stylists can sometimes find themselves caught in the middle of the band managers, the video producers and the musicians themselves, with everyone having their own views on the best look and style.

Catalogue styling
Not always seen as the most creative environment in which to work as a stylist, catalogue work is often highly lucrative. The catalogue is the key sales document for the organisation you are working for so it is crucial that it shows the clothes at their best. The stylist would work closely with the art director and buyer and needs to pay close attention to detail to ensure that every shot looks perfect.

Routes in
A stylist would normally start their career as a fashion assistant – working within a magazine or catalogue team, doing all the administrative work of the business such as keeping the samples organised and arranging for them to be

Stylist internship

Celebrity Stylist and Personal Shopper currently has a handful of international clients that she works with on a daily basis. Building them new images and easing the everyday stresses that come with being in the limelight, by making sure they look good and feel confident!

Length of placement: 4 weeks

Experience gained: The student/graduate will have the opportunity to gain experience of Fashion Styling in all areas, from the fun fittings with clients, photo shoots and fashion shows, to the not-so-fun work that comes before and after the

CASE STUDY:

Hannah is a freelance stylist.

Hannah spent a total of eight weeks at university, studying fashion journalism. She dropped out when she was offered a job as a fashion assistant for a teen magazine. Perhaps surprisingly though, she thinks that going to university was a really important step for her: 'I'd never had got my first job if I hadn't been studying something relevant at a well respected university.' She took a very pragmatic view of the whole thing: she went to university to get a job working for a magazine, so once she had got her foot in the door, she had no need to stay on.

She spent four years at the magazine, first as an intern (unpaid), then as a fashion assistant (mostly sorting out the fashion cupboard), before landing her dream job as a stylist. During that time she did loads of test shoots: 'These are shoots that you plan and organise and get everyone to work on for free, so that you get some great shots for your book.' The 'book' is the stylist's portfolio; you're judged on the images in your book so you have to do all you can to get it looking good.

After four years, Hannah felt that she was in a position to work freelance, so she took her book to a few agents and was taken on. She has now been working as a freelance stylist for some years, spending some time as a long-term contractor at a different magazine and doing bits and pieces of work for a range of weeklies and monthlies. Hannah feels that the profession has changed quite a lot since she first joined, and it is now swamped with 'wannabes' who are attracted by the image and perceived glamour of the role. Hannah points out that, as the stylist, you are not the star, and in her experience one of the keys to being a good stylist is to keep your feet firmly on the ground.

packaged up and sent back to the designers. Stylists are taken on for an individual job either through an agent or, more often, through a contact they've worked with before. Occasionally the stylist would have to pitch for work, and produce a mood board of ideas for their concepts.

Best bits
- ▲ It's loads of fun, you can have a great deal of variety in your job and you work with lovely people
- ▲ You get to shop for a living!

Worst bits
- ▼ You usually have to work for free for a long time before getting your first paid job
- ▼ The higher-end magazines (*Vogue*, *Elle* etc) tend to pay quite poorly

Skills needed
- A love of fashion and a good knowledge of what's going on in the fashion world (if you're asked to provide some outfits in bold tiger stripes, you need to know which designers or retailers are selling them this season)
- People skills – reassuring an insecure celebrity, fighting your corner with a difficult art director or negotiating to get first dibs on the must-have designer items with the PR teams
- Enthusiasm and energy

Study
- Working with clients
- How to choose cut, colour and fabric
- How to create current looks
- Styling tricks
- Trend spotting
- Styling for the media
- PR and its relevance to styling

Links
Drapers Online for general fashion information and inspiration for illustrations. www.drapersonline.com
A range of **entry-level jobs** in the fashion industry. www.arts.ac.uk/student/careers/creative-opportunities.htm

Rating
Average salary: ● ● ●
Entrance difficulty: ● ● ●

Stand out from the crowd
Present your unique fashion personality at the interview, but stress your organisational skills and your broad exposure to diverse fashion styles.

It can be hard to decide where the fashion industry stops and other industries begin. Within 'communications' especially, many professionals combine work in the fashion industry with work in other spheres.

other roles in communications

This article discusses some of the jobs that seem to be on the fringes of the fashion industry, but where you could make your living predominantly, or significantly, within fashion, and where an interest in and knowledge of fashion would really stand you in good stead.

Broadcast journalist/TV presenter
There are a few, just a very few, people who work in broadcasting whose names are exclusively associated with fashion, and a few more whose names are sometimes linked to this industry. There are more 'serious' fashion correspondents who might work for radio or television news or documentaries, and there are presenters who work on makeover shows and as experts on daytime television shows. The explosion in the number of channels and the number of independent production companies has increased this field dramatically, but it is still a very small field.

There are a few different routes into these roles, but they all involve starting in a slightly different place and moving over once you've made your name: for example, working on a fashion magazine, as a designer or stylist, or as a more generic TV presenter or documentary maker. Given that, you will need to think quite strategically about where to start your career, and accept that this kind of job would usually be a long-term career aspiration rather than something you'd get straight into. It's also important to point out that many try and very few succeed within this area, so don't even think about it if you're not really passionate about it, and in any case, it might be worth considering a Plan B.

Advertising
Advertising is an industry intertwined with PR, marketing and journalism, but it doesn't have a section of its own within this book as there's no typical 'fashion advertising' career path. Most ad agencies don't like to limit themselves to working for a single industry and will often sign agreements that they can't work for two competitors within a particular field, so when you get taken on as an account manager or creative contributor of some sort, you are expected to be willing to advertise anything, from Lysol disinfecting wipes to Chanel perfume. Having said that, if you make a name for yourself as someone who is an expert with fashion advertising, you are more likely to win business in that industry, and a long-term relationship with a major fashion client can constitute a significant part of your career.

Musicians
It's rare that a musician would make their living from the fashion industry, but musicians are contracted in a range of

An assistant checks the lighting on a shoot. The right lighting can make or break a photo.

different contexts within the business, and as music and fashion are both industries that are built on networks, if a musician gets known within the fashion industry it is likely that they will be used again and again. Musicians are employed mostly within advertising and for catwalk shows. They need to work closely with the producers or directors and write, choose or perform music that will enhance the image and message of the production.

> *There are many jobs on the fringes of the fashion industry where an interest in and knowledge of fashion would stand you in good stead.*

Set designers and lighting technicians

Catwalk shows are big theatrical productions and depend on experts to get the look and feel of the stage perfect. The set and lighting designers will work with the producers and designers to find the perfect backdrop to show the collections at their best and to complement the brand and image of the design house. They might also be employed working on catalogue shoots and for advertising.

Web designer

Websites are big business. Whether you are a massive multi-national retailer or a sole trader just starting your own fashion label, you need a website. And while most people working in these fields are pretty creative and can turn their hands to many things, they will usually need a web designer

to help them at some point. Web designers would not normally want to limit themselves to fashion websites, but if that's where you build your reputation and get your contacts, then you might well find plenty of work there for you.

Routes in

There are a very few graduate training schemes within journalism and advertising, but unless you are one of the very lucky few, the chances are that you'll need to start off getting to know people in the business, begging for work experience and working for free.

Best bits

▲ These are all very creative jobs, and you might find that your particular kind of creativity is more suited to one of these

▲ You can combine an interest in fashion with a passion in a different field

▲ Your career is likely to be pretty varied as you can dip in and out of the fashion world

Worst bits

▼ Most of these roles (with the exception of advertising) entail a freelance career. This has a certain lifestyle that goes with it (you usually have to be comfortable with uncertainty, instability and spontaneity) and requires a range of skills beyond the creative ones (primarily bookkeeping, self-marketing and organisation) that don't always go hand in hand with the creative mind-set

Skills needed

• Creativity
• People skills
• Determination

CHAPTER EIGHT

education

Fashion is a brilliant and versatile medium for storytelling, and given how much we all like stories it's no great surprise that every year thousands of us are interested in what the study of fashion can teach us. The narratives are diverse and can help to shed light on a great array of subjects.

F ashion is enormously revealing about society: attitudes, customs, values and lifestyles; and through fashion we can analyse our own society as it is now, or any other society at any other time. Fashion can also tell us about technology – from the techniques used to create the Egyptian jewellery of 4,000 years ago, through to the latest ladder-resistant tights, we can use fashion as a way both to understand the history of technology and to build its future. Through fashion we can learn about design, shapes, colours and all the techniques and processes that go together to produce the outfit that you are wearing right now.

A formal gown made from brocaded silk in a floral design, trimmed with lace, feathers, ribbon and beads. It was woven in France and handmade in Britain, in 1755–1760, and is kept at the V&A Museum, London.

Fashion is also a study in people. Why did you choose just those very clothes that you are wearing now? What does it say about your background, values, occupation, age and education?

'Fashion' covers sociology, psychology, anthropology, history, geography, biology, physics, chemistry, design, art, illustration, film and media studies, business and of course, how to make clothes. With this wealth of learning opportunities open to the fashion student, is it any wonder that fashion education is so sought after?

Teaching is the most obvious and direct form of education, but even this is diverse when you take into account the types of students (all ages, from those with learning disabilities through to PhD students, and the practically or academically inclined) and the different areas within fashion (from physics to fine art to tailoring). Beyond teaching there are historians, archivists, technicians and museum staff, all of whom support learning in one way or another.

A student making a three-dimensional study before starting to work with fabric.

Fashion design students listen to a lecture from a visiting professor.

Jobs in fashion education are nothing if not varied. Many involve standing up in front of groups of people talking about your subject, but if this is a side of education that you don't find appealing, don't be put off. There are education jobs that mostly involve one-on-one work or small groups, or roles that are almost entirely behind the scenes (museum curation, archive work or technician work, for example). They all involve putting stories together, but this can be done visually, or verbally, and the focus could be on writing, talking or demonstrating, depending on the particular role.

All roles involve administration to some degree, as work needs to be marked, objects need to be catalogued and rooms need to be booked, but this may be a more significant part of some roles than others.

Routes in

It all depends who you're going to teach. There are very strict guidelines around qualifications required for school teaching. Teaching in statutory education (4–16) requires a degree (in the subject you want to teach for secondary level and above), as well as teacher training and possibly a postgraduate certificate of education (PGCE). Around the fringes (adult education and university teaching as well as technician and museum work), the rules are a bit more relaxed, but formal qualifications are increasingly desirable and are certainly going to improve your chances.

Best bits

▲ It's very interesting – it's not just about the garments and the industry, it's about what they mean and what that tells us
▲ Sharing knowledge about something you love and seeing people grasp the concepts
▲ The culture of the education side of the business can be less cut-throat and competitive than some other specialisms
▲ It's a steady income and the security of this can give you the freedom to take more risks in your freelance or designer-maker career

Worst bits

▼ For those attracted to the glamour of the industry, this is not the area for you

▼ If there is a designer inside you, but you've chosen education for practical reasons, you might end up frustrated that you're talking about things and not doing them
▼ Although you are less likely to have to work unpaid for long (museum work being the exception to this), working within education is unlikely to make you rich

Skills needed

- A talent for explaining things clearly and making them exciting
- Great passion for your subject
- You need to like and respect the people you'll be teaching
- An interest in analysis is also key: not just what people wear, but why they wear it, how the clothes are made and what this tells us

Links

Teach First for general information about teaching. www.teachfirst.org.uk
Graduate Teacher Training Registry (GTTR) for general information about teaching. www.gttr.ac.uk
TES for news and jobs in the statutory sector. www.tes.co.uk
Times Higher Education for news and jobs in higher education. www.timeshighereducation.co.uk

The popularity of courses in fashion, textiles and related subjects means that there is always a need for teachers. You could do all sorts of different kinds of teaching. Opportunities exist at colleges and schools at every level.

teacher

The age of your students could range from eight to over 80 and they may be using the course to help them get the career they want, to improve or diversify their professional skills or just for fun. Your role could be full-time or part-time, or you might work on an occasional basis – contributing a lecture here and there or working on one module of a longer course.

Many practitioners combine a job as a teacher with their role as a freelancer or running their own business, and this can be a great way to get the financial security of a stable income but still have the time available to continue with your practice.

The topics you would teach could range from the very general to the very specific, linked, for the most part, to the level at which your students are studying. At high school level, you would probably be teaching quite generic art and design classes, perhaps with a fashion slant; courses get more and more specialised

A student participates in a specialist one-to-one tutorial.

ABOVE Fashion students undertaking practical design work in the studio.

through foundation and undergraduate level to masters programmes. You could teach short courses for existing practitioners where you might be delivering something as specific as instruction in diamond setting or hat trimming.

The balance of your day-to-day duties will vary depending on the kind of place you end up working. A large proportion of your time will, of course, be spent up in front of a group, talking to them about the particular subject, but you will also need to spend time planning lessons, setting and marking work, offering practical advice and giving feedback. You might get involved in one-to-one tutorials, crits and writing reports. You would also be expected to keep up to date with your subject by reading books, going to exhibitions and attending conferences.

Study

Teaching in statutory education (4–16) requires a degree (in the subject you want to teach for secondary level and above), as well as teacher training and possibly a postgraduate certificate of education (PGCE). In higher education, practical experience is often more relevant, but you may need a masters or phD in your subject.

Links

Teach First for general information about teaching. www.teachfirst.org.uk
Graduate Teacher Training Registry (GTTR) for general information about teaching. www.gttr.ac.uk
TES for news and jobs in the statutory sector. www.tes.co.uk
Times Higher Education for news and jobs in higher education. www.timeshighereducation.co.uk

Rating
Average salary: ● ● ○
Entrance difficulty: ● ○ ○

Stand out from the crowd

Get some experience of working with your chosen student group – do some classroom assistant work, or ask to shadow a lecturer for a couple of days.

Lecturer in Fashion Textiles: Knit

Postion Type: Permanent – Full time
Salary: £40,000–£45,000

This college is one of the foremost centres of fashion education in the world. If you have substantial experience of working in knitwear design development for Womenswear, this is your chance to join a fast-paced and creative team, working alongside extremely talented students in a vibrant environment.

You will deliver our Fashion Textiles: Knit, design development courses at Foundation Degree and Honours levels. This will involve teaching, unit management, curriculum development and research. We will also look to you to contribute to these courses through design development, presentation and 3D realisation.

Routes in

For teaching at primary and secondary levels, you will need a degree and a teaching qualification. To teach fashion at undergraduate level, your professional experience is critical, so you should have several years of experience as a practitioner, as well as a degree in a relevant subject. Colleges prefer to have faculty with teaching experience, but they balance that with the level of experience and special qualifications you bring to the table. (For example, if a fashion illustration teacher was needed, skill and experience as an illustrator would be a primary asset for an applicant.) You will need extensive professional experience to provide training within the industry, but a degree, although preferred, is not always essential.

Many practitioners combine a job as a teacher with running their own business, and this can be a great way to get a stable income.

Best bits
▲ The pleasure of sharing your knowledge with others
▲ Seeing the 'light bulb' moment as your students learn

Worst bits
▼ Occasionally challenging students
▼ Some roles can be very administration heavy

Skills needed
• You need to love your subject and love your students
• You need to be able to explain yourself very clearly
• Empathy

CASE STUDY:

Jo lectures on buying while also working as a buyer.

Jo has what you might call a 'portfolio' career. She is writing a book about fashion buying, she works as a buyer of children's clothing for a small high street chain and she teaches the buying courses at the Fashion Retail Academy.

Jo had carved out a great career for herself in womenswear buying but decided after ten years or so that she didn't want to get pigeonholed, so she took a job buying children's clothing for Woolworths. Just a few months after her appointment, Woolworths went bankrupt and Jo found herself, for the first time in her career, without a job. Her younger child was just starting school and for Jo it was a good time to take stock and think about what she wanted. A job that allowed her to stay in the country and take some time off during the school holidays sounded really appealing so she got in touch with the Fashion Retail Academy to find out what opportunities they had. They were keen on her recent experience and asked her to come and contribute to a couple of courses. The FRA supported Jo to do her teaching qualification and then when an opportunity arose as a full-time lecturer, they asked Jo to increase her hours.

Seven years down the line, Jo felt that she wanted to get back to the front line, so she has now gone back to a full-time job as a buyer but still keeps her hand in with the teaching, doing three or four lectures each term on a buying course. Jo loves the fresh enthusiasm of the students and says that teaching about the process makes her much better at actually doing the job.

The highlight of any fashion design course is the degree show.

There are two key elements to the job of curator in a fashion museum: you need to look after the collection and you need to make it accessible to the public. Herein lies the challenge...

fashion curator

At the summer opening of Buckingham Palace, a curator arranges an evening dress worn by Queen Elizabeth II on the state visit to the Netherlands in 1958.

The job of the fashion curator is to find new, interesting and inspiring ways to make the collections accessible to visitors, while keeping them safe from sticky fingers. One of the main parts of the job is displaying the collection, which involves both the permanent collection and exhibitions. Permanent collections tend to be very large, with even small regional museums having 50,000–100,000 items in their collections, and keeping on top of a collection this size, let alone trying to catalogue it in a systematic way, is one of the more difficult aspects of the role. Curators can also be hugely instrumental in working with donors for fund raising and acquisitions.

Displays in museums are all about stories. The curator needs to think about the kind of visitors they're likely to attract and what would be most likely to interest them. Are they children, women or men? Are they very keen on fashion or just there because it's something to do? Are they knowledgeable or do they need to be informed? The curator needs to tell a story through what is displayed, how it's displayed and what is written. They need to make sure that the audio guides complement the written text, the props surrounding the displays help to make sense of the clothes displayed and the exhibitions feel like good value for money.

Putting on an exhibition is a complex business, and the curator needs to think about the overall concept, which objects to include, how to get hold of them and how to display them and the space and how it should look. Most museums aren't particularly well resourced, so a few staff, often supported by some volunteers, get involved in many different aspects of the exhibition. The lead-in time for an exhibition will vary dramatically, depending on the kind of museum and the size of the exhibition, but on average, planning might start nine or so months before the exhibition opens. In large museums there may be an exhibition

Study

- Fashion
- History
- History of art
- Museum studies

Links

Museums Association (MA): a professional body with useful resources, news and information and job vacancies.
www.museumsassociation.org
Museum Jobs: vacancies bulletin.
www.museumjobs.com

Rating

Average salary: ● ● ●
Entrance difficulty: ● ● ●

Stand out from the crowd

Have a fluent knowledge of fashion history and how it has been affected by social, economic and political events. Be able to discuss the relationship between artistic movements and period fashions.

Curatorial Internship Fashion and Textiles

Hours: 1 day per week, hours 10am–5pm
Remuneration: Travel expenses paid
Start date: October 2010 – 6 months

This is intended to benefit a person who is studying for specific qualifications in relevant subjects or who is actively seeking employment in the heritage sector.

Specific Duties: The intern will work with the Fashion and Textiles Collections team providing general curatorial support but also working on specific projects as and when required.
Ideally the intern will work with the department over an extended period.

department who would work closely with the curators, but in smaller museums the curators would be expected to sort out the nuts and bolts of the exhibition themselves.

Most curators fulfil a public-service duty as part of their role. They answer queries, run drop-in sessions for the public and work with the media, as well as getting involved with the museum education departments, helping to run educational sessions.

The day-to-day job of the curator is varied and ranges from the really high-level and cerebral to the very mundane and practical. In a single day you could be cleaning the floor, making a mannequin to fit a sixteenth-century royal dress and talking to a contemporary designer about their new collection, for instance.

Routes in
To get into curating you would need a relevant degree (such as fashion, history or history of art), ideally a masters in museum studies and to have done lots of appropriate volunteer work.

Best bits
▲ Working with the collections and making it possible for the public to have access to these amazing clothes
▲ Such a lot of variety

Worst bits
▼ There is never enough money to do what you want to do, so the job never, ever, feels finished

Skills needed
• Excellent organisational skills
• Ability to multi-task
• Being prepared to work on all kinds of projects
• Academically and practically minded
• Good communication skills

CASE STUDY:

Rosemary works as a curator at the Victoria and Albert Museum in London.

Rosemary did her degree in the history of art and then did a masters in the history of dress at the Courtauld Institute of Art. Her first role was as a volunteer at the Museum of London in their costume department. She wrote to the museum while on her course and was offered a two-week role to catalogue a slide collection.

Her advice to anyone on work experience is to be useful, adaptable and efficient, and through demonstrating these skills herself Rosemary's experience was extended and she ended up working unpaid for six months. Unpaid experience is more or less essential within this sector, but she found her colleagues very understanding and accommodating, and they were happy to allow her to arrange her hours with them around her paid job. Rosemary learned some really useful practical skills at the musuem, including how to build up a mannequin for a historic dress (as dresses used to be made to fit the owner, curators can't display them on standard modern mannequins so the curator needs to make a mannequin out of polyester stuffing to fit each individual dress), and found that her practical sewing skills were very well received.

Six months later, Rosemary managed to get a job as a curatorial assistant at the museum and eventually worked her way up to a curator. Eight years later, a job came up at the V&A and Rosemary joined the team of 17 curators working with the fashion and textiles department. She loves the variety of the job and really appreciates working with such experts across the musuem.

Exhibition at the V&A Museum in London: 'Grace Kelly: Style Icon'.

The job of the museum education officer is to work with a museum's collections and exhibitions to bring them to life for children. The sessions they run can take place either in the museum itself or as part of a community outreach programme in schools or other institutions.

fashion museum education officer

Education departments don't tend to be very big and even in larger national museums you are likely only to have a small in-house team, sometimes supported by freelancers or volunteers. In smaller museums it's common that there is only one education officer. This has two key implications for those who are interested in carving out a career in fashion museum education. First, it is quite likely that you won't get to focus just on fashion but will be working in a broader capacity. There are very few museums that focus exclusively on fashion, which means that in most cases, the education officer will be putting on programmes that will cover all aspects of the museum's collection, whether that is history (such as at the Museum of London) or other arts (such as the V&A). The second implication is that as it will usually be just you in the education team; you will have to do everything. You will be in charge of all aspects of the education programmes from the high-level strategy, right down to photocopying worksheets for the children, and if anyone needs to dress up as a French revolutionary peasant woman, or don a suit of armour, it will be you.

You will work with the curators to identify themes for an education programme and then come up with some specific workshops, talks and presentations that could help to illustrate the collection and make it interesting and engaging for children. You would write the programme and then liaise with schools and teachers to make arrangements for groups to come in. The workshops will be as diverse as your imagination and the collections, but you might be involved in getting children to draw pictures of clothes in an exhibition, or getting them to try on corsets or decorate paper hats.

Many museums rely on freelancers to deliver some of their programmes so this can be a more flexible alternative to a contract with one museum.

Routes in

This is a competitive area and you will usually need to volunteer before you get a paid job. A teaching credential, although not a prerequisite, is now fairly standard and you will probably struggle to get an interview if you don't have one; some experience of working with children is also useful. A degree in a relevant subject, such as fashion or history, is important. The world of museum education freelancers is a small one and is very much based on who you know, so building your network is very important.

Study

- Fashion
- History
- History of art
- Museum studies

Links

Museums Association (MA): a professional body with useful resources, news and information and job vacancies. www.museumsassociation.org
Museum Jobs: vacancies bulletin. www.museumjobs.com

Rating

Average salary: ● ● ○
Entrance difficulty: ● ● ●

Stand out from the crowd

Get lots of experience working with children in one form or another. Volunteer if you need to, to get the experience. Have a profound love of objects and respect for their history.

DAY IN THE LIFE:
Museum education officer

Deborah manages the educational programmes for the museum of an art and design college. She is involved with both the college's academic programmes within the museum and programmes for regional school systems. Her day might include:

8.30AM TELECONFERENCE WITH SCHOOL STAFF
They discuss the Anglo-Saxon museum exhibit, and plan connections between Saxon artefacts and the literature being studied in the classroom. They schedule dates for the year fives' museum visit.

9.00AM HISTORY OF DRESS CLASS
Deborah assists the professor in teaching the undergraduate course, setting up displays of Charles James gowns for today's class in eveningwear from the 1940s. She handles the gowns with cotton gloves so the students can study the interior structure.

11.00AM MEETING WITH MUSEUM ADMINISTRATORS TO REVIEW PLANNING FOR SCHOOLS' OUTREACH PROGRAMMES
Deborah presents ideas for initiatives aimed at giving students the opportunity to create art inspired by upcoming museum exhibits.

12.00PM LUNCH WITH THE COSTUME AND TEXTILE CURATORS
They celebrate the acquisition of 18th-century gowns from Paris. Deborah also coordinates a visit for sixth-grade students studying *The Great Gatsby* with the installation of an exhibit of fashions of the 1920s.

1.00PM LEARNING TO LOOK TOUR
Deborah leads a group of year three students in an introduction to the museum, teaching observation of shape, colour, texture and materials.

3.00PM TOUR FOR TOTS
An interactive tour with read-aloud story time and gallery activities aimed at pre-school children and parents.

5.00PM DATABASE TRAINING
Deborah guides undergraduate students in utilising the new database to access pieces from the museum's collection. One student requests 19th-century corsets. Deborah demonstrates finding corsets in the costume collection on the computer. The curator pulls several corsets from climate-controlled storage to demonstrate the process.

Best bits
▲ Lots of autonomy
▲ Children can be incredibly responsive, so it can be enormously satisfying to see the impact of your work

Worst bits
▼ Because you end up being quite autonomous it can be easy to take on too much work, and then you can find it a struggle to keep on top of things or to switch off when you get home

Skills needed
• A love of the museum collection
• An interest in working with children
• Good communication skills
• Organisational skills
• The ability to self-motivate

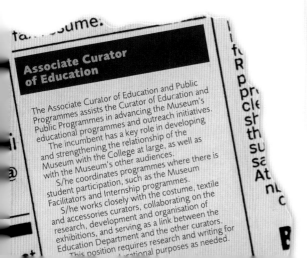

Associate Curator of Education

The Associate Curator of Education and Public Programmes assists the Curator of Education and Public Programmes in advancing the Museum's educational programmes and outreach initiatives.
The incumbent has a key role in developing and strengthening the relationship of the Museum with the College at large, as well as with the Museum's other audiences.
S/he coordinates programmes where there is student participation, such as the Museum Facilitators and Internship programmes.
S/he works closely with the costume, textile and accessories curators, collaborating on the research, development and organisation of exhibitions, and serving as a link between the Education Department and the other curators.
This position requires research and writing for [...]ational purposes as needed.

A relatively new but growing role within the industry is that of an archivist. The archivist will work for a designer or retailer, collecting and cataloguing their collections, and using these archives to support the future of the organisation.

archivist

There are two mains strands to the work of most archivists. The first is to support and inspire the designers. A designer might want to look at a range of garments from the 1920s to help them with a vintage-inspired collection, for example. The second strand of the work of the archivist is to support the marketing and PR functions of the company. The archivist might be required to verify marketing stories or might be asked to speak to journalists, take part in documentaries or advise on costume for a film.

Awareness of the heritage of a designer or retailer is a modern approach to fashion design. Although some collections might have garments and other items from the mid or even early twentieth century, most have only started preserving collections in a systematic and comprehensive way in the last ten years or so.

Collections will vary substantially, depending on the organisation and how important the historical collection is for them, but most will include a range of items in addition to the garments themselves. They might include photographs, sketches, magazine articles, swatch books and brochures. Some archives are displayed in the format of a museum and are open to the public.

Routes in
A relevant background is useful, but that could include a range of degree subjects including anything fashion-related,

CASE STUDY:

Greta is the archivist for Aquascutum.

Greta started her career as a historian, working on the eighteenth century, and her first job after finishing her PhD was digitising a photography collection for a private client. Her next role was to work for a friend of hers who was a stage and costume designer and it was this job that taught her about the history of dress and fashion design. About ten years ago she applied for the job of the archivist at Aquascutum. What is really unique about Greta's position is that it is seen as a commercial role, and Greta is involved in discussions about the designs for the new ranges and the commercial direction of the organisation. This is partly a product of a company whose heritage is such a key feature of its brand but also of the particular skills and passion that Greta brings to the role.

fine art and records management. Jobs are few and far between and unpaid work experience will usually be your route in.

Best bits
▲ Autonomy
▲ Creating order out of chaos
▲ Being able to put your finger on exactly the item that can help someone

Worst bits
▼ As a support function, you have to work hard to get the recognition and resources that you feel you need

Skills needed
• Creativity
• The ability to organise, catalogue and be able to retrieve every item in a collection

Study
• Fashion
• History
• History of art

Links
The Victoria and Albert Museum: one of the world's foremost art and design collections.
www.vam.ac.uk
Museums Association (MA): a professional body with useful resources, news and information and job vacancies.
www.museumsassociation.org

Rating
Average salary: ● ● ●
Entrance difficulty: ● ● ●

Stand out from the crowd
Be really well organised! You need to be able to remember and retrieve information quickly and easily.

The role of the technician is to manage a studio or workshop. Technicians usually work at colleges and are often attached to one particular course – so you would find a footwear technician, or a print technician, for example.

technician

Managing the studio or workshop involves looking after the equipment – making sure it's in good working order and arranging to get it fixed if it isn't, managing the students and making sure that all health and safety checks and policies are in place. The technician would usually be responsible for actually teaching the students how to use the equipment as well as technical skills such as dyeing and pattern cutting.

They would have their own budget and be responsible for ordering new equipment and managing all the consumables that the students need for their projects.

A technician advises a student on practical techniques.

Routes in
Most technicians will have a degree in fashion or some related subject and then will have had some experience working within their sector. This is one of the few areas within the whole business where there is not a culture of unpaid work experience, but new staff are usually started on a short-term contract to see how it works out. Jobs are usually advertised on a college's website.

Best bits
- ▲ Working with the students: seeing them learn and being an important part of their early career development
- ▲ It's a relatively well-paid, relatively stress-free, permanent job with reasonable hours: this is rare within the industry

Worst bits
- ▼ A lot of time is spent on health and safety issues. While you might accept the importance of this work, it won't be the most stimulating part of your role
- ▼ Technicians can sometimes feel a bit undervalued: they are doing a skilled and important teaching role, but don't have the status or salaries of academics

Skills needed
Strong leadership skills to keep the students very well organised and well behaved when working with expensive materials and dangerous equipment. You need to be very skilled and experienced within your field. The ability to get along with all kinds of people is vital: dealing with colleagues, managers, inspectors, suppliers and students.

Study
- Fashion design
- Textiles
- Surface design
- Footwear
- Accessories

Links
TES for news and jobs in the statutory sector. www.tes.co.uk
Times Higher Education for news and jobs in higher education. www. timeshighereducation.co.uk

Rating
Average salary: ● ● ○
Entrance difficulty: ● ● ○

Stand out from the crowd
Know your stuff: you need to be an expert in equipment and techniques.

In addition to all of the job roles explored elsewhere in this book, there is a vast array of other 'backstage' jobs that need to be done to keep the industry moving.

backstage roles

Not all fashion companies will include all the job roles listed here – many businesses within the industry are too small to have the luxury of these kinds of specialist skills within their workforce, but at the other end of the scale, the big retail corporations may have large teams fulfilling each function.

These roles are covered briefly in this book as they are very well documented elsewhere, and to a great extent, the actual job that you would be doing on a day-to-day basis isn't all that influenced by the fashion-specific context. Having said that, if you love fashion and the kinds of people who work in this industry, then you would be working with a product that you are interested in and colleagues who inspire you, which is a pretty good start to anyone's career! So if nothing else in the book so far attracts you, it might be worth thinking a little more broadly.

Human relations (HR)

HR departments will deal with the hiring and firing of staff, disciplinary procedures and inductions for new employees. They may incorporate a training team to help make sure that the organisation has got the right skill mix. HR professionals can come from any background, although a background in a business-related area would usually be favourably regarded. The professional body for HR has a very well-regarded postgraduate diploma, but as it is a very practical, work-related qualification, you would normally be expected to have worked within the sector for some time before studying for this.

Finance

Money is at the heart of every organisation, and the fashion industry is certainly no exception! Every organisation, whatever its size, will have some financial staff to ensure that regulations are being met, money is effectively accounted for and systems are as efficient as possible. Within the finance departments you can find a range of roles from entry-level jobs right through to accountancy roles.

Law

Large corporations will employ their own legal teams who will deal with copyright, contracts and other issues. Becoming a fully-fledged lawyer is not for the fainthearted as lawyers would need to have a degree and postgraduate qualification in law and then need to do two years as a trainee before being considered fully qualified. There are more junior roles within legal departments, such as paralegal work and legal secretaries.

Computer work

No organisation within the world of fashion, whether a designer, retailer or supplier, lasts long these days without a website and computer systems, so organisations will always need to employ staff with up-to-date computer skills, including web development experience. You might choose to get involved in the systems support functions, helping people when their emails stop working and fixing the websites when they stop functioning; or in the research side of things, developing new software to make the processes more streamlined for employees or customers – either way you would usually be expected to have some relevant qualifications.

Administration

Senior managers in all walks of life rely heavily on their executive assistants. Often thought of as the power behind the thrones, executive assistants can be hugely influential, and good ones are highly sought after. Discretion, good people skills and organisational abilities are usually thought of as the key qualities needed, although the role will vary tremendously depending on whom you end up working for. Typical duties may include arranging and minuting meetings, controlling diaries, making travel arrangements, arranging events and anything else that your boss might need.

Office manager

From paper clips to warehouses, someone will be in charge of sourcing the things that are needed to keep the business running. The job may demand some technical knowledge, depending on what you're buying and whom you'd be buying it for, but many jobs in this area of the industry are open to graduates from any discipline. The focus here is on money and negotiations. The goal of the office manager is to get more or better goods for less money, so being comfortable negotiating on prices is the key to success.

Facilities

This covers everything to do with keeping the buildings an organisation occupies functioning effectively. It might include building maintenance (changing light bulbs, fixing door handles, etc), cleaning, security, arranging and supervising building work, sorting out electrical and plumbing problems and ensuring that the lighting and heating are working.

Logistics and distribution

Getting the clothes from A to B has always been integral to the fashion business, but this role is now more important and complex than ever, with raw materials, manufacturers and retail outlets often on different continents. The business advantage to be gained from getting the new styles to your stores more quickly than your rivals is significant. There are a number of career paths, including planning and strategy, management and engineering.

Recruitment

Recruitment within fashion is big business, as retail in particular is very labour intensive and staff turnover high. As a recruiter you might work in-house for one company, dealing with their recruitment needs, or you might work for a recruitment agency, where your role is to marry up clients looking for work with companies looking for staff. In either case you need to understand what skills are required for a particular role and learn ways to identify these in candidates, but in a recruitment agency, you would also have to sell the services of your agency to the employers.

Events and exhibition management

This could include fashion shows and fashion shoots, as well as other events. For example, Fashion Week needs to be coordinated to make sure that the programme goes smoothly, the publicity is sent to the right people at the right time and everybody knows what is happening. Trade fairs are another logistical challenge: people need to sell the stands, book the venues, organise the publicity, work with the exhibitors and manage the visitors.

Routes in

This will vary depending on the specific role, but in general these roles are less competitive than most within the industry. Some require a specific qualification, while for others, the personality and skill mix are more important. In most of these fields, there are career options that start at different qualification levels, so for example you could work as a financial administrator with basic high-school qualifications, right through to working as an accountant, which requires a good degree and a lengthy postgraduate training.

Best bits

▲ You can work for the fashion industry without any particularly relevant background. If you have already established your career in another field but are keen to have some involvement with the fashion industry this is great. This route can also be an excellent compromise for those who love fashion but don't have quite the right skill mix for the more directly creative roles

▲ In some cases these kinds of jobs can be significantly better paid than other roles more directly related to designing and producing the garments

Worst bits

▼ If you are creative and passionate about clothes, you may find it frustrating to be so near and yet so far from the design and production side

Skills needed

• Commercial acumen
• A range of people skills (usually teamwork and the ability to develop good relationships with clients)
• An interest in and a knowledge of fashion and the business of fashion is useful

resources

A selection of websites, institutions and ideas for further study to help you along your chosen career path.

Where to find out more

Skillfast
The sector skills council for fashion and textiles, www.skillfast-uk.org. A great resource for all sorts of up-to-date information and advice about most aspects of the fashion industry.

Canucutit
Produced by Skillfast, this includes profiles of people working in the industry, tips for securing work experience and an overview of the range of qualifications available: www.canucutit.co.uk

Prospects
This is a great resource for information about graduate-level jobs: www.prospects.ac.uk

Skillset
Skillset is the Sector Skills Council that incorporates the media industry: www.skillset.org.uk

Creative and Cultural Skills is the sector skills council for design, with news, information and careers support for designers.

Drapers
Drapers magazine and Drapers Online (www.drapersonline.com) are the key publications for the industry as a whole. But in addition to those, most of the jobs described in the book have at least one relevant trade magazine that is useful to read to keep up to date with that particular specialism within the industry. Specific resources are listed under each job title within this book, but asking advice from people who work in the industry is often the best way to make sure that you are reading the most relevant and current publication.

The Crafts Council
The National Development Agency for crafts: www.craftscouncil.org.uk

Cockpit Arts
A creative incubator for designer-makers: www.cockpitarts.com

The Enterprise Centre
Gives advice and information about all aspects of setting up in business: www.ecca-london.org

Own It
This provides advice and information on intellectual property for the creative industries: www.own-it.org

Where to look for jobs

Drapers
The UK's industry-standard magazine, and is more or less essential reading for anyone interested in any aspect of the industry. Read it to keep up to date with what's going on in the industry and for job opportunities.

Campaign
is the key trade journal for the communications industry and has information and news as well as job vacancies for marketing and PR roles.

Creative Opportunities at the University of the Arts London
– this online vacancy bulletin has a range of entry-level jobs across the industry including work experience, internships and freelance opportunities.

Other university careers service websites have some great opportunities listed – have a look at universities that offer courses in the job area that interests you. For example, Leicester University has a great vacancy bulletin that focuses on museum work.

Company websites
Internships are often only advertised on the company's website, so make sure you keep an eye on those that you are interested in.

Recruitment agencies
There are plenty of these that specialise in fashion, for example www.fashionpersonnel.co.uk and www.fashionunited.co.uk both have a good range of jobs across the sector.

Further study

There are loads of different courses that you can choose to do at college or university. There are more than 30 courses in the UK that specialise in fashion, not to mention all the more general photography, journalism and business courses that will prepare you perfectly well for a career in the fashion industry. In addition to the more traditional courses such as fashion design, or fashion technology, you can also study courses in fashion marketing, fashion journalism and fashion photography, for example. Here are some other related subjects that you may not have even realised existed:

- Clothing Engineering
- Contour Fashion
- Fashion Design Management
- Fashion Design Promotion
- Fashion Imaging
- Fashion Imaging Make
- Fashion Media
- Fashion Merchandising Management
- Fashion Production Development
- Fashion Promotion
- Fashion Stylistics
- International Fashion Marketing

Where to study

There are courses all over the country, and internationally. Here are the main universities in the UK offering directly fashion-related FdAs and BAs:

- Anglia Ruskin University
- The University of the Arts, London (incorporating Central Saint Martins, London College of Fashion, Chelsea College of Art and Cordwainers)
- University of Bedfordshire
- Birmingham City University
- University of Bolton
- University of Brighton
- Glasgow Caledonian University
- University of Central Lancashire
- University of Coventry
- University College for the Creative Arts
- De Montfort University
- University of Derby
- University of East London
- Heriot-Watt University
- University of Hertfordshire
- University of Huddersfield
- Kingston University
- University of Leeds
- University of Lincoln
- Liverpool John Moores University
- London Metropolitan University
- University of Manchester
- Manchester Metropolitan University
- Middlesex University
- Newport, University of Wales
- University of Northampton
- Northumbria University
- Nottingham Trent University
- Robert Gordon University
- University of Salford
- Southampton Solent University
- Southampton University
- Thames Valley University
- University of Ulster
- University of the West of England, Bristol (UWE)
- University of Westminster
- University of Wolverhampton

Don't think this is an exhaustive list! There are a number of FE colleges that offer HE courses, for example Walsall College or West Thames College, so it's worth checking at your local colleges too—you may be able to study a degree in fashion closer to home. In addition, there are some excellent courses at universities that are not mentioned above because the courses are more generic. In some fields (such as photography or marketing) you can get an excellent training through completing a more general degree and then specialise in the fashion side of things later on. For example, City University has some of the best regarded journalism courses in the country; they don't specialise in fashion journalism, but you would still get a first-rate training and access to some very strong networks if you were to study there.

The websites below can help you to narrow down your options:

- www.ucas.ac.uk will help you find out where your course is offered
- www.unistats.direct.gov.uk gives you lots of detailed information about different courses and universities to help you decide
- www.push.co.uk for an alternative guide to choosing a university
- www.notgoingtouni.co.uk for advice and information about other options.

index

credits

Quarto would like to thank the following agencies for supplying images for inclusion in this book:

Courtesy of University of the Arts/© Alys Tomlinson: **p. 1**, **p.12**, **p.15**, **p.18**, **p.19**, **p.20**, **p.32**, **p.33**, **p.40**, **p.42**, **p.44**, **p.47tr**, **p.48**, **p.50**, **p.51**, **p.54t**, **p55tr**, **p.66t**, **p.78cl**, **p79t**, **p.85b**, **p.88**, **p.89**, **p.109tl**, **p.111**, **p.112**, **p.114**, **p.158**, **p.174b**, **p.175t**, **p.176**, **p.183**; Courtesy of School of the Art Institute of Chicago: **p.2** Gina Fama Rockenwagner, photo: James Caulfield, **p.4** Rachel Goldberg, photo: Robert F. Carl, **p.5** Seth Meyerink-Griffin, photo: James Caulfield, **p.7** Grace Lee, photo: James Caulfield, **p.177** Bonnie Alayne, photo: Robert F. Carl; Kitty Dong **p.8–9**, **p.34b**, **p.67**, **p.73**; David Gardner **p.34tl**; Sian Thomas for HOUSE OF BLUEEYES, photo Paula Harrowing **p.52**; Julie Armstrong **p.53**, **p.65**, **p.67tr**, **p.87**, **p.152**; Nicolas Ashburn **p.54tl**; Wallis **p.56bl**; Armani **p.56tr**; Banana Republic **p.57**; Rex Features **p.58**, **p.59**, **p.108**, **p.109tr**, **p.170**, **p.178**; Marks & Spencer **p.60l**; Topshop **p.60tr**; Amin Anthony Philips at Love and be Loved **p.61**; Victoria's Secret **p.64**; Anita Massarella **p.66bl**; River Island **p.67tl**; Antonia Pugh-Thomas **p.67bl**; INDITEX GROUP **P.69**, **p.95**, **p.125t**, **p.127br**; Pringle **p.72**, **p.76t**, **p.77t**; Jerome C Rousseau **p.73tl**, **p.78t**, **p.79br**; Philip Treacy **p.73br**, **p.80t/b**; Daniella Dobesova **p.74**; Leonard of London **p.75b**; House of Fraser **p.76tl**, **p.82**; Stephen Jones **p.81**; Paul Smith **p.83**; Jessica Stuart Crump **p.85t**; Davina Nathan **p.86bl**; Ana Romero **p.86br**; V&A Images **p.92**, **p.174t**; Andrew Meridith **p.118**, **p.119t**, **p.120b**, **p.121**, **p.135**; Selfridges **p.120t**, **p.122-123**, **p.125b**, **p.136**, **p.137**; NHJ Style www.nhjstyle.com **p.138**; ClearView **p.146**; Getty Images **p.148**; Rachel Lerro www.rachellerro.com **p.152tr**; Elliot Siegel www.eliotsiegel.com **p.168t**

Quarto would also like to give a special thank you to Karen Millen, for allowing in-house photography.

All step-by-step and other images are the copyright of Quarto Publishing plc. While every effort has been made to credit contributors, Quarto would like to apologise should there have been any omissions or errors – and would be pleased to make the appropriate correction for future editions of the book.